IN BROAD DAYLIGHT

Also by Father Patrick Desbois

*The Holocaust by Bullets: A Priest's Journey to Uncover the Truth
Behind the Murder of 1.5 Million Jews*

IN BROAD DAYLIGHT

*The Secret Procedures
behind the
Holocaust by Bullets*

FATHER PATRICK DESBOIS

With an Historical Introduction by
Andrej Umansky

Translated from the French
by Hilary Reyl and Calvert Barksdale

Arcade Publishing • New York

First Edition

Arcade Publishing books may be purchased in bulk at special discounts for sales promotion, corporate gifts, fund-raising, or educational purposes. Special editions can also be created to specifications. For details, contact the Special Sales Department, Arcade Publishing, 307 West 36th Street, 11th Floor, New York, NY 10018 or arcade@skyhorsepublishing.com.

Arcade Publishing® is a registered trademark of Skyhorse Publishing, Inc.®, a Delaware corporation.

Visit our website at www.arcadepub.com.
Visit the author's website at www.yahadinunum.org.

The views or opinions expressed in this book, and the context in which the images are used, do not necessarily reflect the views or policy of, nor imply approval or endorsement by, the United States Holocaust Memorial Museum.

10 9 8 7 6 5 4 3 2 1

Library of Congress Cataloging-in-Publication Data

Names: Desbois, Patrick, author. | Reyl, Hilary, translator. | Barksdale, Calvert, translator.
Title: In broad daylight : the secret procedures behind the Holocaust by bullets / Father Patrick Desbois ; translated from the French by Hilary Reyl and Calvert Barksdale.
Other titles: Voisins du crime. English
Description: First edition. | New York : Arcade Publishing, [2018]
Identifiers: LCCN 2017041541 (print) | LCCN 2017043328 (ebook) | ISBN 9781628728590 (ebook) | ISBN 9781628728576 (hardcover : alk. paper)
Subjects: LCSH: Jews—Persecutions—Soviet Union. | Holocaust, Jewish (1939–1945)—Soviet Union—Personal narratives. | Soviet Union—Ethnic relations.
Classification: LCC DS134.85 (ebook) | LCC DS134.85 .D4713 2018 (print) | DDC 940.53/180922477—dc23
LC record available at https://lccn.loc.gov/2017041541

Cover design by Erin Seaward-Hiatt
Cover photo © Imperial War Museum (HU86369)

Printed in the United States of America

CONTENTS

HISTORICAL INTRODUCTION

SEPTEMBER 1941: Eight hundred Jews are shot by a German unit in Pushkin, near Saint Petersburg, in Russia.

OCTOBER 12, 1941: Three hundred Jewish women and children are executed by German customs officials and Lithuanian police in Palanga, Lithuania.

THE END OF 1941: Dozens of Jewish families are killed by a German unit in Naro-Fominsk, forty miles from Moscow.

DECEMBER 1942: Several hundred Jews are murdered by *Sonderkommando* 11b, a subunit of *Einsatzgruppe* D[1] in Naltchik, in the Balkan republic of Kabardino in southern Russia, forty miles from Georgia.

These four mass killings during World War II are geographically linked. They mark the farthest reaches of the Shoah by bullets that was perpetrated by German units in Soviet territory.

Between 1941 and 1944, thousands of executions took place in the Soviet republics of Russia, Ukraine, Belarus, Moldavia, Estonia, Latvia, and Lithuania, over an area ranging from Galicia to the shores of the Baltic Sea and from the Muscovite forests to the Caucasian borders.

HISTORICAL INTRODUCTION

Within the present-day borders of Russia, Belarus, and Ukraine alone, historians estimate the number of Jews exterminated to have been 2.2 million,[2] more than 80 percent of them by bullets, with the remainder having been deported and murdered in camps or gas trucks.[3] It is for this reason that this period of mass murder of Soviet Jews is called the "Shoah by bullets." The criminal "method" of murder by firing squad was employed throughout the Eastern Shoah, regardless of the number of victims. It could be a single Jewish family in a small village or tens of thousands of people in a large Ukrainian city.

From the summer of 1941 through the spring of 1944, the killers repeated the same process over and over: the exterminating the Jewish population—men, women, and children—by firing squad, most often at sites just outside villages and towns. Despite concerns by the Nazis in charge about the psychological health of the executioners, no alternative method was put in place.

Paul Blobel, the head of *Sonderkommando* 4a, the main unit responsible for the September 1941 massacre of the Jews of Kiev in the Babi Yar ravine,[4] was questioned about the process of executing their Jewish victims by Judge Michael A. Musmanno during the trial of the *Einsatzgruppen* in Nuremberg[5]:

BLOBEL: "Everything went very quietly. It took time, of course, and I must say that our men who took part in these executions suffered more from nervous exhaustion than those who had to be shot."

MUSMANNO: "In other words, your pity was more for the men who had to shoot than for the victims?"

BLOBEL: "Our men had to be cared for."

MUSMANNO: "And you felt very sorry for them?"

BLOBEL: "Yes. These people suffered a lot, psychologically."[6]

Certain members of the German units became veritable "experts," congratulating themselves on *Aktions*[7] smoothly carried out. Such was the case of Waffen-SS Herbert Wollenweber, a member of *Sonderkommando* 10a. When questioned about a major execution of Jews in the foothills of the Caucuses, he chose to emphasize his commando's expertise.

"The Jews were fairly calm. Schmitt [the leader of the commando] had organized the operation well. He was a fine man."[8]

The members of the death squads accepted the Shoah by bullets as the only efficient method of extermination over such vast territory (almost one million square miles). Franz Halle, a member of the police and *Sonderkommando* 4a, explained his attitude regarding the extermination of the Jews in Ukraine when he was questioned about the *Sonderkommando*'s actions in a hearing:

"Today, I admit that these proceedings were very misguided. At the point we had reached, we should have found other methods of exterminating the Jews."[9]

Halle betrayed no guilt about killing Jews, nor did he question the nature of the orders he received. For him, only the method to be used in committing murder posed a problem. The murder itself was simply a task to be carried out.

There is a second major difference between the Shoah in the East and the murder of the Jews in concentration and extermination camps, such as Operation Reinhardt.[10] The deportation of Jews to these camps was often done in secret or at least discreetly. Sometimes, in the case of those headed to Auschwitz, the victims were forced to write to their relatives to say that all was well and not to worry.

The Shoah in the East, by contrast, was not discreet. The victims were publicly assembled, albeit often at first on the pretext of being sent to a labor camp or to Palestine. The mass murder then took place in full view of the victims' neighbors, the curious, and soldiers or civilians who happened to be there. The following testimony from a German staff sergeant named Sönnecken, a member of the *Abwehr*,[11] appears in a report on the execution of several thousand Jews of Borisov, shot in Belarus in October 1941:

"In the distance the noise of rifles could be heard all day, the women and children cried and screamed, cars sped through the streets of the ghetto, bringing new victims—all in full view of the civilian population and any German military personnel who happened to be passing by.

"It might have been possible to block off the site in some way, but non-Jews lived the other side of the street and in the streets adjacent. In their eyes, you could read either apathy or horror, because the scenes they'd witnessed were so horrible!"[12]

Maintaining secrecy would have been all the more difficult given that the local population was regularly conscripted to assist before, during, and after the shootings. Sometimes the executioners forced the townspeople to watch the killings; sometimes it was passersby, stopped to ensure that they didn't get in the way, who witnessed the murders. The presence of spectators, whether forced or voluntary, wasn't a concern, so long as it didn't disrupt the efficiency of the operation.

It may seem surprising, then, that this aspect of the Holocaust has remained so little known, when there has been testimony from witnesses as well as from the executioners and survivors among the victims. The reason for this may be that many of these accounts weren't published until 1980, when the *Black Book* by Vasily Grossman and Ilya Ehrenburg became publicly available.[13] Thousands of accounts have yet to be discovered in the Soviet and German archives.

Toward the end of 1942, the Soviets created the Extraordinary State Commission[14] with the goal of recording the human and material damage caused by the Germans in occupied territory. In each formerly occupied district, committees were formed with representatives from the church, the police, and the schools. These committees searched for witnesses to the executions while experts examined the mass graves for medical and legal evidence. More than 25,000 people were interviewed. Several million pages were written.[15] Virtually inaccessible to Western historians before the fall of the Berlin Wall, this material is now available in the Russian Federal Archives.

The German judicial system,[16] which to this day continues to investigate Nazi crimes, has questioned hundreds of thousands of people about the extermination of the Eastern Jews. Their memories are preserved in the regional archives of various states, primarily in the federal archives in Ludwigsburg, home of the central bureau for the investigation of National Socialist crimes.

One would be hard-pressed to find the execution of a Jewish community that was not documented by the testimony of survivors, executioners, or neighbors. It all happened in plain sight. Yet the way in which these crimes unfolded, from the predawn hours well into the night, remains little known to the general public. The goal of this book is to remedy that.

ANDREJ UMANSKY[17]

IN BROAD DAYLIGHT

INTRODUCTION

I was moved recently to discover the beautiful book by Albert Camus, *The Wrong Side and the Right Side.*[1] Since childhood, I've used the terms "the wrong side" and "the right side" to understand myself.

Camus grew up in a poor family under the Algerian sun and I in the warmth of a joyful family, equally simple and full of love. The wrong side and the right side were imprinted within him, as the nervous system of what he would become: "For myself, I know that my roots are in *The Wrong Side and the Right Side,* in the world of poverty and light where I lived for so long, the memory of which still protects me from the two opposing dangers that threaten all artists, resentment and satisfaction. Poverty was never a misfortune for me: the light graced it with riches. Even my revolts were illuminated. They were almost always, and I believe I can say this truthfully, revolts in the name of all."

The wrong side. I spent my childhood and youth with the sense of dwelling, along with my entire family, on the wrong side of what was, for others, the right one.

On my maternal side, the Rivière family, my farmer grandparents lived four and a half miles from the center of Villegaudin, a small village in Saône-et-Loire, on the site of a castle, the Château de la Marche, that had burned down long ago. The property now belonged to a Parisian family. We knew everything about the place: the moats that filled with water and frogs in the summertime, the linden trees

1

whose flowers we had to gather quickly in big white sheets as soon as the weather turned hot, the round pond teeming with fish and bordered with ivy-covered stone benches, and, most of all, the acres of dense forest that, under the guidance of my grandfather Émile, a true woodsman, we tended like a fragile pearl. Everywhere there was light.

My grandmother Victorine embodied the goodness, the smile, and the rigor of the Christian faith. A solid peasant, she not only spoke her native Bressane dialect but also cultivated a French that was refined, almost distinguished. She felt it her duty to serve her landlords when they arrived from Paris to their château. Our farm, our fields, our duck ponds, were for them a place to vacation, a place to spend their leisure time. Victorine called them "our patrons." They usually arrived in the heat of August for their summer vacation. We were their second home.

Once their arrival had been announced to the "Château de la Marche" by telephone, we had to open all the doors in their building as well as the wooden shutters that would sometimes creak, still swollen with winter's humidity. We had to make the beds with big sheets from the armoires, chase away the mice, and then leave discreetly by the little back door behind the kitchen while they came in through the big front door. Therein lay the pride of Victorine Rivière.

The Parisians must have had the impression that they'd left the house only the day before. The moment they arrived, my grandmother closed all of our south-facing shutters for the length of their stay so they could sunbathe undisturbed. Thus, we spent the entire month of August in semi-obscurity, on the wrong side of our landlords' lives. It was a semi-darkness I found hard to bear, because I knew we shouldn't, by our mere existence, spoil their light.

My childhood was spent between town and country; the back-and-forth between Chalon-sur-Saône and Villegaudin gave our life its rhythm, like a metronome.

My parents had a small shop in Chalon-sur-Saône that sold cheese and poultry—foods that, in Bresse, are often found at the same locations. At 47 rue aux Fèvres, "Au Bon Gruyère," life and work were of a piece. In her work clothes, a blue or white smock, my mother practiced the smile she had learned from her mother. "Bonjour Madame, what is your pleasure today?" I heard her repeat this a thousand times.

Inside the shop, we lived in the shade, in the gray light of walls so close together the sun's rays could never reach us. We left the warm light of the country for the cold and lightless town.

The lives of others were our theater; our clients confided constantly. The daughter of one was divorcing, another had lost his dog, a white poodle, and a third had just become a grandfather, at long last! Some railed against the left, others against the right.

My father had given the strict order to smile, serve, and keep quiet. Their "interesting" lives paraded through our little shop like a living carousel.

Sometimes we had to leave the stage and descend a small, rough wooden ladder backward to visit the cold storage room or fetch wheels of Gruyère de Comté or bottles of milk from our basement, which was kept at a constant temperature, like us.

This wrong side was quite amusing to my eyes. We knew everything about the lives of others, who spoke freely. Our presence didn't bother them at all. We were transparent. They came to us without makeup. My father would often exclaim, "It's worse than a confessional in here!" We lived in an opposite time and season from the others.

I gave myself a task: to know all the inhabitants of rue aux Fèvres, floor by floor, building by building. I made it my work and, perhaps, also my game. They were my planet, my encyclopedia, and my life: Tunisians, Italians, Algerians, Jews, all living on my street. In order to better observe them, I asked my parents to give me a little straw-bottomed chair that I placed conscientiously at the entrance to the store, to the left of the door. I sat for hours watching them pass by, chatting, arguing, going home.

I also knew the town well from delivering chickens. The telephone would ring: "Hello, Madame Desbois? I'd like a Bresse chicken, about one and a half kilos [three pounds]. Not fatty! Would you prepare it and have it delivered?" "But of course."

I knew the clients' addresses by heart. The chicken, ready to cook, was wrapped in a pretty sheet of glazed paper with the name of our shop. I was proud of it.

One day, it was raining hard. I had run all the way to my destination on the Grand Boulevard and arrived soaked, protecting the chicken in its glazed paper as best I could. At the entrance to the building, I rang, redid the packaging, and climbed up two flights. The door was opened by a woman, the notary's wife, who said with a grimace, "Oh, don't come in! You smell like wet clothes!" Then, with the proper discretion, she slipped me my ten or twenty centimes tip. I went back out into the rain, freed of my precious chicken, my heart a little pinched.

It must have been on that day, returning to the shop, that I decided to apply myself to my studies. I didn't want to remain the transparent assistant forever, living in the gloom, serving the inhabitants of the right side of the world who leaned so heavily on our wrong side.

A child of public schools, I devoured all the knowledge and opportunities that were offered me, for free, by my country, my republic, the France that I so loved. I went from school to the public arts center, from the poems of Prévert to the songs of Jacques Brel, from the public libraries to the university. I studied mathematics with a passion.

Thirty years have passed.

I have never forgotten the fault line between the wrong side and the right side. Perhaps I have never left it. I couldn't fathom, in my youth, how much being born in the world's backstage would inform my entire life, how the wrong side would shape my quest.

Thirty years have passed.

Faith in God struck me like lightning one Friday while I was studying for my exams in mathematics at the university in Dijon. It happened in the middle of campus. I, the militant atheist, fully conscious, felt myself suddenly overtaken by a certainty, a crazy and unacceptable certainty: God existed. For years afterward, I asked myself what he wanted from me.

I hesitated for a long time between becoming a Protestant or Catholic.

My work with Mother Teresa in Calcutta played a decisive role. After having studied mathematics, theology, and history, I became a priest. As my superior at the seminary would say to the other priests, "Don't forget, he wasn't made in our house, in the Church!"

Having belonged to the world of the little people has given me a specific sensibility. To this day, in restaurants I remain fascinated by the clear, cold line that separates the space of the clients from that of the waitstaff. On the other side of the kitchen door is a different world. There are no more decorations, often; just sad tiles, noisy plates, and anonymous hands washing dishes.

But the transparent cleaning women and the bellhops do see all of our habits and our faults. They move between the wrong side and the right side. Their clients pay to ignore this, to buy into an illusory world, a theater set, where for an hour or two they can leave real life, and the shadows who people it, in the wings. Perhaps these clients can even forget, through disdain or habit, that they are living a spectacle.

My family wasn't even sure of being on the right side's other side. Rather, we had the feeling of existing behind the scenery.

In 1940, fifteen years before I was born, my family found itself caught in the wings of History with a capital *H*, the history of the war. Our farm was first requisitioned by the Maquis, the French Resistance, and then it was taken over by the Germans.

At that time, my Desbois grandparents lived on the island of Saint-Laurent, between the Saône and the Genise Rivers. Marie-Louise, my paternal grandmother, lived less than a hundred yards from the dividing line separating occupied from "free" France.

Victorine, my other grandmother, found herself, like many French women at the time, the sole caretaker of both the farm and the family.

She had to figure out how to face all the challenges of those who refused to accept the German fascists' occupation. Fernande, my mother, told us of having hidden vats of flour under the armoires when the Communists came to look for food and of later being terrified when the Germans smashed the same armoires with their rifle butts searching for Communists!

From her stories, we understood everything, perhaps too much.

The farm had become a hideout as well as an anti-aircraft site. The anti-aircraft batteries of the Resistance, installed twenty yards from our kitchen door, took out two German aircraft, which fell into our fields. Our farm buildings were transformed into interrogation rooms and prison cells for collaborators. The German pilots who were caught and tortured in our stable—or, more precisely, in our pigsty—were buried on our land. I still don't know where. The Alsatian refugees who came to us from the train station slept on our second floor.

Some neighbors denounced us. There have always been such souls in difficult times. The Germans, of course, came to reclaim their own. My grandmother stopped a violent search of the house at the risk of incurring the Germans' wrath and causing hostages—that is, the men of the hamlet—to be shot. This was one of the ways her Christian responsibility manifested itself. She was forever marked by it, conscious not only of history, big and small, but also of the fact that there are days when one has to stand firm. She was, by turns, a servant and a combatant.

I was born ten years after the end of the war. Yet it was as though I had two sets of memories, those of a simple farmhand and those of all the little people who had dared to say no before me. Once the war was over, the worldwide performance ended. The cadavers were forgotten. But my family could never quite return to the wings like before, like the others. The past stuck to our boots like clay.

It is surely this childhood perspective, so damaged by the noise from the machines of war occupying our fields, that led me later to other fields in Ukraine. But even more than the sound, it is the silence. The silence of Claudius, my grandfather whom I loved so much. He was a short, stocky man, a joker, his dark blue beret firmly on his head, a Gitane cigarette stuck behind his ear, and always a blue apron with big pockets. He was the family comedian, at least in appearance. The cheerful one, like Edith Piaf's sad clown, making everyone around him laugh.

But he got quiet whenever anyone brought up his wartime past. Joking stopped as soon as someone pronounced the forbidden words: Rawa Ruska.[2] The site of his deportation in 1942. Camp 325.[3]

As a child at family meals, I would press him, not understanding the reasons for his silences. His wife, Marie-Louise, would leave the table, her glasses fogged. Eventually, I stopped trying to bring it up. But one early morning, in our all-purpose van as we left Chalon to go buy Bresse chickens at various farms, I asked him one more time, "What did you do at Rawa Ruska? Why don't you talk about it?" We were alone that day. Gravely, he offered me these few words: "Patrick, we were locked in a camp with nothing to drink, we ate grass and dandelions, but outside the camp, for the others, it was worse."

Then we drove in silence for a long time. His words are etched in me now like the topographical map of an impossible memory, the equation, the topology of an enigma that has become my own: "Outside, for the others, it was worse." But who were "the others"? And at Rawa Ruska, where was this "outside"?

A few months before his death, knowing he was going to leave this world, Claudius, who was sitting at the head of the kitchen table in his little apartment on Saint-Laurent, asked me, "What are you going to do when I die?" Chuckling, I answered, "Inherit!" He burst out laughing; so did I. I had learned with him to laugh at everything, even when you are crying inside. Even when you are dying.

On that day, I did not gauge the true weight of my response. I *was* inheriting. Inheriting silence.

Much later, in Paris, I met René Chevalier—Maurice's nephew[4]—himself a survivor of Rawa Ruska, Camp 325, and we decided to "return" there.

INTRODUCTION

Early one morning, we walked through the village, which was slowly awakening from the Soviet ice age. I found the French internment camp virtually unchanged. Empty acres with scattered buildings here and there. A Soviet barracks had been built on the site, and one of its walls was painted entirely with scenes from a legend of the Red Army. Farther along, on the outskirts of the town, under thick brambles, we managed to find immense concrete slabs under which most of the 25,000 murdered Soviet prisoners were buried. They were no longer honored in this Ukraine, which by then had declared its independence.

According to the archives, more than 15,000 Jews were shot at Rawa Ruska proper.

We asked everywhere: at the church, at the central market, at city hall. Absolutely no one in Rawa Ruska wanted to talk about Jews. It was the same silence I had known at home growing up, the same leaden lid.

I went to see the mayor, a Soviet, who told me he knew nothing, that the executions were secret. In his little gray second-floor office, he said to me: "*Vive la France, vive Ukraine!*" waving two little faded flags. I went downstairs thinking I would never find the common graves of the Jews.

Thank God, that mayor lost the next election. A new mayor, Yaroslaw, was elected, someone I already knew slightly through my translator, Svetlana.

I was tired of finding nothing. I was lingering at a table at a wedding banquet in a restaurant called Hermès, whose ceiling had been painted by the mayor's wife, when a stranger walked in and came up to me with the words, "They're waiting for you." I didn't get up from the table, thinking, *I've been waiting too, and for a long time, for over thirty years.* The same person came back a few minutes later with the same enigmatic words, "They're waiting for you." Finally, I got up and went outside the building, which was as gray as the weather. A black car with tinted windows was waiting for me. I could see in the driver's seat the impassive silhouette of the new mayor, Yaroslaw.

As I approached the car, how could I possibly know that it wasn't just the new mayor who was waiting for me? And that not only the 15,000 Jews murdered in Rawa Ruska were waiting but the hundreds of thousands, the millions of Jews and Gypsies, who had been abandoned in the bushes? All these, along with thousands of their ex-Soviet neighbors, who were ready to speak.

The car left the center of town on a dirt road, followed a sleepy river, and crossed the long hamlet of Borove. Suddenly, at the end of Borove's deserted main street, I saw more than fifty elderly peasants, very poor, standing at the edge of the village, supporting themselves on wooden sticks. I began to realize who was waiting for me that day: the ones who had helped in the murder of the Jews of Rawa Ruska in 1943. As soon as they saw our vehicle, they walked into the forest in silence, in a slow procession, as if for a burial, their animals following on leashes. We got out and followed them. One had a newspaper stuffed in his boots; another had a white goat on the end of a string.

They led us to the site of a long-hidden common grave. And then they began to speak. One told of the arrival of the Germans, another of the Jews who dug the graves. And then each one left, heavy of foot, alone, weeping.

I felt a "Finally" open within me. I felt like a tired boat coming into port after a long crossing. When evening had fallen, at the end of the stories, I found myself alone in the forest with Yaroslaw. It all could have ended there. *Mission accomplished, Claudius. I found them. The others!*

I started toward the dirt road where our car was waiting for us. That's when Yaroslaw pronounced these words: "Patrick, what I have done for one village I can do for one hundred villages."

I immediately said yes.

INTRODUCTION

I said yes like a gong ringing in the cold air of a country whose ditches are full of the dead. This wasn't the first time my life's course had been decided in just a few minutes. I said yes the way you jump on the train of Providence, without knowing why or how.

Back in Paris, I rushed to rue Barbet-de-Jouy to see Cardinal Lustiger,[5] who told me, "I know the story. My Polish Jewish family was shot in the same way."

I went to Madison Avenue in New York to meet Israel Singer, who at that time was the director of the World Jewish Congress. After I told him of my long hours in Rawa Ruska, he said in Hebrew to his right-hand man, "We've been searching for these graves since 1944 and this guy we don't even know, he finds them." He didn't know I speak Hebrew.

Singer, Lustiger, and I met several months later in a Jewish school in Evry. We began to put together a plan. We needed a structure. We would call it "Yahad," *together.* And "In Unum," *as one,* added Lustiger.

Ten years on, there are more than twenty people who work with us in Paris, Washington, and Cologne. Some are university students, finishing their doctorates. Some are translators or investigators in the archives as well as in the villages. All of them, with the exception of me, are young. All are animated by the same conviction: to find every last mass grave of Jews or Gypsies shot by the Nazis.

What a wager! What folly! To want to build a world of democratic nations that are no longer constructed on top of the mass graves of "others."

In order to find the graves in "a hundred villages" and many more, we had to cross-reference archives with the words of those who knew, who had witnessed. They were still alive, but not for long. There were many of these neighbors to the crime, though at first we didn't know it. But after more than four thousand interviews at the time of this writing, it has become clear that the Shoah by bullets in Eastern Europe was not the secret we have been led to believe for so long. Rather, many people—Ukrainians and Poles, especially—saw it all with their own eyes and sometimes did more. How, after all, do you organize mass death without manpower? How do you keep up a certain rhythm of mass murder without the participation, whether voluntary or forced, of the villagers who have the misfortune to live near the Jews? Who built the ghettos, rounded up the future victims, and dug and then filled the graves? In short, who were the "helping hands" in the crime?

In order to know, we had to understand how the crime took place, the process by which it became concretely possible. This book does not claim to retrace a typical day—no such record exists—but instead attempts to describe how, from the day before a mass murder to the day after it, events would unfold, each time according to a veritable "agenda" on the part of the criminals.

PART ONE

THE NIGHT BEFORE

Chapter I

THE ARCHITECT

Paris, June 7, 2013,
the National Audiovisual Institute, at a colloquium of the
National Center for Scientific Research (CNRS)

Today's meeting bears directly on our work.

It's exactly 9:00 a.m. Since I arrived too early, I'm pacing on the damp, narrow sidewalk. Suddenly, a person appears, walking quickly, key in hand.

The conference room is pleasant and looks out onto a bright patio. Denis Peschanski, the former head of the CNRS, arrives, jovial and bright-eyed. He will serve as moderator. A number of researchers, historians, psychologists, and sociologists have accepted our invitation to attend after having watched our interviews with the "neighbors" to the scene of the crime. Each attendee has prepared remarks. I most clearly remember Peschanski's words. He explains, with a touch of humor, that my interview technique adheres to what he calls the "Smiley method."

"Before going to see a witness, George Smiley[1] gathers all the information necessary to understand the essence of what this witness will say. He must know ninety percent of it. If he doesn't start out with ninety percent and doesn't dominate his witness from the outset, he'll never obtain his missing ten percent and won't even have the keys he needs to understand the missing ten percent."

Yes, I thought, he could be right. The 10 percent is the unknown, or rather the many unknowns in the equations I'm trying to name, to understand little by little as I dig through archives, attend university symposiums, and have meetings on farms.

While Denis continues his presentation under the eye of the camera suspended from the ceiling, my thoughts take flight. I recognize myself in his argument. It's true that often, as I'm walking tiredly through some forgotten village in the heart of these post-Soviet territories, I'm desperately searching for the missing 10 percent. My studies in mathematics at the University of Dijon taught me never to give up when confronting the unknown, but rather to persist in solving a complicated equation, one with several unknowns. It's the same today. Mathematics, it would seem, has resisted Catholic theology.

As I muse about the 10 percent, I'm struck by the memory of an angular face. It's the face of Anton, a very fit old man I met in his farmyard in Bousk, a Galician village in Ukraine. I had already interviewed more than ten people in this pretty town, which lay alongside a seemingly dormant river. They had all brought up the town ghetto, explaining how they'd traded food for clothing with the Jews who had been shut inside. Some had witnessed various shootings from a hiding place in a barn. Through them, we were able to locate the gravesites, down below the Jewish cemetery, toward the river.

One day, I met a former nationalist. He told me how during the war he worked every day in a lemonade factory inside the ghetto. As soon as I saw him standing in his yard, a knife in hand because he had just killed a chicken for Sunday dinner, I knew that, with him, I would find something. I would find the 10 percent we were missing in our understanding of the crimes against the Jews of Bousk.

It was after our third interview, in the cool shade of his upland farm, that Anton revealed his truth to me. He found himself, in 1942, within the walls of the Bousk Gestapo, when he overheard a conversation. It was a phone call from Lemberg, the regional capital. As he remembered it, the purpose of the call was to decide the exact day to kill the Jews of Bousk. According to him, the caller had proposed selecting a precise date.

After several long minutes, I asked him the question: In the end, how did they choose the execution date for the Jews in Bousk?

Calmly, without batting an eye, he answered, "They were proposing something in the next two weeks; the local Gestapo chose the day that was most convenient."

That was it. Simply stated, but horrific in its banality. For the first time, here before me stood a neighbor who had witnessed the selection of the murder date: part of the 10 percent that had been nagging at me for years. For so long, I had asked myself who chose the day of the executions. At Bousk, the local Gestapo administration had settled it. This fact didn't resolve everything, but it did undermine the myth that all was decided from on high.

The 10 percent sometimes defies research, like a stone polished beneath the stream of time, to which nothing can attach. It remains elusive, even after years in the archives and many miles traveled through village after village, all in a quest for the missing piece.

For example, I try to understand who coordinated the labor in the field or clearing that would become the crime scene. This is not an idle question. Every villager I have met remembers with precision the length, width, and depth of the common graves. In other words, the measurements of the killing machine adapted to the number of bodies of its Jewish victims. But who calculates the cubic volume of the dead? Who coldly does the math to find the correct amount of space for the number of living Jews on the verge of being murdered? This question gnaws at me because time and again we discover that the size of the grave was quite accurate. There was someone in the shadows, every day, pencil in hand, calculating the volume of the hole to dig. This person intrigues me.

What determines the size of the graves and their shape? In short, who are the architects and the master builders of the common graves in the villages?

We don't lack for testimony by neighbors of the diggers and the diggers themselves. Some, from their farmyards in the early morning hours, saw their neighbors leaving the village shouldering shovels. Others, children at the time, questioned their fathers when they returned home in the evening, tired from digging all day. Some actually dug. Sometimes they dug several graves. Most of them, all these years later, can remember the dimensions of the graves with precision. Very few, however, mention the presence of an overseer.

These absences, these gaps in memory, when they recur in a number of witnesses, often point to a significant enigma. Recurring silences tend to suggest a very real "unknown," something nobody wants to remember.

As far as I know, only four diggers have addressed the issue of the grave planning with any clarity. The first, Stepan, questioned on April 5, 2007, near Kamen-Kashyrskyi in Volhynia, Ukraine, remembers a German who paced out the perimeter of the gravesite. Our exchange took place in his house, out of the cold:

"The police came to my house and told me to go dig in that place. They gathered us together, about twenty of us, took us there, and gave us the dimensions they wanted. There were Germans and there were police. It was the Germans who showed us what we had to do. . . . They put posts at the corners of the grave we were supposed to dig. It was a place where pine trees grew that we used in construction. They placed pieces of this wood at the corners. They had an interpreter who translated for us what we were to do."

"Did they measure with their steps or with a measuring stick?"

"They measured with steps . . . There must have been five or six of them."

"Did they come by car?"

"Of course. First, the police took us there and then the Germans arrived. The police supervised us while we dug until we were done. . . . The Germans came to show us what to do and then left. But the police stayed."

For the first time, I was getting the profile of a person, or rather several. A German, or rather several German surveyors, showing up in a car. Givers of orders. Accompanied by an interpreter who was anonymous but nonetheless came from the local police, the *polizei*,[2] as they call them there, who stood watch over the diggers and made sure the work was done.

Rarely asked questions are the ones that don't get answered. On that day, I had dared to ask some new questions. And I was rewarded with some sibylline answers. It was as though the witness did not want to remember.

A year later, another digger, Oleg, who was also Ukrainian, seemed to have taken part in a very similar scenario.

January 2, 2008

Oleg: "Of course! A German officer came. He measured the grave out with his paces. I know because I dug it. He had marked it all out. . . . The Germans came from the district of Vyssotsk,[3] and they ordered us to dig the grave. There were twenty of us, maybe more. We were told to bring our shovels."

"How did the Germans measure the grave?"

"They measured it with their steps. He did it himself. He paced it out on the ground and planted stakes to mark the grave."

"So he already knew how big to make the grave before he got there?"

"Yes . . . We worked in tandem, some shoveled the dirt out of the hole and others moved it off to the side . . . with shovels. . . . We had to throw it to either side, since the hole was so deep. They didn't tell us, but we knew it was for the Jews. . . . There were a lot of us, we dug it in one day."

So the "German," as the diggers call him, didn't delegate the marking out of the gravesite to anyone, not to the local police, not to the conscripted labor. It was as if tracing out the grave was too important to the criminal machine to be entrusted to subordinates.

Does this mean that the "German" had the size and volume of the grave in his head before he requisitioned the conscripts? Even before coming to the village in question? I began to think so. We mustn't forget that the grave is not only a tomb but also a killing machine. A number of the Jews would be buried alive there.

Again, in Oleg's account, posts or stakes are planted in the four corners.

January 7, 2009

Iosif, a third digger, in Bibrka, a small town in western Ukraine, remembered that the outline of the grave was drawn with shovel marks in the ground.

"Who gave you the dimensions?"

"The Germans. It was a German from the Gestapo. He stood off to the side while we dug the grave. . . . He had paced it out. The grave was deep: it must have gone down about two meters [six feet]. He simply measured four meters for the length and four meters for the width, and he drew them with his shovel. That's what we dug. It took an hour to an hour and a half. It was easy to dig because it was a sand quarry. It's about a kilometer [about half a mile] from here, near the brickyard."

"The German," as the three diggers call him, appears to be a giver of orders, more a surveyor than an architect.

We don't always know what it is we're unaware of. If Denis Peschanski is right about the Smiley method, I have to keep looking and looking.

The 10 percent will surely never be completely resolved, and this stimulates our appetite to investigate, in the archives as well as in the villages. The unknown 10 percent, so resistant to discovery, drives my search.

The villagers' description of the giver of orders allows us to do little more than sketch a profile; yet the sketch is enough to confirm that such a person existed. He existed, and the local police followed his orders.

Why, then, do the diggers and their neighbors say so little? I see only one possible reason. Maybe, when they recall the German, the diggers can't forget that they knew the terrible secret before the rest of the village: in the spot where they were digging by order of the German, the Jews, their neighbors who were locked up behind ghetto walls, would soon be murdered. A German doesn't come to a Russo-Soviet village to order the digging of a potato silo!

When an act performed by a "requisitioned worker" is described as though "automated," habitual, without a foreign giver of orders, it seems devoid of any responsibility.

Of course, the diggers dig and the fillers fill. But the rare accounts that do describe the presence of the German architect give back a certain autonomy to the conscripts; the surveyor shows, explains, outlines the dimensions of the grave—but, without the skill of local labor, it would never be ready on time. The diggers are not mere labor. They are not simply living excavators. At the base of the hierarchy in the Shoah by bullets, everything is done by hand, everything is human.

The archives themselves say little about the German who comes out of nowhere to sketch with his steps the perimeter of a genocidal crime. However, Andrej Umansky, a researcher at Yahad from its earliest days, did find, in the German Federal Archives in Ludwigsburg,[4] the transcript of a deposition that sheds some light on this enigma.

A certain Friedrich L., in 1964, twenty-three years after the fact, tells this story. He was forty-three years old when he was sent to the East.[5]

"I was the chief of the municipal police in the *Gemeindeschutzpolizei*[6] in Liegnitz.[7] At the end of the autumn of 1941, I was sent East." He became the chief of the police in the small town of Voronovo[8] on the Lithuanian border, with numerous local auxiliary police under his command. "From the beginning of 1942, I had between seventy and eighty-nine *Schutzmannschaften*[9] from the local population in my precinct. . . .These *Hiwis*,[10] as the volunteers were called, were dressed in old black SS uniforms with brown collars and rolled-up sleeves. . . .We got our orders from the regional chief of police from the town of Lida."[11]

To the question of who took part in the mass executions, he answered, without apparent discomfort, "When I am asked if I participated in mass shootings or individual executions in Voronovo, I affirm it. One night in May 1942, the Voronovo police headquarters hosted a meeting in my offices. At about ten o'clock, I got a phone call from the police bureau in Lida."

I'm always astonished by the ease with which killers can recount having participated in murders.

I've read many depositions, but Friedrich's held my attention because he explains in concrete detail how he had the grave dug. The measurements were transmitted to him over the phone; his only responsibility, it seems, was to select the site for the murder.

"I got the order to have a large hole, eighty meters [ninety yards] long, four meters [thirteen feet] wide, and three meters [ten feet] deep, dug before six in the morning. The location was my choice. With the help of the chief of the Voronovo *rayon*,[12] I sent messengers to neighboring villages to conscript the Poles, 'every last one.' Very quickly, between sixty and eighty Poles showed up with their tools, and I had to send some home because there were too many."

The search for the site is described in banal terms, as though he were choosing a spot for a picnic.

"So I went out to look for an execution site, and I chose a place eight hundred meters [half a mile] south of Voronovo, to the left of the highway that goes to Lida. It was an old Russian shooting range about thirty meters [thirty yards] from the road. The grave was done in time, as ordered."

His explanation is terribly simple; he is given two hours before the victims are to be transported to the grave. He chooses the spot, a

Russian shooting range, as if it were simply a matter of common sense. The labor itself is conscripted at the last minute.

Around eight o'clock in the morning, about a hundred German policemen, a squadron of fifteen Latvians under the direction of a Lithuanian *Oberleutnant*,[13] and ten to twelve SD[14] men arrive. This is the beginning of the massacre.

Surprisingly, according to Friedrich's testimony, although he didn't have to go back to the grave he had had dug, he ended up admitting, with some hesitation, that he hadn't been able to resist the urge to return after the shootings, "to shovel."

"I wasn't sent to the execution site. But around twelve, I was given the order to go and fill in the grave. No, I'm contradicting myself. I wasn't given any order. I went of my own volition. After having dug the grave, it felt like the next step. At the edge of the grave I saw a mound of clothes, from which I deduced the Jews had been forced to undress. There was also lime the commandos had brought. The grave was two thirds full. Three thousand Jews, I believe, were killed."

Thus, the common grave was his personal project.

Friedrich's deposition, though a rare find, still doesn't completely deliver what I am after. In the town of Voronovo, Friedrich is ultimately still just a supervisor.

The architect, the one who calculated the measurements, the one who telephoned at ten at night, the one who gave the dimensions of a hole that could swallow up three thousand people, didn't come in person, it seems. He simply telephoned from Lida.

Does this mean the size of the grave was calculated, then ordered from a distance, from an office? But how does the architect know from a distance the number of Jews to be killed?

The German that Stepan and Oleg saw arriving at dawn to sketch the perimeter of the grave was most likely another intermediary, one who chose the site of the crime. But, if that was the case, who was the architect?

Chapter 2

THE REQUISITIONS

NewYork City, July 4, 2012, Independence Day

The streets are swarming with tourists, rushing, despite the city's crushing heat, to hit the holiday sales. The New Yorkers themselves are apparently seeking cooler weather out of town. An absence of cars in the streets gives Manhattan a certain weightlessness. The metal shutters of many stores remain rolled down and locked. Nonchalant pedestrians drift across the avenues with little caution.

How, in my lectures in the United States, in modern American culture, will I be able to communicate the reality of the Soviet requisition and the truth of who was requisitioned in the occupied territories? Today, many of the young Americans I meet barely know what a kolkhoz or a sovkhoz[1] was. So how to explain?

I decided to reread and watch again interviews of two villagers who were requisitioned: two men who could not have been more different. The first was Ivan, a living memory riveted to a body. During the war, he performed the gravest acts. The second was Gregory, whose family saved several Jews and received recognition from the State of Israel as Righteous Among the Nations.

When I give a presentation in a university or community here in the United States, the same question arises quickly and frequently:

THE REQUISITIONS

"Weren't the 'requisitioned' collaborators?" It's not so simple to explain that requisition was part of daily life in Soviet villages and that people were not given a say in the matter.

Ivan. I revisit an interview conducted by Alexy Kosarevskyi, a Ukrainian member of the Yahad team, in Volhynia, on May 1, 2012. Alexy warned me: This witness is totally unique, he speaks without taboos, and he acted during the war with virtually no scruples. Moreover, he was requisitioned many times on the days of shootings. I decided to follow Ivan in his account in full consciousness of his lack of moral restraint.

Ivan has a distinctive appearance. His thick white mustache gives him the air of an artist, and he wears big Soviet glasses that are round and very thick.

Even though the interview was conducted in his own house, he never took off his large hat, which he kept pulled down quite far over his head.

The interview took a long time. The video was interminable, the transcript twenty-eight pages long. It took place in the small town of Ozeriany, not far from the city of Kovel in northwest Ukraine. I listen. I watch. I talk to Alexy. It's nauseating.

It's nauseating because Ivan, a Ukrainian born in 1927, had a hand in everything—from the construction of the ghettos where the Jews of his village were confined to the decontamination of their common grave in the aftermath of the murder.

It's nauseating because, according to Ivan's account, there was no possibility of escape. He presents the story of the shootings and of his own participation in them in minute detail. He captures them the way the stop-motion photography of Étienne-Jules Marey captured the movements of a galloping horse. Ivan was subject to many requisitions throughout the process of the extermination of the Jews in his town. He gives the precise names of the materials used, describing the acts performed with a simplicity and a roughness so basic and without veneer that he projects you into the materiality of events sixty years in the past. This is all the more surprising in that, at the time, Ivan was just fourteen.

"Requisitioned." This term beats like a metronome throughout Ivan's long deposition. Who is Ivan? He is among the many requisitioned people whom we have questioned in Russia, Belarus, Moldavia, Poland, Romania, and Ukraine. But what are we talking about when we use the word "requisition"? What does it mean to be requisitioned on the day of the shooting of one's Jewish neighbors? What does it mean coming from the mouth of a young Soviet peasant who lived under the German Fascist occupation?

Requisitioning is very often one of the hidden faces of the military occupation of a country. In France, we well know that houses, apartments, and town halls were requisitioned to house German military and police. But property was not the only thing requisitioned. People were, too. Bus drivers were requisitioned to transport Jews on the days they were rounded up and also to drive them to an internment camp in the south of France or toward the Drancy transit camp.

Requisition wasn't solely the prerogative of the Germans; the Communist underground in Bresse commandeered our barns. Food, especially flour, was frequently requisitioned by the Resistance. We were of course on the side of the Resistance, but perhaps not to the extent of giving them all our flour! A person whose home or goods have been requisitioned sees himself as dispossessed of the right to make everyday decisions. His life is a series of struggles and attempts to diminish the diverse pressures exerted by the occupation as well as by the Resistance.

Requisitioning could also arise when the local administration placed refugees fleeing the bombardment near the front lines in one's home. This happened to my family. We housed Alsatians. I remember them coming off the train, when it was still functioning in those days, at the tiny station of Villegaudin at a spot called "Les Quatre

Chemins," the four roads. My whole family recalls that among them were nuns wearing cornettes.

Requisitioning during an occupation often affects the daily lives of common people. It is a forced cohabitation, a breach of the sanctity of one's home.

Having grown up with my own often-told family stories about requisitioning, I wasn't very surprised, upon visiting Ukrainian farms for the first time, to hear our translator Svetlana tell me in French what the peasants were recounting. They had experienced multiple requisitions, not only from German units but also from the local administrations. However, the Soviet requisitions were different from the ones I knew about. In France, we are used to a unified, centralized administrative system. Every commune has its mayor, its municipal government, its rural guards. Each French department has its prefect, its police, its police stations. From one village to the next, the structures and nomenclature are virtually the same.

As French people, we tend to project similar structures onto other countries and take centralization for granted, especially in authoritarian regimes. But in the immense rural territory of the former Soviet Union, there was no single system.

When the peasants first told me about a *staroste*[2] installed by the Germans during the occupation of Rawa Ruska, I immediately imagined that this person must be the equivalent of a mayor. Other farmers recalled not a *staroste* but a *soltous*,[3] also put in power by the Germans.

Most of the people who were requisitioned told us they had been under the orders of either a *staroste* or a *soltous*. However, as I began asking more pointed questions—"Was it really the *staroste* who came in person to knock on your door on the morning of the requisition?"—some of the villagers answered, no, it was the *desiatnik*.[4]

I consulted the people working with me who spoke fluent Russian and Ukrainian and were familiar with rural Soviet political structures.

They told me that a *desiatnik* was a figure dating back to the seventeenth century who traditionally obeyed the *staroste*; his name derived from the number ten, *desiat*. There was a *desiatnik* for approximately every ten households. The structure came into focus: the Germans put *starostes*, sometimes called *soltous*, in power. Beneath them were the *desiatniks*, sometimes also called the *dejourny*.

Our investigations and interviews continued from village to village, from region to region, and from country to country. The deeper we went, the more opaque and less heterogeneous the situation seemed. In a single district comprising several villages to this day, half of the inhabitants well recalled a *staroste* and one of these infamous *desiatniks*. The latter was often a neighbor, an older man put in charge of carrying out the requisitioning of milk, eggs, and meat, in the name of the *staroste*.

Yet in the next village, when I asked, "In your village, during the war, were there *desiatniks*?," the farmer would show with a shake of her head that she had never heard of such a person, before, during, or after the war.

"So who requisitioned you then?" I asked.

"The police, the *polizei*, the Germans, the *staroste*."

After having interviewed more than 3,800 witnesses, we met in Paris, at Yahad headquarters, to reflect. Given witnesses who did not at all remember the same administrative structures from during the war, how were we to understand what actually happened? It became clear that we needed historians to answer the following questions: In 1941, when German units took over in Ukraine, Belarus, and Russia, what kind of rural governments were in place? How did the Germans structure the administration of the occupied villages?

The questions were crucial. In each account of an execution or the construction of a ghetto, the witness is only able to refer to local authorities. So we decided to organize a forum in Paris in which to reflect on this issue. We invited several historians, some of whom specialized in the Nazi occupation. We also invited scholars of the history of the Soviet Union, tsarist Russia, and its neighboring countries.

THE REQUISITIONS

Our goal was to answer the following questions: Who was in power in the typical Soviet village when the Germans arrived in 1941? Who did the Germans find at the administrative level? Who did they then put in charge? And who was installed in their place once the Soviet Union took back command?

Who came to get the peasants to dig the ditches? Who gave the recruitment order at the town hall? Who knocked on the peasants' doors? Was this kind of requisition a German creation or a continuation of a Soviet tradition? Was it a rupture or not?

I understood that any discussion of the requisition directly raised two questions: that of the public nature of the executions and that of the participation, voluntary or forced, of the peasants. Those requisitioned were the crimes' first spectators, not only passively, but also through their actions; without the requisition, there would have been no helping hands in the villages on the days of the shootings, no shovels, no wheels, no wagons. The availability of labor and materials allowed the Germans to appear suddenly at dawn with their convoys of military vehicles and guns and to leave again the same evening for their base.

The requisition of villagers is the hidden face of the *Einsatzgruppen*, the special German mobile units. The Germans could be so mobile thanks to an immobile local population that was always there to do their dirty work.

As the Germans took over the Soviet territories, they put in place their own men in the town halls almost systematically. These German municipal authorities were usually called *staroste*, which in Russian can mean both "elder" and "he who will govern the group." The *staroste* became the point person on the lowest rung of the administrative ladder, charged with relaying the orders of the occupying power. His role was tragically crucial on the day of the execution of the Jews, his mission being to find and furnish "the help."

It was an old Soviet, Andreï, originally from Rokytne in the Rivne region of Ukraine, who gave me the clearest explanation of the work of the *staroste*, his staff, and the *desiatniks*. The interview was conducted by Alexy.

I can still see Andreï, corpulent in an armchair and proudly wearing a dark green jacket covered in Soviet medals.

"In this village I'm telling you about, the *staroste* was named by the Germans. Then the *staroste* appointed the *desiatniks* to go to people's houses to collect a sort of tax. The *desiatniks* didn't have any power. They received orders, which they then transmitted to the population: what had to be given, where, when. . . . As for me, I was asked to provide meat for the front. 'Organize a requisition of meat. Make sure people bring us their livestock as well as their reserves.' So, having done what we were told, we were able to go back to the *desiatniks*, and we said to them: 'We went to every house asking: what livestock do you have? How many head? How many could you give for the army?' With our help, the *desiatniks* were able to collect the livestock, thirty-six head in all. . . . I remember that everyone knew they were *desiatniks*. They didn't have a chief; they were under the command of the *starostes*. The *staroste* was in charge of the entire village, whereas the *desiatniks* worked only in small neighborhoods, usually the ones in which they themselves lived. Each had a specific number of villagers for which they were responsible. The *staroste* called the *desiatniks*. . . . There was also a staff that went to get the *desiatniks*. This staff was made up of villagers called for service on any particular day. One day, it was the turn of two people, the next day, two different people."

Andreï thus broke the local administration down into three categories: the *staroste*, the rotating staff of villagers, and the *desiatniks*, who carried out orders on a street or neighborhood level. To these we must add the *polizei*, an omnipresent auxiliary militia, present even in the smallest villages. Clearly, in the collective memory, the municipal administration is perceived as a potential requisitioning force at any moment: of food, clothes, wagons, and also labor.

During his interview, Andreï recounted the imprisonment and execution of the Jews through the lens of his own requisitions. It was full of surprises. As he began describing how the ghetto was constructed, he suddenly revealed that he had personally helped to build it. This was not the first time I noticed a witness begin generally, "The men in the village were requisitioned . . .," only to slip unconsciously into the first person, "I."

"The ghetto was surrounded by dense barbed wire. There was about twenty centimeters [eight inches] between the wires. The size of the ghetto was fairly large; I'd say, twenty-five to thirty meters [eighty to a hundred feet] long. The barbed wire formed a wall about three meters [ten feet] high."

Seventy years after the events in question, his memory of the dimensions of the village ghetto was intact. The length, the width, the position of the gate. The same was generally true for the ditches.

"Who enclosed the area around the warehouse with barbed wire?"

"It was the villagers. The men of the village were requisitioned to install the barbed wire."

We could have left it there and gone on to discuss ghetto life. But Alexy, who was experienced in these types of interviews, knew that in 1942 there was no enterprise in the village that made wooden barriers or installed barbed wire. All this work had to be done by hand, by the villagers themselves, by men and women requisitioned by the town for collective work. So, Alexy asked the question: "Who requisitioned them?"

"The *Golova*[5] got them together and told them what they had to do. There were at least a dozen villagers who worked on building that enclosure. They planted posts every five meters and then they put in the barbed wire."

Alexy persisted, the way you might continue to push a door that is stuck half-open. "Was anyone in your family requisitioned to install barbed wire?"

Finally, Andreï admitted that he himself helped to build the ghetto walls of his village. He was quite embarrassed by his answer. "Yes, me, I may have done it. Our *Golova* was really violent. He said his blood was eighty-five percent German and he beat people to make them obey. He came along with the *polizei* and he beat me."

"Did he show you how to plant the posts and what area to fence off?"

"Yes, he told us we had to put posts in the ground, and he showed us where they should be using tree branches."

To my knowledge, this was the first time a witness not only described how the barricades and the barbed wire were put up around the ghetto but also admitted that he helped build them with his own two hands. His story continued, becoming more and more precise.

"We cut the trees down in the forest behind the village and we made the poles."

"Who gave you the barbed wire?"

"The Germans came by car and brought enormous rolls of barbed wire. Two men would take a roll of wire on a stick and unroll it. They were enormous, around fifty kilos [one hundred and ten pounds], hard to carry even when there were two of us. I think we used six big rolls. I remember that some villagers stole one to build a fence. They spent three days looking for it, and finally they found it, hidden in the valley."

"How did you put up the barbed wire?"

"We unrolled it and nailed it to each post. We had rubber gloves to protect our hands, and we unrolled the wire a little at a time."

"Was it the Germans who provided you with the rubber gloves?"

"Yes. They brought a big bag of gloves and we could take what we needed. The rest of the equipment, like the hammers and the pliers, we brought."

In rereading Andreï's deposition, I caught my breath. They had built the enclosure for the Jewish ghetto exactly the way my family used to build holding pens for cows on the farm of my childhood. These were actions I myself had seen performed many times.

I can still see my grandfather Émile, a forester, and his son Jacky, my godfather, going into the forest in search of young trees whose trunks were not yet too thick. We cut them down with axes and removed the bark. The fresh sap smelled good. We sawed the trunks to get them all to the same height. Then, still in the middle of the forest, we lifted them into our cart harnessed to one of our mares. We sank our posts equidistant from one another with a sledgehammer that resonated with the blows, a sledgehammer we had made ourselves, with a tulip-wood handle.

Andreï was fifteen when he was requisitioned along with the other young men of his village; he performed the same tasks I once performed. Only in my case, it was in order to build a pen for cows, horses, or sheep; in his, to enclose his Jewish neighbors.

How many witnesses, women and men, neglected to describe these barbed-wire fences surrounding the houses in the ghetto? Up till now, I had never understood that the barbed wire of certain ghettos was attached to fresh wooden posts, cut hurriedly by the village youth.

In 1942, in Soviet villages, the fences around stables were not made with barbed wire. Everything was built by hand, often with finely interlaced twigs forming a sort of trellis between posts. Since Andreï's village wasn't very far from the town of Kovel, the Germans had the rolls of barbed wire transported from Kovel by truck. The barbed wire was the only material imported from the city for the purpose of imprisoning the Jews.

No, that's not right. The Germans also furnished gloves.

Rubber gloves . . . The Germans brought boxes of rubber gloves so the local peasants installing barbed wire in the ghettos wouldn't cut their hands. To this day, such a detail still sounds wrong in these tiny villages. It's hard for me to believe the Germans were sensitive to the working conditions of requisitioned villagers. I would be more inclined to believe that their concern was one of efficiency. A wounded villager slows the job down.

As I listened to Andreï's words, I thought, *How many hammers, pliers, and posts fashioned hastily in the forest did it take to build all those thousands of ghettos in Soviet villages? How many hands put up barriers of death*

*wrapped with how many bales of German barbed wire? How many boxes of
rubber gloves were circulated?*

Andreï was the first to describe what happened simply, without
narrative detour. I now understand better how hard it was for him
to say what he had done. Harder than admitting to digging a ditch.
Because when you dig a ditch, you can always tell yourself the hole
has some other purpose: to stockpile corn, potatoes, or cabbage. But
when you put up barbed wire around the houses of your Jewish
neighbors, there is no room for doubt. The wire is going to shut in
human beings, neighbors no less.

He continued to speak at length, unperturbed. Sometimes he
pushed the limits of decency. And then suddenly, he wasn't talking
about the requisition anymore. He was unveiling his personal initiative, his own responsibility, in the crime against the Jews.

He told of how he had gone to barter in the vicinity of the ghetto.
One day, while he was loitering just outside the barbed wire, an old
Jewish neighbor called out to him, "Give me some bread!"

To his starving neighbor Andreï replied, "If you give me your
watch, I'll give you bread."

"I brought him bread in exchange for his watch."

I had often heard of bartering between villagers and Jews shut in
the ghetto, but never of such a trade!

Today, Andreï calmly recounted the transaction, seemingly devoid
of all compassion or feeling. He related everything in the same tone,
from the imprisoning of the Jews in the ghetto up till their mass murder by shooting. It brought to mind a statement made by Abraham
Foxman, president of the Anti-Defamation League, as he was award-
ing me a prize in New York in 2008: "I would ask Patrick Desbois to
suspend his moral judgment so that we can collect the greatest possible amount of proof of the shootings of the Jews by the *Einsatzgruppen*." Listening to Andreï, I felt the full weight of Abraham Foxman's
words on my shoulders.

Andreï continued with anecdotes that revealed the utter violence to which he had been both witness and accomplice. He spoke of his neighbors the way we speak of animals: "There was a rich Jewish merchant who owned several businesses. He said, 'Why are you taking me to the ghetto? Kill me here!' So, they killed him along with his family: his wife, his brother, and his sister-in-law. They took the bodies to the Jewish cemetery where they threw them in a ditch. I saw all this. I was right there. The police let us watch."

Andreï is truly the worst sort of eyewitness.

Alexy conducted the interview calmly, opening one door after another, careful not to reveal his own feelings.

"So, these Jews were killed right before the others were locked up in the ghetto?"

"Yes. All their goods were pillaged by the villagers. They had horses, cows, sewing machines. People took everything."

The imprisoning of Jews in the ghetto of Rokytne went hand in hand with their neighbors' looting of their houses. This sort of thing wasn't rare. To have it told so baldly, now that was unusual.

"The Jews said to us, 'The dark days have come,' but we already knew this. If they were being locked up in the ghetto, it was so they could be exterminated. We guessed what was going to happen. . . . The police who saw us bartering with them said nothing. . . . Half the village came to barter."

The neighbors in this village of Rokytne weren't merely spectators; Andreï wasn't simply a docile, submissive conscript. Everyone felt authorized to commit violence, to steal, and to loot. He was no exception.

"Did the villagers also take furniture?"

"Yes, each took what he needed. People came with wagons and loaded them up with furniture. Sometimes, they even took the doors."

Pillaging—or, more precisely, the carving up of Jewish households—happened not just publicly but as a collective act by the people of the village. You can't load a horse-drawn wagon up with furniture in a small town without everyone being aware of it. The phrase resonated in my head: *Half the village came to barter.*

"People from the surrounding area came too. Some Jews hid in houses. Once, I went into a house and climbed up into the attic. A Jew was hiding there. When he saw me, he attacked me with a knife, and I escaped. As I was running out in the street, I bumped into a *polizei*. He asked me why I was running, and I told him that a Jew had tried to kill me. The *polizei* found him and shot him."

In France, we feel the weight of the thousands of denunciation letters that landed in the offices of the French police during the German occupation. These thousands of pages, written and mailed, were thousands of hands personally aiding in genocide from the shadows. Andreï denounced a Jew in broad daylight in the middle of the street. He discovered this man because he was searching Jewish homes one after the other at the very moment that the column of Jews was being marched toward the ditches where they would die. The pillagers were escorting the killers.

"Did you go into several houses to see what was inside?"

"Yes, we did the rounds of the village."

"So, during the three days that the Jews were shut up in the ghetto, the villagers emptied their houses?"

"Yes, people took everything. . . . I didn't follow the column to the ditches. I saw them leave, and I went into the houses. I thought I might find a watch, a knife, or some other useful object. . . . I went with a few other boys. And then we joined up with the Jews."

Without wasting any time, Andreï looked for whatever he could scrounge from the Jewish houses, then ran to join the column.

Seventy years after the fact, Andreï's conscience seemed to feel nothing beyond the collective abandon that was authorized on the day of the shootings. The collective act seems to have abolished any sense of personal guilt.

While he may have been conscripted by force to build the ghetto, he himself was responsible for trading a piece of bread for a watch. And no one forced him to raid Jewish homes with his friends, while the Jews themselves were being marched to their death in a common grave.

The appetite for gain is rarely so explicit in the testimony of a witness to genocide. We will never know the principal motivation for these criminal acts: the desire to steal the possessions of the dead? The profound anti-Semitism that poisoned the air? Dire poverty? Authorization by the "forces of order"?

Andreï described the shootings with the same coldness and the same striking indifference that he showed his Jewish neighbors as they were killed before his eyes. However, when it came to the German shooter, whom he did not know, Andreï watched him closely and retained a very detailed memory of him. He recalls the way his uniform stayed clean, the strain and fatigue on his fingers as he was firing, his need to eat and take a break. For Andreï, the Jews stopped existing, were already dead. The hero, the one who was fascinatingly alive, was the killer.

It should be noted that in this village a single German, in one long afternoon, killed more than seven hundred Jews!

"The German shot them in the head. Sometimes in the forehead, sometimes in the neck. He didn't aim too carefully. . . . He shot from very close, about a meter away from the Jews; just far enough to avoid the blood splatter. . . . He had cases full of bullets in the truck. . . . When the shooting was over, the truck drove to the edge of the ditch to collect the clothes."

"Did someone load his gun for him?"

"No, he had the full magazines in his pockets. Each magazine held seventy-one bullets. The German loaded them as he went. . . . First the Jews stood on one side, and then when there was no more room, the German switched sides. This way, the bodies fell from both sides, headfirst. There were also babies in their mothers' arms. The German

37

shot the baby and the mother. We were right next to him. We saw everything."

Andreï couldn't recall any one Jew in particular, not one face, not one name. For him on this day the Jews were not neighbors. They weren't even human. They were simply "Jews."

However, he hadn't forgotten that the shooter, tired out from working all alone and hungry, asked for some buttermilk. The shooter murdered the Jews because they were Jews and then paid the local farmer for his milk because the non-Jew remained human. Andreï's intact memory of the killer brings fully to light the fracture in humanity that is genocide.

"He stopped to drink some buttermilk, and he paid the man who gave him the milk. There were women and men from the village by the ditch. He said he wanted buttermilk. About fifteen meters away lived some people who brought him the milk. He was thirsty because he'd been shooting so long without a break. He drank a whole bottle in one gulp, then he took two deutsche marks from his pocket to pay the villager."

"While the people were gone getting him the milk, did he continue shooting?"

"No, he waited. He was exhausted. He had already killed half the Jews in the column. It was very hot and he was thirsty. He drank the milk, and then the shooting started up again."

I lower my eyes. My parents, in Chalon-sur-Saône, sold fresh milk and also buttermilk. I myself sold a lot of it. I know from the inside what Ivan describes. I know that to drink buttermilk in high summer quenches thirst. With all my strength, I want to resist the horrors described by Andreï, especially since they are woven with simple, shared, human acts, acts that have been my own.

Andreï has not one word for the hundreds of Jews awaiting their death while others lie in the ditch. The shooter drinks buttermilk.

What is tragically clear is that Andreï only feels empathy, understanding, admiration, and human fraternity with the German killer, the murderer.

It is a true challenge for us to meet someone like Andreï. We want to understand what happened and to be able to picture the scene of the crime. But at what cost? It is very tempting to show signs of outrage, to exclaim, "You are a racist and an anti-Semite!"

Without a doubt, this was true. And perhaps it should have been said. But we chose not to show our emotions in order to know more. So that tomorrow young people from all nations, hearing these accounts, would understand how the human genocide machine was built from town to town, from village to village, partially from the consciousness of certain neighbors.

Andreï recalled that the shooter didn't wear gloves. He worried about the shooter's hands just as the Germans seemed to worry about the hands of the peasants who were laying barbed wire.

"No, it's just not practical to shoot with gloves. He didn't have a smock or an apron either. He was wearing a uniform . . . with a chevron in the form of a skull on his left arm. It was so hot that people were mostly wearing light, short-sleeved shirts. They started around noon and the shooting lasted until evening. There were one hundred and eighty people. The German had pressed down so many times on the trigger that his fingers hurt. . . . The only break he took was to drink that milk. In the evening, he climbed into the truck and went back to Kovel. . . . I couldn't help but notice he had a really good car. All you had to do to start it was to push a button. To start our cars, we had to turn a crank. By five in the afternoon, it was over."

Listening to Andreï, one might be forgiven for forgetting the fact that the German's work consisted of systematically killing hundreds of people.

He did however relate one instance of revolt by the last of the Jews; a refusal to obey that was punished with horrific violence. Here again, he speaks without restraint.

"He had chosen five Jews to fill in the ditch with dirt, but they refused. So the German caught one of the Jews with a spade and tore open his stomach. His guts spilled out and the other Jews tried to stuff them back inside. . . . Then he shot them."

"So who filled in the ditch?"

Suddenly, Andreï was ill at ease. After this litany of horrors recounted in the coldest of terms, he was forced to admit that he himself was one of the ditch fillers.

"They requisitioned the people from the neighboring villages to fill in the ditch. It was a bloodbath; the smell was unbearable. . . . I also filled in the ditch. . . . I would throw in some dirt and the blood would soak through it. The odor was nauseating; I fell to the ground. So the German came to give me a cigarette. But the tobacco was so strong that I fell again, so the German sent me away. I took my shovel and left."

The German took pity on Andreï and freed him from his work. Andreï recalled the killer as capable of compassion for a young man who couldn't stand so much blood. Andreï seemed to have memorized everything about this man, his words, his gestures, the way he ate and dressed. Even the way he started his car. The German remained indelibly in Andreï's memory as the only real person at the scene of the crime.

A man requisitioned for a task remains a responsible human being; he can sometimes choose between better or worse, even while forced to perform certain acts. Some, like Andreï, extorted goods from starving Jews, combed through their empty houses, denounced those in hiding. Still, many Germans, on trial after the war, never stopped repeating, "We were just obeying orders."

The conscripted population was at the bottom of the genocidal ladder and probably the most constrained. However, Andreï's testimony is that of a man responsible for many of his actions. The claim of total constraint appears to me to be camouflage. The fact that he was obeying orders does not erase his complicity.

THE REQUISITIONS

To illustrate my point, I would turn to the story of another requisitioned man, a certain Gregory. Gregory was interviewed by Andrej in August 2012. He lived in Transnistria, a region that was occupied by the Romanians. Today, Transnistria is Ukrainian and is one of the most rural parts in the whole country; its roads are often difficult to navigate.

Months after the interview, Andrej was still moved by the thought of Gregory. Gregory had been requisitioned to transport Jews who arrived by train from Odessa at the station in Berezovka, a small town in the north country. The interview took place during a heat wave. The night before, on August 2, Andrej had interviewed a Jewish survivor whose mother had thrust her into the arms of a Ukrainian woman when she emerged from the same train at Berezovka. An exhausted mother had saved her daughter, who was raised by a Ukrainian family as one of their own. An investigation like ours is made up of historical research, of course, but also of encounters that touch the depths of the soul.

In January 1942, Gregory had to go to the station in Berezovka in order to transport the Jews by sled. His story is very different from Andreï's. First of all, he recalled the bitter cold and the poor state of the people disembarking from the freight car at the station:

"The winter was brutal. It was minus thirty-five degrees [minus thirty-one degrees Fahrenheit]. A *polizei* came to our house and told me to . . . go to the Berezovka station. When I asked what I was supposed do there, the *polizei* answered that I would receive my orders on arrival. In total, they requisitioned twelve people from my village; there were twelve sleds between us. It was snowing hard. . . . We arrived at the station at around ten in the morning. We asked the police there what we were supposed to do. They answered that we should wait. . . . We were at the station and we were waiting for the train to arrive. . . . We saw exhausted people sitting in freight cars that were normally used for transporting coal. They looked worn out and frozen. There were women, children, and old people. . . . They were dirty from the coal dust in the wagons, and the police told them they would be taken to the baths. They brought them to the hose that they used to fill the locomotive and they turned the water on. It was minus thirty-five degrees. Some people froze on the spot."

For Gregory, the people getting off that train are not "Jews," but women, children, and elderly people who were being mistreated before his eyes. As he attempted to describe the people he had to drive through the cold, his eyes sparkled with emotion.

"Then they told us to load as many people as we could fit onto our sleds. On my sled, there were twelve people: two men, one boy, and nine women. The people we carried were the weakest. The others had to walk to the village. On the way, I saw people frozen to death on the other sleds. Because they'd been forced to rinse off in cold water at the station, in negative thirty-five-degree temperatures, a lot of them died from the cold along the way. It was horrible. I saw frozen corpses falling from the sleds on the way there."

Gregory's kolkhoz was called Kondrachov. The women in the village had also been requisitioned. They were given the job of building an enclosure. "During this time, the *polizei* requisitioned the women to cut down trees in the forest in order to make posts. Then they had to surround the stables with the posts. The stables were empty because the Germans had already stolen all of our livestock."

Gregory's family decided to take the twelve people on his sled back to his farm.

"These people were exhausted. It was so cold that I took pity on them. So I decided we would lodge the twelve people who were on my sled. I brought them home with their suitcases. I asked my mother to welcome them and to light the stove to warm them up. They stayed in our home to sleep. My mother cooked them potatoes and *mamalyga*.[6] All night long, the villagers worked outside. First, they surrounded the stables, then the entire village, in barbed wire; they created a ghetto. This way, the Jews could move around within the confines of the village, but they couldn't get out."

Listening to his testimony, I thought: a requisitioned man who took the initiative to shelter Jews in his home. Between the stories of Andreï and Gregory, there was an abyss—the abyss of human responsibility.

The village was suddenly transformed into a provisional prison for all the Jews living there. Gregory and his family shared their home with those they saved for three months. "There were twelve Jews and we didn't have any beds available. So we brought in hay, and they slept on the hay on the floor. Early one morning, the *polizei* came. They asked the Jews with a certain irony if they were comfortable. The Jews thanked us for our warm welcome."

Like Andreï, Gregory was called up several times by the *polizei*. They came to get him for a second time to transport Jews from Berezovka. "A while later, another train full of Jews arrived, but I refused to go." This surprised me. During our investigations, we have encountered very few villagers who resisted being requisitioned.

"Did other men go in your place?"

"Yes, they took my horses, which belonged to the commune anyway, and they requisitioned other men to go get the Jews at the station. Eventually, the whole district was populated by Jews. . . . Over two or three days they brought almost two thousand Jews here. . . . They came in January and stayed until March."

Gregory witnessed several shootings carried out by the *Volksdeutsche*,[7] who were Soviet citizens of German ancestry. The Jews in his kolkhoz in Transnistria were shot by the *Volksdeutsche* of a neighboring town. "During all this time, on Sundays, the men from the village of Kartakaï,[8] a German colony, went around to the villages; they were the *Volksdeutsche*. They came to the villages where the Jews were being held, and every Sunday, they shot a group of Jews in one of the villages. Every Sunday, they shot around two or three hundred people."

I couldn't help but think, as I listened to this testimony, about the Sunday hunting parties. The role of German citizens in the Shoah remains very poorly known.

"On March 29, 1942, the Romanians came here and surrounded our village. . . . Then the *Volksdeutsche* came in wagons. They told the locals that the Jews were to be taken somewhere else. They had rifles, guns, and a machine gun. Right away, the Jews knew this wasn't about a simple move. They knew they were going to be shot. Not far, there was a clay quarry that was about eight meters [twenty-five feet] deep."

Gregory's family had to say goodbye to their lodgers. "When they came to get them, we said goodbye to the Jews. They had been with us for two months, and we had become friends."

Gregory's mother sent him to see up close what became of their protégés, hoping they might somehow escape.

"We were worried. So my mother told me to go and see if 'our' Jews had been able to escape. We knew that it was practically impossible to escape because the column of Jews was surrounded, but some brave men had gotten away nonetheless. The column of people stopped on a wasteland in front of the quarry. There they had to take off their clothes. Some stayed in their underwear, others were entirely naked. Then they were taken by groups of ten or fifteen toward the quarry."

Andrej pressed on in the interview, sensing that Gregory must have gotten very close to the quarry.

"Did you get closer to see what was happening?"

"No, I stayed a hundred meters from the quarry. I was scared to get too close."

"But you could see that the Jews were getting undressed?"

"Yes. The young children were simply thrown into the quarry. They took them by the feet and threw them to the bottom. Among the Jews, I saw those who had been living in our village. I was pretty far away, and the Jews were undressed so that I couldn't recognize them by their clothes. So I got closer and hid behind a stone wall not far from the quarry."

Gregory ended up admitting his attraction, his desire to see the crime up close.

"There were others watching, but I was the only one who got close. The others stayed back. At the time, I was brave and reckless, so I got up close. I saw the Germans drinking eau-de-vie. They took drinking breaks between shooting. They had planned everything; they had brought a jug full of eau-de-vie on their carts. They would go up to the cart and take turns drinking their alcohol from a tumbler."

Gregory watched the victims as they got undressed, but also the killers; they were neighbors, seeking comfort in alcohol. The killers were not professional criminals, they were neighboring German peasants. These civilians, amateurs, often murdered the Jews with boundless brutality.

Suddenly, almost inadvertently, Gregory began to tell the story of the rescue of two Jewish women. Most people who have saved Jews barely mention it in their interviews.

"Toward evening, the Germans were drunk. Suddenly, I saw two women walking in the direction of the quarry. They were Jewish. When I saw them, I said, 'Run away while the Germans are drunk!' They came toward me and I told them to lie down on the ground. I covered them with leaves and I went to get some clothes because it was still cold in the month of March. . . . I gave them the clothes I found."

"What were these women called?"

"Their names were Lucia and Tania. . . . They were fairly young. They were three or four years older than I was. . . . They were in a state of shock, terrified. They weren't hurt. God spared them. I asked myself where I should take these women. I told them I would go ask Lidia Kondrachova, the mother of my friend who had been lodging them up till now, if she would take them back. It was dangerous. We had been warned that those who hid Jews would be shot along with them. I went to Mrs. Kondrachova, and I told her everything. She really didn't know what to do. Then she asked the advice of her daughter, who told her she should take in the Jews. So I brought these two young women to the Kondrachov family."

Gregory was a boy of fourteen who was probably considered a simple young man capable of odd jobs. Yet, he decided to step forward and save two Jewish women, despite the risk.

Andreï and Gregory, two young Ukrainian men who underwent the same requisitions. Two cogs in the genocidal machine.

And yet, two radically different people.

Can we affirm that belonging to a criminal machine neither negates a person nor absolves him of responsibility? I have come to believe that a requisitioned person can chose to be a killer or a savior. Andreï denounced a Jew in hiding to a *polizei*, knowing full well that the Jew would be shot. Gregory saved two young Jewish women just feet from the grave that was waiting for them.

It can be hard sometimes to perceive the least "important" people, the neighbors, the helping hands, as actually responsible. But they are responsible. For the worst as well as for the best.

Chapter 3

THE DIGGERS

June 29, 2012, Chicago

On the eve of a conference, the sky has suddenly darkened. The cars have put their headlights on and are speeding across the little metal bridges that span the river. It's twelve thirty, and darkness envelops the skyscrapers. A violent storm threatens to break over the city. Unperturbed, air conditioners churn, ignoring the angry sky. The screen of my iPad lights up the laptop on my dark wood desk. The light outside is pale.

The words won't come. My screen is blank.

Something is bothering me, blocking me. I try desperately to write, holding onto the keyboard the way we used to grab our pens in school. Next to me is a thick file: Soviet archives, translations of Ukrainian testimonies enclosed in a red folder. Written across the front in black ink are the words: THE DIGGERS.

Certain types of manual labor that are perceived as grubby are too often substituted for the names and stories of those who perform them. A "grubby" job designates the person who does it as a tool. My own approach to the diggers suffered from this.

When I first listened to Soviet men and women talking about digging the mass graves of the Jews, I thought, *Incredible, this is a digger!* It was as if I'd discovered a new species, a human tool. In my mind, the repugnance of the job was so strong as to forever mark the person who did it, no matter how briefly. It gave them a name. It achieved a sort of branding. In murder cases, it is not uncommon for the media to name the perpetrators after their crimes. Last week, the French headlines were full of stories about "the cutter."

It took me a while to see that the "diggers," despite their repetitive movements, had personal histories, often involving their Jewish neighbors, and that these histories were part of the larger human story of the genocide of the Jews. Without the digging of a grave, there could be no mass shooting.

It might seem difficult, even indecent, to want to know about the people who dug the graves where the bodies of the Jews and Gypsies were thrown. Nonetheless, I chose to tell their stories in the same fashion as those of the people who had been requisitioned.

Not to tell their stories seemed to me a way of getting rid of them and thus forgetting a basic genocidal act. Failure to include them would be to reduce their act to a mechanical task, as though they were nothing more than human excavators, devoid of responsibility.

Why did it take me so long to dare to write this chapter? Perhaps unconsciously, I thought of "diggers" the way we think of gravediggers. They're the people we would prefer not to face as we leave the cemetery in tears. We would rather imagine that gravediggers have no place in our family—indeed, that they have no place in history at all.

In French, a gravedigger, a *croque-mort*—the literal translation is "eater of the dead"—carries associations that are disgusting to our modern sensibilities. We use sanitized terms around death like "mortician" and "undertaker." They sound cleaner. Gravediggers are barely visible; when a family arrives at the cemetery, the grave is usually prepared; it has been dug.

I am going to try to face the men and women who dug, in all their ambivalence, in order to address the questions they raise. And through them, I will look at the interweaving of genocide into ordinary village life.

Perhaps this chapter is particularly difficult for me for personal reasons, too.

Local Soviet archives rarely lie about the execution of Jews by "Fascists." I reread a document in which a forest warden recalls, in 1944, having seen French prisoners from Camp 325, digging large graves for more than 15,000 Jews. Camp 325, Rawa Ruska, is the camp where my grandfather Claudius was held.

In this document, a certain Stefan Alexeievitch Pelip is questioned; he witnessed the French prisoners digging.[1]

"From working as a forest warden and living seven hundred meters [half a mile] from the site of the shooting of the Jews, I know all the details of the shooting of the Jewish population by the Germano-Fascist monsters. In the month of November 1942, within this perimeter, French prisoners dug a huge grave, thirteen meters [forty-three feet] long, eight meters [twenty-six feet] wide, and four meters [twelve feet] deep. On December 5, 1942, early in the morning, seven trucks carrying Jews, men, women, and children of all ages, guarded by the German police, drove up to the ditch. At that moment, I was on a hilltop, about two hundred meters from the ditch and I saw the shooting happen. The German police put the Jews in rows of six, making no distinctions of age or sex, and made them advance to the edge of the ditch where there were six machine-gun shooters."

In November 1942, my grandfather was already imprisoned in the camp at Rawa Ruska. Was he a "digger"? I cannot bear to think about it. Or rather, I can think of nothing else; it all comes to the same thing. What if I am the grandson of a digger? My thoughts take flight, or rather they crash into one another. You can study for years, visit thousands of villages, and still there is a question you cannot ask yourself, a personal question you encounter, far from home, after years of work. In the corner of a forest. On the page of an archive. Your question: *Was my grandfather implicated in the genocide of the Jews while a prisoner in one of the most repressive camps of the Third Reich?*

You cannot change your origins, nor can you erase your own links to genocide. Did my grandfather perceive my premonition when I asked my question, with such insistence, as we traveled the roads of my native Bresse? "Did you do anything bad in Rawa Ruska?"

On that day, he, who never got angry, started to yell at me.

How could I have understood? Maybe his will was forced, his moral conscience twisted like metal, by heat and hammer. How to understand his fear of being judged and misunderstood upon his return to France? The situation at Rawa Ruska was so complicated to explain at home in the West. What he lived through—what it was I will never know—both guides and cripples my research.

It's as if I were desperately seeking to understand what happened to him, and to us.

Who is the human being caught, either voluntarily or in spite of himself, in the mechanism of genocide? Genocide is of course first and foremost the creation of mass murderers. Nonetheless, it is made possible by the participation, voluntary or forced, of thousands of people. Armed men are not sufficient to commit genocide. It requires so many arms, legs, shovels, and wagons—so much labor. It is the deeds, as well as the conscience, of these minor actors in the crime that I seek to understand and hear today. I want to keep asking hard questions in the hope that tomorrow the leaders of genocidal governments can't find help so easily.

These thoughts, while sitting at my desk in this stifling hotel room in Chicago, take me back to the winter of 2008. To Serniki, in the Rovno region of Ukraine.

It was cold. It was January 2, 2008. My entire team and I were looking for mass graves. It was hard for us to wish one another a happy New Year. The archives we were working from were hardly clear. They estimated the number of Jews shot at 850, in a grave somewhere outside the village. I knew an Australian investigative team had already been to Serniki. In 1990, right before the crumbling of the

Soviet bloc, they came as part of the prosecution of a *polizei* who had taken refuge in their country.

The hotel where we were sleeping in Rivne, the regional capital, was one of those gray Soviet buildings, with ice-covered concrete steps. The impassive face of the receptionist hardly lent the place a festive air.

We'd left early in the morning. After about an hour of travel, we found ourselves standing in snow, next to an icy road leading into Serniki.

Serniki is a small Ukrainian village near the border of Belarus, embedded in a thick, dark forest. While we were passing through the sleepy town, a workhorse appeared. It was brown, heavy-footed, pulling a wagon covered with yellowed corn husks. An old man was sitting on top of the pile of husks, legs hanging, hooded, a thick coat covering him. Svetlana, our translator, stood on the side of the road, immobile in the cold, as though she were hitchhiking. She waited for the cart to approach. The driver pulled on the reins and the horse stopped. Svetlana started a conversation that none of the rest of us could follow.

I never quite understood what she said to the old people in the villages. All I knew was that after a few minutes she would become a part of the Soviet fraternity. She would tap into its empathy, open its communal memory. I saw the driver of the cart point out a house to her. Svetlana came over to me. "In the house over there, there is a woman; her name is Anna. Anna saw everything."

I reread the page in the archive: more than 850 Jews had been shot not far from Serniki in September 1942. We made our way, trying not to slip on the snowy road taking us to a cold and silent farmhouse.

Anna appeared standing in her yard, dressed all in black. She came toward her painted wooden fence. Svetlana pushed open the gate, which screeched under the weight of the snow. From out of sight, a dog barked loudly. Svetlana exchanged a few words with Anna before turning to us. "She says she agrees." Agrees to give the interview.

Anna invited us into her home. The door to her kitchen opened, and when I went in, I saw her with her husband, Pavel. He was very thin, as though he had shrunk to protect himself from the cold, and perhaps also from gazes and memories. There was almost no difference between the temperature inside and outside the house.

Very quickly, they assumed the positions in which they probably spent most of their day: sunk as though drowsing in two low chairs on either side of a large, unlit, blue-and-white tile stove.

Anna wanted to talk quickly; her sullen husband rarely let out a word, and when he did it was in spite of himself.

In September 1942, on the day of the execution of the Jews in Serniki, Anna and Pavel were not yet married. They were fourteen years old. Anna had seen the arrest and the columns of Jews. Her older brother, Ivan, had been conscripted to dig the graves.

Anna, with her somewhat cold, impassive face, spoke of herself very simply in the typical manner of older Soviet peasants. "I was born in November 1928. I have always lived here. And I will finish here. . . . We had two cows. I had no father, only my mother. We were three children, myself, my younger sister, and my older brother, born in 1925. I took the cows out to pasture."

"I took the cows out to pasture," she repeated several times. I thought, *How many Soviet cowherds have helped us in our search?* While following cows to the pastures, they were able see, from afar or up close, the murder of the Jews. Few admitted to having temporarily abandoned their herds, but I know very well that cows fear the sound of gunshots and the smell of blood.

Anna spoke calmly, her face often turned downward. Her grandparents lived in the "Jewish neighborhood," as she called it. The Jews were not foreign or unknown to her. "We knew Jews because my grandparents lived in the Jewish neighborhood, which was at the center of town. I went there often; all the Jews knew me." Anna was a child who lived among Jews.

Suddenly, the tone of her voice changed. She recalled a certain boy named Aizik.[2] When Aizik's mother was confined to the ghetto, she sent him to Anna's mother for safety. Aizik's mother also left clothes in Anna's house; perhaps to protect them from German theft, or perhaps to pay for her son's lodging. Aizik was not there very long. "He spent two weeks at our house. He slept in the same bed as my brother, Ivan."

This was the same Ivan requisitioned to dig the ditches in which the Jews were to be shot. Sixteen-year-old Ivan, a digger, slept in the same bed with a young Jew, Aizik, who was hidden in his house. I had to concentrate not to let my expression betray anything. A digger and a Jewish child hidden on his farm, in the same bed!

When Aizik's mother learned that Ivan, the son of the family where she had sent her own child for safety, was digging a ditch, she ran to the farm to question him. "Ivanko,[3] they've forced you to dig a ditch? A ditch for us? What ditch have you dug?"

Such an awful question. The scene described by Anna was surreal. This wasn't the first time a witness had told me about Jews leaving the ghetto to ask, "Is the ditch for us?"

Before all this research, I thought that worlds were distinct on the day of a genocide: that there would be a farm where the digger lived and another farm that sheltered Jews. This was the first time I was confronted with the knowledge that a digger and a victim lived under the same roof. Here in Serniki, a young Ukrainian named Ivan left his house in the morning and returned in the evening shouldering a shovel. Along with other peasants, he dug. Then he returned home, sat at the family table, and played with another young Ukrainian from the village lodging with them.

Anna clearly remembered the anguished dialogue between Aizik's mother and Ivan. "My brother answered, 'I don't know what to say.' Then she asked, 'What does the ditch look like?'" Ivan used hand gestures to show this Jewish mother the shape of the ditch he had dug.

In an instant, Aizik's mother understood. It wasn't a silo for corn or an anti-tank trench. The ditch Ivan dug was a grave for the Jews.

Suddenly Anna's husband Pavel interrupted her. "Eight meters [twenty-six feet] wide, forty meters [one hundred thirty feet] long! I dug it!"

My thoughts froze for an instant. So the taciturn Pavel, sitting here to the right of his stove, was also a digger. What a family, what a farm!

Ignoring her husband's remarks with a nonchalance that was probably habitual, Anna continued impassively. "So this woman said to my mother, 'Give me back my clothes. I have to go. Where is my son?'"

Anna's mother tried to keep the Jewish boy hidden in the house. Was it to hold onto the clothes? To save the child? She certainly knew that her child was digging ditches to swallow up the bodies of her Jewish neighbors.

The boy's mother insisted, "We have to go!"

So Aizik left the farm and returned to the ghetto. Anna started to speak more slowly, her voice quavering. "So they left. A week went by. Maybe less than a week. One day, I had taken my cows out to pasture. I'll never forget; it was a Wednesday. You see, I forget everything these days, because I was so young at the time, but that I will always remember. They brought them on a Wednesday. My mother had heated the oven and was getting ready to bake bread. I was out with the cows. Suddenly, I heard a noise. I turned around and I saw them: it was like a black cloud. . . . Once I saw them, I didn't wait for them to reach me. I took my cows and I ran to the house. My mother hadn't seen anything. I told her, 'Mommy, they are taking the Jews to kill them.' So, they took them out and soon they started to shoot them. We cooked our dinner in tears."

Anna finished her story with her head lowered, her eyes wet with tears. I too was moved. This was the first time I heard a witness tell of running home during the firing. Instead of watching her Jewish neighbors be slaughtered, she brought her cows home. Then she cried with her mother while they cooked. During the shooting.

At this point, Pavel indicated that he wanted to speak. He did not appear at all emotional. Since the beginning of the interview, when he did speak it was to try to show that he knew more than his wife. He had been a digger.

The cameraman pivoted in Pavel's direction. Pavel kept his hands crossed on his knees while the crew installed his microphone.

His face nervous and suddenly animated, Pavel began to explain what happened. First, there was a German officer who came before the diggers began work. He had paced out the dimensions and demarcated the size and placement of the ditch. He had marked the four corners with posts. The ditch was rectangular, with a dirt staircase at each end so the Jews could get into the ditch rapidly from both sides at once. The Jews were supposed to lie down head to toe, making two lines down the ditch and leaving an aisle in between.

The shooters circulated in the aisle, shooting the Jews from left to right. "There were three shooters. They relieved one another. . . . At the beginning, the shooters were outside the ditch; then they went down into the ditch to shoot. Here is the ditch!"

Pavel began to draw, or rather to trace with his foot on the red carpet, a large rectangle, to show how the Jews lay across the length of the ditch in two rows. "The heads faced one way, the feet the other. Then the next group lay facing the opposite direction. The shooters walked here, between the two rows of bodies, shooting in their heads."

"What uniforms were they wearing?"

"The SS ones with the skull."

Rereading his testimony years later, on a computer screen in the Chicago heat, I can analyze it. But sitting on a low stool in a farmhouse, in stocking feet so as not to dirty the floor with mud and snow, it was hard to find the necessary distance. When I revisit my conversation with Pavel, I become aware of my compulsion to understand the mechanics of how the crime could have unfolded. I realize I wanted to verify his testimony by grilling him with practical questions. Overwhelmed by the tides of information coming at me through the chill of that awful house, I concentrated on the "functional aspects" of the mass grave. This was the first time a villager had described a ditch with two staircases. Here is our exchange:

"So, there were forty meters between the two staircases?"

"Precisely," Pavel answered.

"Did the shooter stand on the stairs?"

"No, he walked from one end of the ditch to the other, and he shot the heads," Pavel said, imitating the action of shooting from one side to the other, between two lines of bodies. Then he added, "They positioned the next group in the same formation, naked, but with their heads on the feet of the bodies underneath them. Then the other shooter passed through. That's how they did it. . . . If they had shot from above, the shooter would have missed the ones that were farthest from him. And if they had only had one row of bodies, they would have had to dig down six meters [twenty feet]. This way, they only had to dig three meters [ten feet], and even then we had to do it in shifts. . . . Depending on the position of the heads, the shooter would go down one side or the other. If the heads were facing the inside of the ditch, he would go along the middle. Otherwise he went along the edge. Do you understand?"

Pavel was giving us a lesson in the workings of mass graves. In his explanation, the stairs were there to allow the Jews to get down more quickly.

I can still feel my profound unease on that second day of a new year as I got back into our van with our silent crew. Anna's testimony was calm and moving. Pavel's was cantankerous. His scenes were like layers of a hard lava flow from an ancient volcano, technical, bitter, and cold.

These two elderly people in this freezing farmhouse were from two very different families. Anna's family had housed a Jewish boy and tried to help his mother, even while Ivan, the eldest son, was digging their common grave. Neither Anna nor her mother had wanted to see the Jews murdered. Pavel came from a vastly different place. He dug and stayed to watch the crime. Then he waited with his horse-drawn cart, which was requisitioned to carry the clothes of the murdered Jews.

Were Anna and Ivan from a family of diggers? Saviors? Paid hosts? Forced witnesses? And Pavel? Was he a digger, a witness, a transporter of clothing?

I continue to believe that to be requisitioned to dig a grave for your Jewish neighbors marks your identity and your memory indelibly. Some families remember with tears the names of those killed. Others recite the measurements of the ditches, describing their architecture and their workings. Yet the names of their Jewish neighbors have left no trace in their memories.

I will end this chapter here. The streets of Chicago have been nearly flooded by the storm. I have to go meet my team at the Holocaust Museum in Washington.

Chapter 4

THE NIGHT

It is late, but sleep won't come. Our investigation has been moving forward, and I can't stop going over the testimonies we've been gathering for what is now ten years. We have interviewed more than 3,900 people in seven Eastern European countries. Little by little, we are able to take apart and analyze the different stages of the crimes from the dawn arrivals of the German convoys through their evening departures. We have been cross-referencing Soviet and German archives with the testimonies. And now, even as the work progresses, I suddenly feel that something isn't right. It's like a small clanging sound in a running motor.

You hear it little by little, as you recall witness after witness, men and women. The villagers who saw the execution of the Jews seem to talk about everything, or almost. A silence, or perhaps several silences, can be heard.

Silences, by definition, say nothing. But this one was different. It was like a gap in the chronology of the murders.

Suddenly, I was struck by the memory of the testimony of a Jewish survivor from the ghetto of Zoludek.[1] Her name was Irena. Irena not only survived the arrests and raids in the Zoludek ghetto but managed to keep an intimate journal about her experience. Her statements stayed with me for two reasons: the precision of her memories and the

58

depth and intensity of her response to the daily extermination of the Jews taking place before her eyes.

She testified at a hearing after the war. In the middle of her long deposition, during which she translated her Polish journal into German, a bell went off in my head. This was the moment all the witnesses we interviewed seemed to have forgotten. Irena explained that the crime began not at dawn, but the night before.

"Last night, they surrounded the ghetto and didn't let anyone out of their houses. The shutters had to remain closed for twenty-four hours. That evening, they gathered sixty horse-drawn carts belonging to the villagers, as well as people and shovels. They bivouacked all night beside a fire in the park, next to the police station."

It took me some time to understand the implications of what she had written. Irena understood that if the neighbors were requisitioned outside the ghetto, with tools, it meant that the next day they were going to murder the Jews; this confirmed the Serniki testimony. When the Jews saw their neighbors with shovels and wagons, they knew the shooters were coming to the village. The requisition of the villagers was often understood by the Jews as a sign of their impending death. The conscription of the diggers was like a black crow presaging their utter misfortune.

Yet no one had ever told me about a nighttime requisition. Sixty villagers are called and forced to wait all night outdoors. An unknown and invisible requisition, either forgotten or condemned to silence in the words of the witnesses. The aim of this requisition cannot be in doubt. The men have shovels. They are here in order to be ready first thing to carry off the Jews, the old, the sick, but also the healthy. They are here to bury them.

They were called up at night so as not to waste any time at dawn. The Germans, the *staroste*, must have figured that it wasn't certain the cart drivers would be awake and ready on time. They preferred to make them come the night before in order to have them "at hand."

We're not talking about a small group of people gathered in secret. Sixty villagers! That's a lot of horse-drawn carts. I know from experience what a horseshoe sounds like on a road, paved or dirt, and I know the squeaking noise of wheels. Sixty carts driven to the center of the village at the end of the day could in no way pass unnoticed. And it is impossible that the families or neighbors of the cart owners would not have asked, looking out their windows, "Where are you going with your wagon at such an hour?"

Village life is like clockwork. The herds of cows leave at the break of day and return to their stables in the evening. Always at the same time. When people see the cows coming home with their cowherd, they know they should stop work soon because night is going to fall. Their comings and goings are like walking timepieces. The carts that carry the fertilizer out to the fields and return laden with hay or potatoes are also regimented by the hour, day, and season. How many *desiatniks* did they have to send to the town hall to get all those drivers to come? To convince them not to go home but to spend the whole night outside with their horses?

And yet nobody, absolutely nobody, after so many long years of interviews, told us or even hinted that anyone—himself, his father, or his neighbor—was forced to come with his horse and cart to spend the night just outside the ghetto walls. A forgotten requisition. Occulted. Silenced. But for what reason?

Why such a veil over something that ultimately, compared to the rest, could seem insignificant? Banal acts that have been collectively silenced in the narrative of a crime can, once discovered, elucidate a whole part of the commission of that crime that everyone is trying to hide. Often these acts prove serious.

April 8, 2009, Belarus
The green Volkswagen van drives off from the hotel into the main thoroughfares of the town of Brest.[2] It is seven in the morning. The sun's rays, still cold, slowly illuminate the Soviet buildings. The parks

are covered in frost. It is already our tenth day investigating in this region. Despite refrains of Vera Brejneva blaring from the little radio that belongs to our driver Andreï, the team dozes. But I prefer to keep an eye on the road. I'm too aware of potential surprises, like wandering cows.

After leaving the town and its endless gray concrete periphery, we head for Bronnaya Gora. It is eighty miles from Brest, a solid two hours.

On the seat of the van is a file. I page through the archives that have been translated for this trip until I get to the Soviet Extraordinary State Commission's interrogation of a Polish police officer from Bereza Kartuska,[3] Josef Chidlovski. Chidlovski recounts the process of shooting the Jews of Bereza Kartuska in May of 1942[4]:

"When Pitschmann[5] arrived in the morning, he gave the order to gather the police in addition to the members of the Gestapo who came with him, about five hundred people. When we, the police, were assembled, they gave us the order to stand guard near the houses where the Jews lived. The cordon was organized in the following manner: one policeman and then one German from the Gestapo. They positioned us three and a half meters [eleven feet] apart behind the Jewish houses. They gave the order not to let anyone in or out of the houses. I should correct myself and say we actually encircled the Jewish houses that evening. I was in the police cordon. We stood guard near the Jewish houses until the morning; at sunrise we saw the trucks arrive and the Germans started to force the Jews out of their houses and make them climb into the trucks."

Josef, in his capacity as a local policeman, is one of those called upon to surround the Jewish domiciles until their killers arrive. For the whole night prior to the execution, the ghetto is methodically sealed off and guarded by armed men. But why? The shooting won't take place until the next day. Why do the guards surround the ghetto the evening before and not at dawn, as they normally would for a police arrest? What is it that happens during this night?

The van accelerates. We are alone on a long straight road crossing through a dark forest. I ask myself . . . The surrounding of the ghetto on the eve of the crime at Bereza Kartuska seems to happen quickly and silently. Was this the case elsewhere? I cannot recall any witness, not a single Ukrainian, Russian, or Belarusian farmer, mentioning this lockdown. Yet, in Bereza Kartuska, it wasn't a team of just a few police officers scattered around the ghetto but five hundred uniformed people encircling an entire neighborhood. This couldn't have gone unnoticed.

In the spring of 1942, in this small town, 3,000 Jews were crowded into the ghetto houses. To go out into the street was to risk being humiliated or beaten by guards. The extermination of the Jews had started; the peasants were asleep and saw nothing of the maneuver.

Through foggy windows, I look out at the landscape. Villages, enshrouded in thick morning fog, pass before my eyes in a slow country rhythm. No, I thought, it wouldn't be surprising that the local Belarusians would have seen nothing of the nocturnal lockdown of the ghetto. I take up my archival reading again. There is another town, Novogrudok, southwest of Minsk; there was a ghetto there, too. Here is the testimony of a Jewish survivor Mordechai Meirowicz, recorded in Tel Aviv in 1960.[6]

"On the night between August 7 and 8, the ghetto of Novogrudok was hermetically sealed by German units along with local police. In the morning, all the inhabitants of the ghetto were gathered in the square in front of the *Judenrat*.[7] They had received the order to bring one piece of hand luggage and been told they were being taken away to work. The trucks advanced and the people were loaded onto them. . . . Then the victims were taken to Litovka, undressed, and shot and buried in mass graves."

Here again, the surrounding of the ghetto took place at night. But why?

I see a rusty blue sign for Pinsk. I am reminded again of the report[8] from November 1942 written by Helmut Saur, the chief of the

10th Company of the 15th Regiment of the German police, which recounts the liquidation of the ghetto in Pinsk.[9]

"The blockade that was ordered began at 4:30 in the morning. Under the command of the chief of personnel, given in secret, the barrier was finished in little time, making any escape by the Jews impossible. According to orders, the combing of the ghetto should start at 6:00 a.m. But because it was still dark, it was postponed to a half hour later."

The testimonies converge. The execution of the Jews took place within full view of all. However, the surrounding of the Jews took place at night, with speed and secrecy. Was the secret truly unknown or was it a known secret that was well kept? And for whom?

I see painted wooden houses emerging through the fog. The road is bad, and the van has a hard time avoiding potholes. I'm no longer paying attention to the music crackling on the radio, going in and out as we cross through the high pine forests.

Secrecy. In our interviews, secrecy was rarely mentioned. By contrast, it was evoked frequently by witnesses describing the arrest of their neighbors by the NKVD.[10] A black vehicle would arrive in the middle of the night and several members of the NKVD would emerge and quickly and noiselessly arrest the designated person and force him into the car, so that his fate was lost in the dark of night. All this happened in silence, in secret. No one knew what became of the person they had arrested, not even the family.

When I first came to work the ground in Rawa Ruska, I discovered, with the aid of the mayor at the time, that there were living witnesses from the camp where my grandfather was interned. There were also living witnesses to the shooting of the Jews. I asked myself, what if this were the case elsewhere? I quickly realized that, in most of the Ukrainian villages I was passing through in my rusted Volga, there were elderly people who had been present at the executions. Before Rawa Ruska, I was under the illusion that the Shoah had taken place in secret. But no, our research showed us that the genocide of the Eastern Jews happened not in secret but in broad daylight, in the presence of local witnesses.

The actual arrests of the Jews took place during the day, amid the yelling of the Germans or the police, the barking of dogs, and the cries of distress from the victims. The secrecy of the nocturnal encirclement of the ghetto clashes with the rest of the process of the Nazis' execution of the Jews. What then was the point of this encirclement the night before?

In the archives, it is clearly stated that the ghetto was sealed off in order to prevent the escape of the Jews, who might try to flee when they saw the Germans or local police arrive. The lockdown constituted not only a threat but also a mortal trap. In the course of one night, the ghetto was sealed off. No one could go in or out. Any attempt to escape was punishable by death. Either Germans or police, armed with rifles or machine guns, were posted around the ghetto. A vise closed in on the Jews as dawn approached.

I turn the pages of the file with reddened fingers; outside the cold is arctic and the van's heater is struggling. My eyes linger on a particular testimony. Another German, Rudolf F., a member of an SS cavalry unit, describes his role in the liquidation of the ghetto of the Belarusian town of Stolin.[11] I glance at the map of the region spread out in front of me; Stolin is a few miles east of Pinsk.

"I know we were woken up during the night. That evening, there was a rumor that an intervention was really imminent. We marched to the market square, where we took our positions at dawn. They announced that the ghetto was going to be evacuated. I was posted as a machine gunner, with Walter B., in the market square. It was our duty to make sure that none of the assembled Jews could escape."

I lift my eyes to the landscape, still frozen in the frigid morning. Why won't the local people we interview sixty years later talk about this? What is so weighty, so terrible, that after over half a century none of them will broach it? The secret . . .

Various hypotheses swirl through my mind. Perhaps it's simply that we never asked the right question. Can this explain the silence? No, in the light of our many investigations, it seems instead that the silence of the witnesses is due not to an omission but rather to a feeling of guilt.

I look again at our document from the village of Bereza Kartuska. Between 250 and 300 local police were conscripted the night before the execution to surround the ghetto until the Germans' arrival.

The local police didn't reside in barracks; they lived on their farms with their families, their wives, and their children. How is it possible not to see so many police, with their guns and armbands, heading for the ghetto one evening? I can recall a little Ukrainian village called Inhulets, in the Dniepropetrovsk region, where one evening the return of a herd of cows shook up the entire community. In this countryside, where the slightest unusual movement was an event, where everyone knew everyone, how could the departure of 250 to 300 men be achieved in secret? At the very least, the families of the police had to be aware. Ghettos were rarely on the outskirts of town. The inhabitants of the houses near the ghetto of Bereza Kartuska couldn't be unaware of this many people moving through, of the human barrier that was isolating the Jews of their town.

It's eight in the morning. We're still driving. The sun appears above the tree line and slowly begins to warm the road in a monotonous yellow light.

I continue to search in the archives for anything that could illuminate the motivation for such a general silence about these nighttime requisitions. Then I recall the report from a police battalion about the extermination of about three hundred people in Sabolotje (or Zablocie),[12] in the Belarusian region of Brest. It took place over September 22 and 23, 1942.

"The company received the order to exterminate the locality of Zablocie, situated in the northeast of Mokrany. . . . Units 1, 2, and 3 arrived at the western exit of Mokrany at about six in the evening, with their own trucks."[13]

Here we are again. This is the same timing as at Zoludek. The killers' trucks leave the evening before, at six o'clock. In the month of September at six o'clock, the night is approaching but there is still daylight. More vehicles will join them.

"After a short discussion about the situation and the dividing up of the men, we started to march in the direction of Zablocie at around 11:00 p.m."

And here was the clue I was looking for:

"The ninety-three carts mobilized for the action were left aside to be called upon later, and were guarded by a quarter of the commando unit."

This was surely because the Germans knew that the farmers would try to return home to sleep. So, before the police battalion even arrived in the village and then headed to the extermination site, ninety-three carts had already been requisitioned. "Mobilized," as is written in the deposition. This statement aligns perfectly with Irena's deposition. It even appears that that they weren't used right away but were stockpiled for later. The carts were put at the disposal of the killers, whatever their needs.

Ninety-three carts, with at least as many horses and drivers! A veritable armada. It suggests at least ninety-three requisitions. In 1942, there was almost no outdoor lighting in these parts. It is understandable that Irena has the impression of seeing a bivouac. The *Aktion* begins at dawn:

"On September 23, 1942, at two in the morning, we reached the outlying farms of Zablocie. While most of us continued on toward the village, the isolated farms were surrounded by a commando. . . . The *soltous*, who was also present, was ordered to be at the edge of the village at five."

We have met so many requisitioned people who have described fifty different jobs given them for a day or even a few hours. Not one of them remembers a nighttime requisition! Some recall having dug graves, sold clothes, pulled out gold teeth. So why doesn't anyone want to talk about what happened the night before?

Why is it so hard to say that you were forced to come with your cart at six p.m. on the eve of the murder?

The answer—or at least one of the answers—is perhaps found elsewhere. The folder that I had in my hands in that rattling old van held the deposition of a certain Alfred Metzner. He was German, originally from the Baltic states. The Nazi word for such colonized Germans living now in the territories of East Germany was *Volksdeutsche*. Since they spoke Russian and had good knowledge of the Soviet Union, they were often recruited to the ranks of the *Einsatzgruppen* to serve as interpreters. The most zealous among them, like Alfred Metzner, became shooters. In 1947, Metzner recounts the liquidation of the ghetto of Slonim, not far from the road we are currently on.[14]

"At this extermination, about 10,000 Jews were liquidated. The night before the *Aktion*, the protection and the sealing off of the ghetto had already been ordered. Protection against the partisans had been ordered by the commander of the town. At four in the morning, the ghetto was surrounded by the local police. All the Jews who tried to escape were immediately shot. The Jews had learned ahead of time about the execution and that is why they had tried to dig holes in the ground at various places in order to escape the encirclement. The ones who did escape were turned in by the local population and shot on the spot. The extermination of the Jews took place as follows: when the Jews refused to leave their houses, they were either forced out and then shot or shot inside their houses. During these *Aktions*, particularly sadistic people threw lit flares at the living Jews; they caused serious injuries. Men with machine guns were stationed outside the ghetto to counter any attempt to escape. The Jews were not led to graves but shot right on the spot. The night before, women had been raped by the police and then shot. The police bragged about the number of women they had abused in this manner and tried to outdo one another. Later, when no one was coming out of the ghetto anymore, the troops were formed up to go inside."

Not only were the Jews in the ghetto of Slonim guarded all night, on the eve of their death, but they were also preyed upon by their guards. It had never occurred to me that such violence would have been perpetrated on the eve of the executions. It was as though nothing held these men back because the Jews were going to be killed the next day.

I don't know if this happened anywhere other than in Slonim.

Is this how we explain and interpret the silence of 3,900 Ukrainian, Russian, and Belarusian witnesses about the night preceding the shooting of the Jews?

The extermination machine is not just for killing. It authorizes all forms of cruelty so long as they don't interfere with the strict timing on the day of the genocide.

The van stops. Andreï, the driver, turns to me and shows me the sign for the village of Bronnaya Gora. I gesture for him to drive on to the center of town. A new investigation begins.

Chapter 5

THE RAPES

It was July 2008, and Andrej had just returned from a long investigation in Belarus. He called me from Cologne, Germany, where he currently lives. "I had a very long interview with a witness. In Russian. It's amazing what he told me. . . ." I could tell from his voice that something had happened, something unexpected and shocking.

Some time passed. As usual, the recordings were sent to Paris, where they were digitized and filed. Several months later, witness number 100B was assigned to a translator, Anna, who day after day gave us access in French to the words of a certain Léonid.

Léonid was not a neighbor. Léonid was Jewish. He lived in Minsk, the capital of Belarus. In this country, where more than seven thousand villages were burned, Hitler's troops met an unusual degree of resistance.

Because it was too long to be translated in one day, I received Léonid's testimony in pieces.

One morning, I took the time to reread it in its entirety. As I went through it, I understood why Andrej hadn't told me more when he first called. At the time, he had explained that Léonid wanted to talk at a hotel, safe from the gaze of his family, behind a thick curtain that surrounded the lobby. He spoke for hours.

It was only behind the curtain that he could return to the Minsk ghetto, where he himself had been imprisoned. Where the common graves had reportedly been.

The interview was not only long, it was also intimate.

First, he told the story of his father's death. Then his mother's. It is always something to hear the voice of an old man, who became an orphan long ago, describe the murder of his parents by young men who'd come from Germany.

Here is that testimony.

"June 28, 1941, the Germans came to Minsk. I remember their arrival very clearly. They came in cars and on motorcycles. . . . My grandmother, who remembered the Germans in Belarus during the First World War, always said of them, 'The Germans are a cultivated people. They are cultivated, they won't do us any harm.' We had no idea what was going on in Poland, where the persecution of the Jews by the Germans was already in full force at the time. We didn't know that Hitler had made the extermination of the Jews his stated goal. Ten days after the German Fascists arrived, they ordered the creation of the ghetto.

"So we had to leave our apartment, find someone to help us transport our things, find a place to move in. It was horrible! I remember that I myself didn't cry—I was fourteen—but my mother and grandmother cried quite a bit. We had to leave so many things for which we had worked so hard and which we needed so much. We couldn't bring the bed or the armoire or the buffet. We had only ten days. It was clearly posted that those who had not moved within ten days would be shot. . . .

"Once, in the spring of the year 1942, I was with my father. There were no longer any sidewalks. People tried to avoid the streets. We mostly went in between houses to avoid walking in the streets. But on this day, I was in the street with my father. All of a sudden, the *Kommandant* of our ghetto and another German appeared at the corner. My father didn't have time to take off his hat. I myself didn't have a hat on. The German came up to my father and asked him: 'Why didn't you take your hat off?' In the meantime, my father had taken off his hat and tried to explain to the man, 'I didn't see you coming.' The

German answered him, 'I'm going to teach you how to see.' He took out his pistol and shot my father on the spot, merely because he hadn't taken off his hat. The German laughed. He said to me, 'Now you'll know *Die Mütze muss man abnehmen!*' One must take off one's hat!"

Thus, his father was murdered before the child's eyes simply for having forgotten to take off his hat for a German.

Suddenly, Léonid seemed to stumble into a memory of a day when he had been protected by his family, pushed deep into a bed on the pretext that he was sick in order not to be taken by the Germans.

"Worst of all was that, in the Minsk ghetto, we had no peace, day or night. At night, the Germans and the police came into the houses. I think it was during the day that they decided which houses they would go into. They raped the young women, looked for objects of value, and then killed everyone. . . .

"Right before the second raid, the Germans had massively invaded the ghetto, which made people panic because they knew there was definitely going to be an *Aktion*. My mother ordered me to get into bed and forbade me to get out. By this time, people already knew that whoever was taken by the Germans would never return home. So, I was in bed and my mother wrapped my head as though I were sick. There was a window with curtains. Of course, I wanted to know what was happening out in the street. On the second floor of our house lived another family. Every house had two families. In this family, there was a young girl. She was maybe fifteen or sixteen. She was very pretty; she wore a very long braid. I can remember it well. Her braid went all the way to her waist and was very thick. She was walking in the street. The Germans captured her. One of them tore off her dress and her underpants, threw her on the ground and started to rape her. Of course, she started screaming. Her mother came out of the house. I saw it. I couldn't understand what was happening. I had never seen a rape before. Her mother ran out of the house screaming. She was running toward her daughter when one of the Germans who was there shot her."

I reread these words slowly, in silence. His testimony was clear, implacable. Léonid spoke with his child's eyes, his adolescent eyes, of what he himself had seen in the Minsk ghetto. Germans went into the ghetto on the days of the *Aktion* to rape the young Jewish girls and, if the families resisted, they were murdered on the spot. The Germans chose a family, raped, stole, and then killed.

Right away, the question came to me: do we need to talk about this? Do we need to write on this subject? I thought about it a lot. How many people must have stayed quiet, out of respect for their daughter, their mother, and their sister? Do we need to talk about it now?

Ten months later, I was giving a lecture in Rochester, in northern New York State. The weather was nice. The university auditorium was filled with people of a certain age. In the middle of my speech, I started to say that there had been rapes in the ghettos and not only in the ghettos. All of a sudden, someone got up. I don't know who it was and I never will. He said to me in a firm voice, "That's impossible. Never would a German, an SS soldier, touch a Jewish girl. It was forbidden."

His words struck me. Forbidden. It was forbidden.

For the following two weeks, I considered this. Many people must surely think the same thing. Many believe that dictators adhere to the morality of their dictatorship; that genocidal murderers follow the creed of their criminal ideology. How many times, from high on podiums, had the Nazis railed against transgressions with people of impure blood as the surest route to the destruction of Germany!

Léonid was not the only witness to rape. But he had seen it from the point of view of the victim, as a Jew, as a young person.

The words of the Bousk villagers began to reverberate in me. They recalled sexual slaves imprisoned by the Gestapo, selected by the Germans, then shot by a neighboring unit from Sokal; by the end of the year, most of them were pregnant. The guards standing outside the ghettos of Brest, in Belarus, recalled that the Germans went in every night to rape young girls, in full view and in full knowledge of all.

Everyone knows that rape is a form of murder.

The story of the Jewish women in the towns and ghettos of the German occupied Soviet Union remains to be written.

A few weeks ago, Patrice Bensimon, a member of our team, was participating in a seminar in Los Angeles at the University of Southern California, organized by the Shoah Foundation. Their theme was violence against women. Several times in the invitation, it was specified that the seminar would be confidential.

Sixty years after the fact, should we say it or keep it quiet?

My sense is that it's essential to recognize that the Germans who marched in front of their insane leader through Nuremberg Square with robotic expressions on their faces were—once they were far from Berlin and in the Russian towns they believed they were colonizing—nothing more than criminals, murderers freed from any moral obligation. Theft and rape were of a piece with the genocidal crime. Of course, in the *Einsatzgruppen*[1] reports they'll count the number of Jews murdered. Of course, before the courts they'll try to minimize their responsibility. They did nothing but obey orders! They surely would never admit that they were also thieves, that they were also rapists.

This brief passage in Alfred Metzner's testimony, spoken with no particular emphasis, comes back to haunt me: "The night before, the women had been raped by the police and then shot. The police bragged about the number of women they had abused in this manner."

What if this were one of the reasons for the silence of witnesses concerning the nighttime requisitions? During the night watches, the Jews found themselves at the mercy of the Germans, but also of the local police.

Some questions leave such a bitter taste in the mouth! This hypothesis seems plausible but has to be verified.

The entire village knew that the Jews were to be shot in the morning. It's not hard to imagine the appetites, the discussions among the families, the desires for pillage and rape, especially since the German commando hadn't arrived yet.

This is only a hypothesis. Will it ever be possible to know what happened during those terrible nights of guarding the ghettos, during the several hours spent waiting for the *Einsatzgruppen* vehicles to arrive?

PART TWO

THE MORNING

Chapter 6

BARRIERS

It was the festival of the Greco-Catholic Church in the village of Bouse, in western Ukraine. The popular Palm Sunday. Children came out one after the other with pretty decorated bunches of budding twigs. Their color lent joy to a landscape slowly emerging from the sadness of winter. Once the mass was over, Lydia appeared on the church steps. She was well dressed, with her black hat and mantilla, as one should be to attend church in a rural village. I had no inkling, as she approached the microphone held out by a member of our team, that her testimony, her memory, was going to open up a whole new vista of questions that to this day remain without convincing answers.

Her parents were merchants in Bousk, more precisely "meat merchants in the town center." As a child, she saw the ghetto; along with her mother, she had several times exchanged food for goods with the Jews imprisoned there. She talked about it at length. She was one of the first people to describe for me the comings and goings of the Soviet farmers around the ghetto fences. The villagers exchanged and bargained with the Jewish families, who often had no choice in the matter. Until then, I had pictured the ghettos hermetically sealed. She explained in detail where the places of exchange and passage could be found, out of sight of the police who guarded the Bousk ghetto.

I saw her again several times. She didn't give up information easily. Or rather, she reflected a lot before she spoke.

As our conversations progressed, shielded from her neighbors' gazes in her well-decorated house, she ended up telling me that every day of the German occupation she went to her primary school via a long street called Chevtchenko. Suddenly one morning, all traffic was cut off, including for pedestrians; a guard, a *polizei*, stationed in the middle of the street, said to her, "No school today."

There was "no school" because in Chevtchenko, not far from this guard, to the right, in the cemetery, the Jews from the ghetto were being murdered.

So Lydia had a "vacation day." But she didn't turn around. She didn't go home to her parents but instead found a way to see what was going on up close, despite the guard. She wanted to see with her own eyes "the crime" of the ghetto Jews, the same people with whom her mother had traded food just a few days earlier.

This is what sticks in my head: why did the young Lydia from a merchant family decide, despite the guards apparently posted all around the site of the shootings, to play hide and seek with armed policemen? Wasn't she playing hide and seek with her own death in the event the police decided to open fire? Why wasn't she really afraid of Ukrainian guards?

For that matter, what did these guards do?

We find them present at every stage of the crime. Many of them were interrogated in the postwar German trials. The terminology they employed was often that of the police: "locking down the ghetto," "the raid," "the inner cordon of guards around the ditch (or the grave) and the Jews," "the outer cordon to block all traffic." They could be German, Ukrainian, Russian, or Belarusian, made up of mobile units or local ones.

Their deployment apparently had only one objective: that the Jews have no possibility of escape or revolt, that they walk toward the graves through a storm of blows and threats, and that no neighbor get close enough to disrupt the shootings.

We shouldn't picture these guards as being like the Parisian police who block traffic when there is a protest in our capital. They are in no way simple keepers of order. If a Jew doesn't obey a command, the guards have complete discretion over whether the Jew lives or dies. If a Jew tries to escape, they are going to shoot to kill.

In his testimony before the East German authorities, Joseph H., a member of a mobile unit of the Stanislau[1] Gestapo, clearly describes the division of duties among the guards during the extermination of the Jews in Drogobytch,[2] Ukraine:

"After rounding up all the Jewish people of the town, one group of guards was responsible for keeping watch on them in the main square with the fountain, which had been designated as the site of the roundup. Another group was responsible for directing and protecting the transportation of the Jews to the site of the shooting, and a third group for guarding the victims waiting beside the ditch as well as accompanying them to where they would be shot. . . . Their stated mission was to stop all attempts at flight from the ghetto by the victims, and, with their firearms, to shoot any fugitives."[3]

When I read Joseph H.'s deposition, I cannot help but think of Lydia; she was only a few yards from the site of the shootings, despite the fact that she'd been banned by a guard with the authority to shoot . . . to shoot Jews, that is.

Does this imply that the guards separated the space of the crimes from that of the ordinary villagers? I would be inclined to think so. The perimeter that they set up in Bousk is the line between life and death; inside the perimeter, all the Jewish inhabitants—men, women, children, babies—will be killed. On the village side, outside the fence, the guards simply have to push back overly curious neighbors. They stand there with their arms out, defining for a few hours the circle of genocidal rupture between the citizens of the same town. They constitute a human enclosure around the scene of the crime against the Jews. They are to the shootings of the Jews what the barbed wire is to the concentration camps.

Should we think then that young Lydia, the daughter of a merchant, isn't really afraid of the guard for the sole reason that she knows she is not Jewish? Terrible question. With a terrible answer.

Lydia is not unique. Many young neighbors to the crime, whom we met sixty years after the fact, had no hesitation about confirming this. All of it, the guards, the Jews, the shooters, was a horrifying spectacle for them, but it remained, after all, and perhaps more than anything, a game, a child's game, an attractive game.

Patrice, on his return from the Ukrainian region of Khmelnitsky, told me the following facts.

In Derajnia, a small town known for its train station, he had met a certain Maria. Like Lydia, she knew the Jews of her town personally; she spoke of them with smiles and emotion: "There were a lot of Jews. We went to school together; we were friends. They were very good people. If a Jew gave his word, it was sacred. Everyone would confirm that for you. . . .

"Most of them were artisans. They sewed boots, dresses, linens, etc. Some were merchants: they had shops. There were also musicians. I remember at the end of the street, there was a house with a veranda. . . . There was always an old Jewish man there playing the violin. We would go listen to him."

She has no hesitation in naming the *polizei* of the village and in denouncing their violence. She knew them. "I'm sure they were very aggressive. For example, Dioma[4] Podnevitch was ferocious, to the Jews and to the Russians. There was also a certain Kassiane."

Like Lydia, before the shootings Maria went willingly to the boundary of the ghetto many times to exchange food with the Jews enclosed behind the barbed wire: "I took milk and I went there. I passed it through a hole because the whole Jewish quarter was surrounded with barbed wire. It was called the ghetto. I came and I set the milk down. The Jewish woman glanced around to make sure no one was watching, then she came to pick it up. Sometimes, they asked if we could bring potatoes or other things."

She recalls in particular one of the Jewish friends she visited, Sara. But on the day that all of her Jewish neighbors were exterminated, including the old violinist and her childhood friend Sara, what does she do? She takes all kinds of risks in order to watch the murders, to witness the massacre of the very same families to whom she has been bringing milk:

"On that day, we children were watching our herds near the ravine. People came running. 'They're taking the Jews! They're taking the Jews!' they cried. We climbed trees to see what was going to happen. Once we were already up high, a German or a policeman started shooting at us with a machine-gun pistol. We jumped down from the trees. Where should we go? The field had just been plowed, and the most recent tractor grooves were deep. Bending down, we walked along the furrow, and we found ourselves facing the execution site. In order to escape notice, we put down clods of earth between which we left enough space to be able to see. That's how we saw everything."

A guard fires at her while she is perched in a tree, a young, educated girl. Does she run and take refuge at home? No, she goes and hides in a deep tractor groove in a field and makes loopholes to peer through, as though she were building a dirt fortress. The way a child on summer vacation might build a sandcastle on the beach. Rereading Maria's words, I saw myself as a small boy in Bresse, walking in my big tan plastic boots inside the deep tractor grooves in my grandfather Émile's freshly plowed fields; some of the grooves were so deep that one could indeed hide in them. Maria and her friends continued this childhood game for as long as it took to murder their Jewish neighbors, the groove becoming for them like the crenellated wall of an earthen fort.

And yet, what she describes is not a childhood game but an absolute horror.

"Two young women tried to give something to a German in order to be allowed to keep their nightgowns on. . . . But he didn't permit it. They started to hit the girls, and they tore off their nightgowns, and they were naked like all the others.

"They forced the Jews to line up along the steps that had been made on either side of the ditch. They fired with a machine gun, and all the Jews on one of the steps fell. Then they shot the Jews on the other step. This way, they all fell headfirst toward the middle. I can't talk about it. It's extremely hard. Can you imagine, for the child that I was! It was a nightmare. After having seen all this, I couldn't sleep or eat or do anything at all. . . . There were some mothers who had babies in blankets in their arms. They were told to put them down around the ditch; they did it. That's when Dioma, the policeman, came. He kicked all the babies down into the ditch; they were alive."

The guards, who made a cordon around the men who were murdering the Jews with such violence and cruelty, appeared to those outside as security guards for the villagers. I'm afraid that, on that day, they led the neighborhood children to understand that they were not at any great risk.

In Derajnia as in Bousk, there were guards rather than barbed wire around the graves. In places like Belzec, Sobibor, and Treblinka, barbed wire cut humanity in half. On the inside, Jewish human beings were corralled to die in artisanal gas chambers; on the outside, their Polish Christian neighbors could approach, sometimes watching through binoculars, standing on a hill, as the Jews entered the gas chambers. Outside the barbed wire of the extermination camps, as outside the circle of the guards around the common graves, the neighbors knew that they lived on the right side of humanity. The side of life.

Ultimately, didn't the sight of the armed guards at Derajnia signify to Maria that she was going to live? So why do Lydia and Maria stay so long to watch the massacre of their neighbors and friends? Is there a certain pleasure in watching one's neighbors tortured and murdered as long as one knows that one doesn't belong to the group of "others"? Is there such great pleasure in watching "others" die because we've been authorized to live? A pleasure such that neither Maria nor Lydia would want to avoid the spectacle? On a day of genocide in a village, is Sade the expert in human behavior?

I reread with terror the last lines of Patrice's report upon leaving Derajnia.

"Throughout the village, the witnesses were paradoxical. They all had many Jewish acquaintances with whom they got along very well. One of them had even been taken in as an orphan by a Jewish family; still another had a Yiddish accent. . . . And yet, they all went to watch the incredibly violent execution. . . . The witness who had the Yiddish accent was . . . very, very calm, a teacher wearing sunglasses. During the interview, she seemed both present and absent, as though deep in her memories. But she didn't cry."

In the end, the local guards who surrounded the Jews on the day of the murder reassured all the others. The authorization to live, the pleasure at seeing the "others" die on a day of genocide, seems to obliterate for a number of us all human ties with the condemned. They become a "spectacle," both horrible and alluring.

Chapter 7

THE COLUMN OF JEWS

Jerusalem, 1999

As a young priest, recently named secretary of the Conference of French Bishops for Jewish Relations, I find myself in Schlomo Street, not far from the Great Synagogue. I am walking with Father Bernard Dupuy, an erudite Dominican who was the first secretary of Jewish relations for the Church of France. I have a hard time keeping up with him despite his age and weight. He knows where he is going; with a greeting in Hebrew, he enters the shop of an old bookseller. The owner, *kippah* over white hair, raises his eyes behind small round spectacles. From his look, I can tell that Father Dupuy is a familiar face here. The owner isn't at all surprised to see the priest dive into the back of the store, stand on a wobbly stool, and begin searching through shelves that look as ancient as the books they hold. Still busily intent, Father Dupuy goes into a small room lit by a single lightbulb hanging from a wire. He looks for, or rather he rips from the shelves, the works he thinks are essential for me to understand Jewish tradition. The Mishna translated into English. "Patrick, you have to have this translation. It's hard to find in Paris these days." Then he hands me a volume on Hasidism.[1] In his cheerful, intelligent way, he tells me, "It all starts with Baal Shem Tov, in Medzhybizh. He's the one who founded the Hasidic dynasty. But you also have to read the works of those who opposed the Hasidim, the Mitnagdim, but also the history of the secular Jews, and also . . ."

We had to return to this little shop several times carrying big bags, for we had bought about two hundred pounds of books—which got me into some heated negotiations a few days later at Ben Gurion airport as I was checking in for my El Al flight.

Medzhybizh, 2008

Years later, I find myself in Medzhybizh, the home of Hasidism. The place where Hasidic Jews from all over the world come to pray at the tomb of Baal Shem Tov, who died in 1760. Back when I was listening to Father Dupuy's quick, precise words in Jerusalem, it never occurred to me that one day I would actually find myself here, in this holy site of the Jewish faith.

We are in a van weaving between muddy potholes and frantic geese crossing the road, hopping and honking. After half an hour of research in the village of Medzhybizh, the investigators, the people who search out witnesses, come back to get me. "We found a grandmother," says Denis. "A young Belarusian. She saw the column of Jews being led to the shooting. The column went along this street," he adds, gesturing with his hand to the street where we stand. Denis looks determined. Our research would be impossible without investigators of his caliber. Before the camera crews arrive, teams of investigators, a few men and women, tirelessly scour roads and villages, knocking on doors in search of elderly witnesses to genocide. Today again, Denis has discovered an important witness. He has the gift not only for finding them but also for reassuring them.

He takes us to a blue-painted house. Olga is sitting there. Her memories are a child's, and it shows in her gaze. From the moment Denis begins speaking to her, we can see that a scene has begun playing out before her eyes. A scene she witnessed decades ago that remains engraved in her memories as a little girl. It is not at all rare for witnesses to take on a childish vocabulary when they speak to us.

This is what Olga will do today, sunk into her armchair, covered in a thick red blanket.

Just moments into the interview, Olga tells us, "The first shooting took place on September 21, 1942. The second one happened the next day. People said it was Judgment Day. We lived not far from the paved path on which they took the Jews to the shooting. My memories of that day, and my feelings, are still those of a child. . . .

"The Jews walked calmly; they spoke slowly; they talked among themselves; some even smiled. However, there was a sense of worry in the air. The path was paved with little blue stones. The Jews walked and their footsteps made a rustling sound. They moved along slowly, without hurrying. . . . It made such an impression on me that even now the feeling I had as a child rises up in me. People said, 'They aren't out for a stroll, walking like that.'"

Olga's gaze is lost in the scenes of her memory. I have never heard a witness remember the color of the paving stones on which the column of Jews walked, nor mention the sound of their feet as they advanced toward death. But her strongest memory is that of thinking she was witnessing Judgment Day. For me, as a priest, the idea is especially striking.

The Last Judgment. I had already heard this expression from a witness to the shootings in another village, an old man. We had just begun our research. It was only 2004, and yet it seems a century ago. We've accumulated so many testimonies since then. We were standing at the entrance to a small Ukrainian village in the region of Lvov. The old man, dressed in a gray shirt that was too big for him and a light-colored beret, was standing by a wooden fence. In front of us was a small hill that he gestured to with his hand. "Look, the Jews went up to Golgotha."

"How's that?"

"You don't see? It's like in the icons!"

And he pointed to a small road, or rather a twisting path up to the top of the hill. It was the path the Jews had taken to their common grave. The old man insisted, "You know, I saw it on the icon!"

As a priest, these little phrases impressed themselves upon my memory first as shock, but also as a question. From Father Dupuy, and from my teachers like the doctor Charles Favre,[2] I had learned that the Catholic Church had broken with the Accusation of Deicide.[3] The Jews had been perceived for centuries by the Church, with public opprobrium, as having committed the unpardonable crime of murdering Jesus, or God himself.

For my part, I have always refused any religious interpretation of the Shoah. Perhaps this is thanks to my roots in French secularism, but more likely it is the inherited determination of my grandparents; we didn't theologize about Nazism, we fought it.

Here in Medzhybizh, I listened to Olga tell me that as a young girl she thought she was witnessing the Last Judgment as she watched a column of Jews, her neighbors, walking to their deaths under the blows from the German guards.

For a long time, I wondered. How can you believe you are at Judgment Day watching the Jews of your own town die murdered before your very eyes?

Throughout my travels in the former Soviet Union, on farms in Russia, Belarus, Ukraine, and Moldova, I have seen countless small icons, painted and gilded, representing the Virgin, Jesus, or some saint, often simply glued onto little white boards, decorated with fabrics embroidered in regional or national colors. I can recall a small red-brick house in the Donetsk region. Along the angle of one wall was a series of icons arranged vertically, surrounded by dried flowers on wallpaper that had yellowed with age. I remember this scene in particular because just below the icons, sitting on a varnished coffee table, was a portrait of Leonid Brezhnev.

Despite years of Sovietism, the countryside of these nations has not lost its deep attachment to the Christian religion. In the 1940s, the Biblical scenes portrayed by the icons were, it seems, still very much alive in the eyes of villagers.

Thus, Olga, as she watched the column of Jews leave for the shooting, believed she was witnessing the Last Judgment. What can this mean? The Jews are condemned to die by occupying armies with the famous inscription engraved on their belts: *Gott mit uns.* God with us.

The death of Christ, for a Christian, is first and foremost the liturgy of the Stations of the Cross. I have never forgotten the little church of my childhood in the village of Villegaudin, in Bresse. Having traveled several miles by bicycle, following, as best I could, my grandmother on her black Solex moped, we would go inside the parish church, planted in the middle of a cemetery, where the priest was waiting to lead us through the Stations of the Cross. Station after station, we followed the progression of Jesus being put to death. His arrest, his humiliations, his fall, the idiotic remarks of the men guarding him. We followed these stations of public execution by walking through the interior of the church along the walls of the nave. The path was not very long, and we crammed together to get closer to each station, closer to Jesus's suffering. In the narrative of the Passion, not only does Jesus die in public, but he falls in public, is humiliated in public. And this public, prior to Vatican II, was very often designated as guilty of murder. The guilty ones, the public, were Jews, we were told. Jesus went onward, surrounded by Roman guards amid the Jews.

The Germans often inverted the Bible to explain their crimes. I can recall a small town south of Ternopil, called Monastyriska. The Christians in this town had been informed about the arrest of the Jews. They were told to get wooden crosses to affix to the lintel of the doors to their farms. Wherever there was a cross, the Germans would not enter. Wherever there was no cross, the Germans would enter, pillage, arrest, and kill the Jews. An inverted Jewish Easter!

It seems to me that the same thing happened in Medzhybizh. Olga sees all the Jews being marched in a column under the blows of a brutal occupying army and circulating among the local Christians until they are put to death. She believes she is seeing the Stations of the

88

Cross in reverse, the Last Judgment, God's answer to what happened to Jesus.

Other witnesses in Medzhybizh, on seeing the Jews wearing yellow circles inscribed with the German word *Jude*,[4] thought they were reading the name of Judas, the apostle in the Gospels who betrayed Jesus. "The Germans put discs with the inscription 'Jude' on the Jews' clothes. Who was Jude? Jude was the traitor of Jesus Christ. So the Germans believed that whoever was Jude was kaput."[5] So, every Jew had these discs sewn on his clothes: some on the chest, some on the back. And on these disks was written "Jude."

The arrest of the Jews, their humiliation, their being put to death . . . Olga wasn't the only one to believe that she was seeing God's response to Judas. His response to the Stations of the Cross, to the Passion of Christ, to the betrayal of Jesus by Judas! God's personal response to the deicide committed by the Jews. Thus, the column of Jews heading for their mass graves was perceived, somehow, as a religious procession. Like a liturgy. Like an act of God himself.

How many little Olgas, in thousands of Eastern villages, believed on the day of the crime that they were witnessing the Last Judgment? Is it possible that in Western Europe, certain Catholics likewise perceived the raids, the camps, the trains bound for Auschwitz as an act of response by God himself? Was not Séverine Drumont, the wife of Edouard Drumont, the all too well-known pseudo-Catholic author of the anti-Semitic tract *La France Juive* [Jewish France], the guest of honor at the exhibit on the Jews organized in Paris by the Vichy regime?

Medzhybizh is not an anomaly on the map of Jewish murders. I have heard more than twenty elderly women whisper off camera, after having recounted the horrors they witnessed, "But they killed Jesus!"

This could explain in part—and only in part—why so many neighbors chose to go watch the executions of the Jews. The way you would watch Jesus's death until his last breath.

I remember a teaching of the philosopher Gerard Israel, speaking before a group in Judeo-Christian dialogue in Lyon, many years ago:

"If the Christians, or rather certain Christians, didn't reach out to the Jews in a brotherly fashion, might we not wonder if, when they saw the deportation and the humiliation of the Jews, the humiliation made public, they couldn't help but think that they were witnessing God's vengeance in some way?"

Did the occupying Germans realize that Soviet children and adolescents, standing on the roadside or hiding behind the fences of their farms, believed they were seeing the enactment of a religious scene as the column passed? It is far from impossible.

This could explain in part why the execution of the Jews wasn't hidden from the villagers. The Stations of the Cross in reverse were not only public but on view. Since meeting Olga in Medzhybizh, I now frequently ask the witnesses I am interviewing, the neighbors, "Did you make the sign of the cross when the Jews passed in front of you in their columns? Did you make the sign of the cross while the Jews were being shot?"

The answer comes, simple and implacable: "Of course!"

It took me years to dare to ask this question. We all have our blind spots, especially when our own identity is at stake. But the Christian faith that was transmitted to me during my childhood cohabited with the Resistance. Not with anti-Semitism.

The Germans in the Eastern territories could not be unaware that the gawkers who rushed to see the Jews murdered, sometimes up to the grave's edge, crossed themselves over and over. Consciously or not, they organized a tableau vivant, a living picture, of an inverted representation of the Stations of the Cross. The Christian representation of the Jews' unpardonable guilt regarding Jesus sent certain spectators to the scene of the crime on the day of the Jews' murder by the Nazis, not only as curious neighbors but also as pseudo-Christians.

Chapter 8

THE GIRL IN LOVE

October 1, 2009

We are in Monastyrchchina, in the region of Smolensk, a large city on the Russian border, near Belarus.

Autumn has already robbed the trees of their leaves. Everything is dressed in gray. We are staying in Smolensk, near a big park, and each day we leave early in the morning to explore the villages of the region. The days are already short in the month of October; night falls quickly. This morning, when we left Smolensk, it was still foggy.

This is our first research trip to Russia. After five years of inquiries in Ukraine and Belarus, we have decided to begin investigations in the enormous Russian territory, or rather in the Russian territories that were occupied by the German army. The Germans made it as far as St. Petersburg to the north.[1] To the south, they got as far as 125 miles from Baku, in Azerbaijan. The immensity of the territory to be traversed makes your head spin. Yahad consists of a small team of about fifteen employees in Paris, and it's a real challenge to cover not only Ukraine and Belarus but now also the parts of Russia that were once under Nazi occupation.

Our initial choice for a Russian region was Smolensk because we already had the archives needed to prepare our investigations in order to gather testimony. According to these archives, the German occupiers had many victims: Jews, Gypsies, Communists, and prisoners of war, but also Russian civilians.

On this October morning, we found ourselves in the home of Alexandra. Denis, our Belarusian interviewer, had found her at the market. She was a woman of a particular stature, very strong and determined, wearing a large, dark smock, her cheeks highly colored by the morning cold. She had had a very interesting career as a police colonel.

Everything in her house suggested sobriety. There was a large, white-tiled wood-burning stove, an armchair upholstered in a gingham print. She held herself erect and held a white handkerchief in her hands. Tears came often to her serious and sometimes stony face.

She agreed to hold the interview in her heated home, which was a stroke of luck for the team. How many interviews have we conducted in glacial winds?

She sits down on a couch draped in a brightly colored woven rug of the kind often hung on walls in rural houses.

Within the small room, her discomfort is palpable. Alexandra appears focused but sad, with her gray hair in a ponytail. From her very first words, I understand that the war was not the first tragedy to strike her family.

Before the war, her parents were designated as "kulaks" and condemned by the Soviet regime for having too many possessions and refusing collectivization in the kolkhoz. They were, as they say locally, "repressed."

"Yes, de-kulaked. It was the collectivization of the times. We were de-kulaked during the collectivization. My parents were fairly well off. . . . Life set us apart. My parents owned four horses and some livestock. They took everything from them. They wanted to send them to Siberia; my father left for Leningrad and my mother for Smolensk. As for me, they left me with my grandparents. They took everything from us: our house, all our possessions, and they forced us into the *bania*."[2]

THE GIRL IN LOVE

Once the German occupation came in 1941, Alexandra's family was dislocated. She went to live in Smolensk but couldn't remain there, because, as with many others, her house was bombarded. "In Smolensk, the house we were living in was destroyed by a bomb. So we came running here, to Monastyrchchina. Our maternal grandmother came from Leningrad, whereas we came from Smolensk after the destruction of our house. . . . Here we lived in the center of town."

In Monastyrchchina, thanks to a Jewish family for whom her father worked, they moved into a house that had belonged to a Jewish kolkhoz, emptied of its inhabitants by the Germans.

"My parents had a Jewish acquaintance. When they did carting, they transported this Jew's merchandise. . . . When we arrived here in Monastyrchchina, he met my grandmother and said to her, 'Come live with us in our house.' They were about to be moved into the ghetto. They left us their house, their big house."

"We arrived with nothing. . . . His [the Jew's] wife was sick. He would have left. . . . But he couldn't because of his wife. Some police came and took them away. At that point, we weren't yet living in their house. He had just made us the offer to move in. We moved in later, about a week after they left. The house was open and no one was going in. At the time, people didn't pillage. . . . If I recall their leaving, it's because they had a son six years older than I was. I went to visit them two or three times and we became friends. His name was Ziama."[3]

She speaks of Ziama hesitantly, with the precaution and shyness of the ten-year-old girl she had been. One day, a policeman arrested Ziama and his family to imprison them in the ghetto. Clutching his rifle, the policeman had pushed open the house's wooden door. He had seized Ziama by the collar and brutally dragged him outside while his parents begged for mercy. The whole family had been taken to the ghetto.

At first Alexandra tries to tell me that she hadn't seem Ziama again after the arrest. Most likely, this is also what she once told her family.

"Did you see your friend?"

"No. We just talked through the fence."

The translator insists, "So you saw him several times through the fence?"

"Yes, not many times; just a few times. They locked me in the house. I would say I went a dozen times. What could we have talked about? He asked me to bring him things to eat. We talked about the pieces of bread that we shared with them and brought, passed through a hole according to our private signal. The ghetto was entirely surrounded by a fence and barbed wire. The Jews put a branch between the planks. That meant that they could lift the plank at that spot and get whatever we had brought for them. In summer, it was easier. In winter, with all the snow, it got harder. We talked about a bottle of milk and the best time to bring it. I do have to say that there were some good police. They sometimes let us give food to the Jews: we went to the ghetto gate and gave the food to the Jews."

It is my turn to insist. "Do you remember the last time you saw him? Did he have a sense that something was going to happen? Or did you not talk about that?"

"No one talked about it back then. Nobody talked about anything; everyone was scared of everything. Something happened every night: either it was the police who came or it was the resistance fighters. They all wanted something. We were afraid."

This fear seems never to have left her. Her retelling is made all the more difficult by the insistent ringing several times of a white telephone on the table. Each time, she picks up the receiver, answers briefly, and hangs up. Then she resumes her testimony.

Finally, she admits that she was there when the Jews were arrested, on the day they were taken to their mass graves.

"It was wintertime. January, I would say. I don't recall the exact date. I know that it was the beginning of the month of January. They were being taken in groups."

She was there as usual to bring food and possibly to see her friend. "That day, we got to our agreed-upon spot just at the moment they were being taken out by group. They were guarded; there were Germans everywhere, and police. I saw Ziama and I wanted to go to him."

Alexandra is reliving her life as a small Soviet girl; how could she have known that far away in Berlin, in comfortable and well-heated villas, it had been decided that her Ziama was no longer to be considered a full-fledged human being and must be eliminated from the surface of the Earth? For her, he was not primarily a Jew. He had a name. His name was Ziama.

She got so close that she was almost swept up into the column of Jews. "The policeman almost took me. But the women along the street screamed, 'What are you doing, she's Russian!' They are the ones who pulled me out." Recalling that moment, she sighs deeply, as with regret. As though she still didn't realize, sixty years later, that she might have died on that day. Or rather, as though she still loved her Ziama.

She takes up the thread of her memories again. "They were put into rows, but some of them could walk while others needed to be helped. It was a tragedy. . . . How to describe it to you? They didn't walk in regular columns, but there were about five people in each row. Some held others by the arm. . . . Ziama's mother was sick. He and his father held her up as they walked. This is what I saw. Then I was pulled out of the column."

Her words are seared into my memory. I was struck by the complete difference between her recollections and those of the vengeful anti-Semites. On that day, she did not see a Jew. . . . Her childhood love was being marched to his death. Did his murder influence her professional choice to join the police, eventually to rise to the rank of police colonel? This thought crossed my mind.

Finally, as if summing up, she remembers the punishment her mother gave her when she learned that her daughter had risked getting shot with the Jews from the ghetto. "My mother came from somewhere and hit me and brought me back to the house."

How many Ziamas and Alexandras must there have been in Soviet lands?

How different it is to see the Shoah from an airplane or a satellite than to see it from a Belarusian farmyard!

I hazard a last question: "Did he also see you?"

"Yes [with sadness]. Yes."

I have never forgotten my interview with this woman, this retired police colonel in Monastyrchchina. Whereas for the Germans, the Jews advancing in their column were already considered dead, for Alexandra, Ziama stayed a person to the end.

The young girl she was awakens slowly in her testimony, as her first love and her great risk come back to her. Her face lights up as she evokes her memories of Ziama. Their story could have ended there. The story of two Soviet children in a kolkhoz; one Jewish, the other not.

A fence was put up between them on the orders of people who believe in shattering the human race. Alexandra sighs again, as though she has just returned from that rupture. I am conscious of the fact that her biggest regret, even to this day, is not having stayed with Ziama. Without the intervention of her neighbors and her mother she would have been killed along with him by the Germans. She was made to live because she was not Jewish. He was not allowed to live because he was Jewish.

What the fence boards of the ghetto could not separate, bullets could.

I leave Alexandra's house with a sadness of my own. I look at the distant fields swept by the autumn wind. Her words resonate in my head: "I barely had time to get close to him when the policeman pushed me into the column. The others started to scream and got me out. We weren't able to exchange a single word. It was very stressful. I couldn't understand what was happening. I was already used to all kinds of suffering. There was a punitive detachment in our area. We saw all kinds of horrors. But we never thought they were going to take all these people to be shot."

On that day, I understood that, despite it all, despite the too numerous common graves, despite the bullets, Hitler had failed. Alexandra loved Ziama as a young girl loves a young man. The Nazis' intended fracturing of the human race could not touch their love.

Chapter 9

THE DIRECTOR

OF THE TRUCKING COMPANY

Rawa Ruska. For me as a child, Rawa Ruska was nowhere. I didn't even know what country it might be in. And then one day, a very long time ago, I found myself with my friend Steven Goldstein in Cracow. I will never forget it.

He lived in Geneva and sold duty-free chocolate in the shape of gold bars. They could be found in all the airports as the Goldkenn brand. It is doubtless with him that I began my journey. He had told me that his parents got married in the Cracow ghetto, then fled with the promise that, if they survived, they would find one another.

I walked with Steven through the streets of the Cracow ghetto, the medieval ghetto of Kazimir, and then of Podgorge, where the exterminations took place. With his guidebook in one hand and his phone in the other, he called his mother, who was in a retirement home in the town of Netanya, north of Tel Aviv. He had suddenly come upon the place of his parents' marriage, now an ordinary spot on a middle-class street.

The neighborhoods were still not entirely rebuilt, and one could easily get through half-broken-down gates, into courtyards, to look around and to ask questions. When we found the place, I didn't know what to say. Steven's wife could barely walk, not because she was tired or old but because it seemed that at every corner she might still meet the Germans. Across from us, on other side of the street, was a sign in big letters for OPTIMA, a chocolate brand. As Steven realized that his parents were married across from a chocolate store, he was struck by the symmetry of his having spent most of his life selling Swiss chocolate in the shape of gold bars. Since then, he has gone into the health food business.

We went to the Cracow train station. At that time, it was an old Soviet station with small, seemingly faceless ticket windows and long lines. We went because we knew that many Jews had left from there.

I looked at the big departure boards where the letters spelling out destinations turned with a loud mechanical noise. Suddenly, a new destination appeared: the next train was leaving for Rawa Ruska.

I couldn't believe it. Rawa Ruska, the mystery town, was displayed on the board at the Cracow train station. Unable to resist, I waited in line at the window and asked where Rawa Ruska was. The Polish rail employee said to me, "We've just reopened that line. It's at the Ukrainian frontier."

For the first time, Rawa Ruska was an actual place.

It took me about ten years to finally take the road leading to Rawa Ruska. It's not easy to go to the site of such a painful family memory, even if it's not your own but that of a beloved grandfather, even with the passage of time. How many times since that first visit have I passed through Polish and Ukrainian customs?

When we did go, we weren't just passing through Rawa Ruska— we were staying there. The adjunct mayor, Yaroslaw, housed our team. The place was strange, located just inside the border. There were numerous gatehouses where one could change money, euros and dollars, into *hryvnias*. We wondered why there were so many of these gatehouses, because the exchange rates from place to place didn't vary. Still, each of the women sitting in these poorly heated booths would try to attract any obvious tourist getting out of a truck or car.

We made our way through this succession of little huts. Each one was more or less falling apart, their paint peeling, crowded together behind the forest. Suddenly, a little sign pointed us to a hotel decorated with red-and-green painted wooden dragons. A small structure served as the hotel lobby. Just inside, a man, apparently a trucker, was focusing all his energy on a game machine that he was shaking desperately in order to get his coins to fall in. A young woman gave us our keys and led each of us to a little wooden cabin. Here we stayed for a long time, put up by the mayor at minimal cost, as we had almost no budget. The furniture was basic; there was a white electric radiator always set on high because it was so cold, a small bed whose sheets often went unwashed, a rudimentary bathroom. But we were grateful to be somewhere in Ukraine that offered us a base for our investigations. Without Yaroslaw, without this surreal setup in Rawa Ruska, not far from Camp 325 where my grandfather had been a prisoner, we would never have been able to go as far as we did in our research.

At the border crossing, there was a big forest and a no-man's-land between Poland and Ukraine. I have made the crossing in all sorts of weather, fog, snow, sunshine. At the beginning, I couldn't have known that one day I would discover in the archives that a certain Josef, head of a trucking company that was operating under the German occupation, had made this same crossing with his trucks full of Jews bound for mass graves. I couldn't have known that this pretty forest at the frontier still conceals, to this day, the unknown tombs of more than ten thousand Jews.

It was 2012 when Andrej called me on the phone. "I've found the testimony of a German civilian who was working in Rawa Ruska." Each time the veil lifts a little more from over Rawa Ruska, my mind reels. Andrej went on to give me Josef's testimony.

Josef Liefers was interrogated after the war by a German court as part of a trial of Nazi war criminals. He was from the town of Essen in the Ruhr Valley. Before the war, he was a truck mechanic. At Rawa Ruska, he was hired as the director of the trucking arm of the German company, Bermann. He had previously worked for the company in Hamburg, Germany.[1] "I got a contract to work and a pass that allowed me to come into the country without hassle. Once I arrived in Rawa Ruska, I took on the direction of the company's entire inventory of trucks. The garage was located at number 6 Potiliczerstrasse."

One day, at ten in the morning, Josef got a special order for trucks for the following day. The trucks had to be ready early, at six on the dot. "I saw that the orders were blank. So I couldn't tell where the vehicles would have to go. Also, it was expressly stated that the drivers had to be German, although their copilots could be Ukrainian." Josef learned that thirteen other private German transport companies had received the same orders. Every truck in Rawa Ruska was mobilized.

On that day, Josef only had two German drivers at his disposal. His three other trucks would have to be driven by Ukrainians. He went through the usual motions: putting in the orders for five vehicles, asking for their gas tanks to be filled, for snow tires and chains. It was December.

"Since the trucks had been reserved for the entire day, I assumed that they were being used for a long trip. I told the drivers that they should bring food and have the tanks filled for a four-hundred-kilometer [two-hundred-fifty-mile] journey, meaning two hundred kilometers each way, which corresponds to one hundred and twenty liters of gas in the truck. I had them take double the usual number of spare tires and put on chains for the snow. My trucks were ready for an all-terrain journey."

The next morning at 5:30, Josef heard the vehicles leaving the parking garage. It was still pitch dark at that hour on December 20, 1942. At 8:30 a.m. he arrived at his office, where he learned that none of his Jewish workers had showed up. He rushed to the center of town, which today is a big square, not far from the Polish Catholic church. There he watched the arrest of the Jews, who had to get into all the trucks.

"By that time, the first three trucks had been called and filled with Jews. There was an SS guard on each truck step, submachine gun in hand. An open car, with two SS officers, started to drive in front of the three trucks. A. and I went to the military town-planning center. There we learned that no one had been told ahead of time and everyone at all the other companies had been just as surprised. The military planning service had simply given the order to make available to the *Kreishauptmann*[2] as many trucks as possible for a special mission. We concluded that we were powerless and could do nothing but wait. So we turned around and headed for our office on Potiliczerstrasse.

"At around ten in the morning, the Bermann trucks came back to the garage, much sooner than anticipated. The first driver, H., who was from Cologne, was pale. He couldn't speak. It was B., the second driver, who told us, 'Once our trucks were full of Jews, we still didn't know where we were supposed to go. On each of our truck steps was an SS guard with a loaded submachine gun ready to fire. We started to drive once the three trucks from the Stickel, Charlottenburg Company were full. We went down Judenstraße, to Lembergstraße, then we turned right down Lublinerstraße. After two kilometers [a mile], we turned off to the left, behind a small forest, and took a dirt road. We kept going until we got to an old Russian anti-tank ravine. At the edge of the ditch was a large number of SS with submachine guns, and here and there we could see actual machine guns. The Jews had to get out, and were immediately surrounded. The Jews wearing good quality clothes were forced to take them off. Then, they were ordered down into the ditch in groups of ten to fifteen people, with no difference made between the young and the old or between men, women, and children. Once the first of them were in the ditch, the SS started to shoot. Already on the trip, the Jews who had tried to resist had been immediately executed. People were trembling, many on their knees praying. The SS were pitiless and pushed them into the ditch. Then we came back here. We won't go back.'"

Josef then went to assess the state of the trucks and saw that they were full of blood.

"This is the report made to me by B., our driver from Hamburg. I inspected the vehicles, filthy with blood, and gave the order to clean them. I sent the driver B. home. Around two o'clock in the afternoon, the other three trucks returned, also full of blood. I again had them cleaned and parked. I had decided not to let my vehicles go again, and I succeeded."

The drivers from Bermann, along with the thirteen other transport companies in Rawa Ruska, were neither military nor police but German civilians, small and medium-sized companies that had voluntarily expatriated to occupied Soviet territory.

Reading over this report, I thought, how many German civilians, how many small businesses, were "used" for the murders of Jews in Soviet territories? Without Josef's deposition, would we know that thirteen German trucking companies had been directed to carry the city's Jews to their death? And who could have told us that so many Jews were gravely injured or murdered in transit? Never again, after reading this deposition, could I travel the road between Rawa Ruska and the forest without thinking of the Bermann Company's German trucks.

Later, the Rawa Ruska Gestapo must have realized how many German civilians were used as part of the machine of genocide. They were made to sign a pledge of silence at the headquarters of the Rawa Ruska Gestapo.

"On the Gestapo's orders, all the Germans in Rawa Ruska had to meet in the German mess hall," Josef continued. "The Gestapo chief, Späth,[3] made a speech in which he explained that the threat of typhus had been very serious in the town of Rawa Ruska and that it was for this reason that the action had been carried out. . . .At the end, he said that no one could leave the room until he had signed a paper. Späth then read us what it said. The content was basically, 'I guarantee, by my signature, that I will keep a strict silence regarding the procedures and actions taken in Rawa Ruska and its surroundings. I have been informed that I would expose myself to severe sanctions were I to talk about this.' That was pretty much it. As we went out, there was a table where we all had to sign, about four hundred fifty Germans, men and women."

Four hundred fifty civilian Germans! Just in the town of Rawa Ruska, 450 German civilians were used by the genocidal machine, or at least had knowledge of the crime and had to sign an oath of secrecy. In one town, 450 German civilians knew. I ask myself, how many thousands saw or participated in the genocide of the Jews and stayed quiet for the most part, going home and saying nothing?

Apparently, killing units weren't afraid to publicly murder Jews in front of Slavic populations, but they didn't feel the same way with respect to German civilian employees. Practically, it would have been impossible for them to murder all the Jews in Rawa Ruska without using the available German labor. Still they tried, with signed documents, to reduce the German civilians to silence, so that in Germany itself, both during and after the genocide, nobody would know the full story. Josef's deposition is proof in itself that the pledge of secrecy did not fully work. After having read it, I walked differently through the streets of Rawa Ruska, asking myself how many German civilians had lived during the occupation in these houses I passed, witnessing or actively participating in the massacre of the Jews.

Chapter 10

THE TRANSPORTERS OF JEWS

I t is spring 2012.

We are far from Moscow, far from Berlin. We are in Krasnodar,[1] a large Russian city founded by Cossacks in 1793.

As soon as we arrive here, I am struck by the animated, colorful little markets, with their Armenian and Azerbaijani merchants sitting on the sides of their trucks, calling out invitations to buy potatoes in burlap sacks. On the outskirts of the markets is a peaceful calm, like a village. There is an air of the South in these streets.

We go to Armavir,[2] named in honor of its Armenian founders. Armavir is known for its pretty nighttime lighting; one would think it was Christmas. Garlands, in the form of pines, flowers, and giant rabbits line the main street, lending a joyful air when the sun disappears. We come home late every night and leave early in the morning, so for several days we see the city only in this lantern light.

In the immensity that is Russia, we drive many miles to get from one place to another. We know from archives that many Jewish shootings occurred in this region of the Northern Caucasus. The victims were not all Russian. Many among them were refugees from Poland, Ukraine, and Belarus. We often forget that the Soviet Union took in many refugees, Jews and non-Jews alike, hoping to escape the German army. Most of them were eventually caught by the commandos of the SS.

The documentation we have on Nazi crimes in the Caucasus is thin, and the German reports from the period are less than complete. The region is very far from Berlin and by the time the Germans were here, they no longer felt certain of winning the war. The occupation here did not last long; the German military invaded some villages in November 1942 and left in March 1943. Five months. What is five months but a blip in the history of the twentieth century? But this occupation was long enough to allow *Einsatzgruppe* D[3] to murder Jews, Gypsies, and Communists, sometimes in the same grave.

We returned several times to the Caucasus.

On April 10, 2012, our team visited a hamlet near the village of Temir-goyevskaya, in the region of Krasnodar. According to his neighbors, a certain Alexander had much to tell about the execution of Jewish refugees during the war. As we walked into his yard, our eyes needed time to adjust to the universe we were entering.

Alexander is sitting on the ground, shaping pieces of white wood with which to repair his gate. All around him are fresh wood shavings. Alexander has a lively air about him; he is dressed in blue and reminds me of the old *kibbutzniks* I met in Israel.

"It's almost Easter!" Alexander exclaims. "We have to spruce up anything that got damaged during the winter." In many villages, I have often seen families repainting their garden walls, often blue, at the approach of Easter. At the back of the yard, Alexander's wife is also sitting on the ground. She is mixing wet earth with dried hay.

Without interrupting his own repair work, Alexander explains that his wife is making bricks to fix the walls of the chicken coop, which were devastated by rain and snow. There are, in fact, many red and white chickens wandering around in the yard; they peck around for stray corn kernels or grains of wheat. On the left, a small staircase gives them access to the branches of a large tree where they can find shelter at night. Alexander notices us looking at the setup and comments that when chickens sleep up high, they are protected against

German soldiers preparing to raid the Kovno ghetto as its Jewish residents look on. Lithuania, 1941–1943. (United States Holocaust Memorial Museum, courtesy of George Kadish/Zvi Kadushin)

Ukrainian Jews on their way to register with the German police. Many were subsequently executed by the German and Romanian occupiers. Odessa, October 22, 1941.

The Jews of Krivoi Rog leaving their village en route to the site of their execution. Ukraine, 1941.

Jews wearing circular badges are marched through town as they're deported from the Krzemieniec ghetto. Ukraine, 1942. (Institut Pamieci Narodowej)

Guarded by Germans, Jews walk through the streets of Kamenetz-Podolski toward the site of their execution outside the city. Ukraine, 1941. (US Holocaust Memorial Museum, courtesy of Ivan Sved)

Jews assembled before their execution at Fort VII in Kaunas, Lithuania, 1941. (Bundesarchiv, B 162 Bild-04135 / photo: O. Ang.)

In Tluste, a small village near Zaleszczyki, Ukraine, Germans force the Jewish inhabitants to undress before shooting them. 1941. (From the Archives of the YIVO Institute for Jewish Research)

Jewish women guarded by German soldiers before being shot. The caption
in German on the back of the original reads: "They will be massacred."
Skvira, Ukraine, 1941. (Museum of Jewish Heritage, courtesy of the Yaffa
Eliach Collection donated by the Center for Holocaust Studies)

Jews forced to dig their own grave in Zborov, Ukraine, 1941.
(Bundesarchiv, Bild 183-A0706-0018-029 / photo: O. Ang.)

Members of an *Einsatzkommando* unit firing on a group of men standing in a trench in front of them. USSR, 1941–1942. (Dokumentationsarchiv des Oesterreichischen Widerstandes)

Members of the German police prepare to execute naked men and young boys lined up at the edge of a common grave. Eastern Europe, 1939–1943. (Bildarchiv Preussischer Kulturbesitz)

The Mass Grave

A mass grave containing the bodies of several thousands Jews, Proskurov (Khmelnitsky), Ukraine, 1941–1942. (US Holocaust Museum, courtesy of Muzeum Wojska Polskeigo)

A man rummages through the piles of clothes belonging to Jews murdered in Vinnitsa, Ukraine, 1941–1942. (From the Archives of the YIVO Institute for Jewish Research)

German soldiers rummage through the clothing and belongings of Jews murdered at Babi Yar, Kiev, Ukraine, 1941. (US Holocaust Museum, courtesy of Julius Schatz)

lice. I recall my grandmother Victorine's guinea fowl in Villegaudin. They also slept in a tree, a weeping willow, and they woke us up at dawn with their little cries.

Everything in this yard speaks of the simplicity of traditional rural life. This universe is familiar to me. Our little house in Bresse, where my maternal grandfather Émile was born, had only one room at first. The walls were also made of cob, the mixture of mud and straw that for so many years served to build the farmhouses of Europe.

Alexander spoke calmly, for a long time. Hanna, our translator, would tell us later that he was one of the easiest witnesses to translate.

Alexander was an adolescent when the war broke out. He talks about it with the freshness of a young Soviet, proud of his country. "When we found out that the war had begun, we were enthusiastic. We were kids, and we were convinced that we were going to win easily. For us, this was a chance to demonstrate the greatness of our country that we had read so much about in books. At the time, I was twelve and this was an adventure."

With the same vivacity, he recounts the arrival of the Jewish refugees in his kolkhoz. The trucks had to pick them up at the train stations and divide them up between the local families.

"They brought the Jews here on the train and lodged them with the inhabitants of the surrounding kolkhozes. We lived in harmony. But I don't know where they came from. . . . The district administration just gave the order for the trucks to be available to drop the Jews off in the kolkhozes. The people here thought the Jews wouldn't stay long and that they'd return to the west afterwards."

The history of these evacuated Jews taking refuge in the Asian republics of the Soviet Union is very little known. At the time of the evacuations, sometimes planned, sometimes spontaneous, the traces of many families are lost in the East.

Alexander continued his story. Suddenly he was struck by the memory of a Jewish childhood friend named Sergueï. We asked, "Did your friend Sergueï live in your house?"

"No, he lived over there, but I never went to his house. He came over to mine often. We were friends and we got into mischief together; we were only twelve at the time. We would go swimming in the river in the summer, in August 1942. We played 'whites and reds,' where you had to break through team lines and take your opponents' flag. We also played tag and hide and seek. Sometimes, we got up to mischief and snuck into the village orchards to steal fruit. We also went into the forest a lot. We were very curious."

Memories of a Soviet childhood. On our side of the curtain, we were playing cowboys and Indians, while on the other side they played whites and reds. Games inspired by national myths.

Sergueï's parents, Jews from the West, seemed a bit strange to Soviet peasants. They were city folk, unfamiliar with working the earth. "Sergueï's parents didn't work. They only stayed here for about a month, not enough time to work. It was the month of August and we often saw them on the riverbank. That's where we met."

For Alexander, the arrival of the Germans was an adventure, a game tinged with fear. When the Wehrmacht invaded the village, most of the inhabitants hid in the forest. Alexander was very worried about his father.

"My father was standing there and a German pushed him from behind with his machine gun. I don't know what got a hold of me, but in a flash of rage I jumped on the German and grabbed onto his gun. The German was surprised by this unexpected action, and he looked at me without moving to see what I would do next. I pulled with all my strength to get his gun away from him, but he was a big strong man, and he didn't budge one millimeter. I stayed holding on, suspended in air. He laughed, set me on the ground, and said, '*Gut, Kinder.*'"[4]

Alexander's story could have ended there. Memories of a very brief German occupation. It was nothing much. But then, Alexander's face darkened at the recollection of another man, a Russian-speaking German. He arrived at the head of a train of carts, each with a horse and driver. Alexander climbed aboard the cart the man was driving. This German would deceive the whole village, for he was preparing the massacre of the Jews.

"It was two weeks or maybe even a month after the Germans' arrival. One morning, at around nine o'clock. . . . I saw a column of between seven and nine empty carts arrive. On the first cart, there was a German, a young man. When he saw me, he signaled me to stop and asked me where the Jews were. I told him the Jews lived near the barns. He told me to go with him. I tried to refuse, but he forced me. I asked him who he was. . . . He spoke Russian with no accent. He told me he was German but had lived a long time among Russians.

"I later learned he was in charge of taking the Jews to the ghetto. We went to the area where they were living, and, I admit, I was curious to see what this man was going to do."

Alexander accompanied the German from house to house. For Alexander it was a game, but the German was counting the Jews.

"He went into one house after another and asked if there were any Jews. All he had with him was a notebook and a pencil, nothing else. I tried to see if he had a gun, but I couldn't find anything. In his notebook, he had a list of the Jews with the names of the people who were housing them. If all the Jews on his list were present, he told them to load all their possessions onto the carts. He said they had to leave for the ghetto, that their departure was set for five o'clock. We went around to all the houses, and the Jews loaded their things."

The list of Jews was easy to find. Anyone who lives in the Soviet Union has to register, so all the Jewish refugees were known to the local administration. All the Germans had to do was get hold of the registers; this is how the German had the list of names and addresses in hand. From nine in the morning until five in the evening, Alexander would accompany the young German. In Temirgoyevskaya, the Jews were not promised removal to Palestine but rather a transfer to the ghetto. The height of the German's treachery was that he took a nap at the end of the afternoon, right before the massacre.

"We were talking, and he was laughing. I couldn't possibly imagine that he was taking the Jews to be shot. We went to a woman's house, and the German asked her for some milk and a duvet. He drank the milk, then he laid out the duvet in her garden and went to sleep."

How could the Jews have been afraid of a young German accompanied by a kid from the village?

Alexander had no idea what was about to happen. While the Jews had loaded their possessions on the carts and were themselves sitting or standing, Alexander insisted on taking a cart ride the German had promised him. "I asked him if we could take a ride in a cart. He said yes. After the ride, I went swimming with the other boys."

Sergueï came one last time to Alexander's house. Alexander's father seemed to know what was going to happen but kept quiet. "Before leaving, my Jewish friend Sergueï came over. My father gave us something to eat and looked at Sergueï with sadness. At the time, I didn't understand why my father was looking at him like that. I think he already knew what was going to happen. We were at the river until four o'clock, then we went straight to the carts. They were all loaded. The German *Kommandantur* had given the order to round up all the Jews and bring them to the ghetto.

"At five in the evening, all the Jews got onto the carts. The German counted them. I noticed that our driver didn't talk to anyone. Maybe he knew what was about to happen. The German got onto the first cart and gave the order to leave. Along with thirty other boys from the village, I climbed on with the Jews, for fun. The line of carts headed off in the direction of Temirgoyevskaya." The killer would eventually have to put an end to the game the children of the kolkhoz were playing, but up until the very end, the children played with this convoy of death.

The drivers, for their part, said nothing. Their silence intrigues me. It is obvious that they knew. Throughout all of our research, we have met very few people who transported Jews. The diggers, the fillers, even the sellers of stolen clothes will speak. Why do the transporters stay quiet? From experience, what usually engenders silence is the theft of belongings. Were the drivers compensated? Did they partake in pillaging at the time of the arrests? Or did they rob the Jews they carried? How to find out . . . ?

Alexander goes on with his terrible story: a game on the fly for the kolkhoz kids, the road to death for the Jews.

"The carts left the village, and after about a hundred meters [a hundred yards], the German stopped the column. He had kept his promise to give us a ride, but now it was time for us to go home. He inspected each of the carts and made all the village children get down; then he got back in his seat and the line of carts began to move forward again.

"We wanted to ride some more. We chased after them and jumped back on the carts. He looked at us with a smile and said nothing. Five hundred meters [a third of a mile] farther along, he stopped the procession again and this time he told us firmly to go home."

It's terrible to realize that this line of carts, full of Jews, was perceived by the children of the village as a mobile carnival ride. Terrible to know that the requisitioned drivers were aware. Why did they stay walled in silence? Had they received threats? Money? Goods in exchange? The children played on the carts until the last minute. The German led the procession. The drivers went on without a word.

When the carts had finally disappeared, the children started to play again. "The carts left and we stayed where we were and played a game of reds and whites."

But Alexander's childhood is over. It snaps like a cut cord.

"Suddenly, we heard women's voices, then German voices, and then the sound of motors. We heard a crowd screaming, but we didn't see anyone, and then there were volleys of gunshots, and then more women's cries. We got scared and ran toward the village.

"The next morning, I still didn't realize what had happened the evening before. I went to the river because I had left some fishing lines out, when suddenly I saw the corpse of a little boy in the water.

He was kneeling, naked, his head in the water. All you could see was his back. I had seen the bodies of Russian and German soldiers before, but I had never seen a dead child. I didn't dare to touch him with my hand, so I turned him over with my foot, and I saw that it was my friend Serguei."

Alexander can no longer speak; he is sobbing. He cries like the child he was, the child he will never be again. Up until now, he has been able to hold together the illusion of the drama and the game. But all at once, no more games are possible. No tag, no reds and whites. The body floating in the river was not that of a stranger. Nor was it simply the body of a child. It was Serguei's body.

So many peasants have told us, in tears, how they saw their class-mates, whom they can still name, arrested, transported, then shot before their eyes because they were Jews. It has always seemed to me that these former children formed simple bonds with their Jewish friends, and they have never recovered from witnessing their murder. The young Alexander, within a few minutes, grasped everything and understood too much.

"When I turned him over, the current carried him off. It was at this precise moment that I understood that all the Jews had been shot. I don't know what came over me. I started to run without stopping and, even when I reached my house, I couldn't stop running; it was as though I had lost my mind. I ran in circles around the yard, in a state of shock. My father came out of the house and told me in Ukrainian to stop. . . . I could hear his voice, but I couldn't obey him. He caught me and asked me what was happening to me. I told him they had shot the Jews! As I spoke, he put his hand over my mouth and carried me into the house. . . . He forbade me to go outside for the next three days."

The father's action speaks volumes. Alexander, like the transporters of the Jews, like his own father, is going to have to be quiet. Quiet out of fear. The German units also murdered Communist partisans.

"Sometime later in the village, a handwritten announcement began to circulate. It said: 'Citizens, if you discover the body of a German soldier, you must inform the *Kommandantur*. If you find the body of a Russian soldier, you must bury it. However, if you find the body of a Jew, do not touch it!' Then two or three weeks later, the bodies of the Jews started coming to the surface of the water. That's how we knew they shot them in the river. When the other boys and I came to swim, we saw the bloated bodies floating. We saw our neighbors, Katia and Aunt Dounya. We pushed the bodies as far away as possible, waited an hour, and then went swimming. . . . Nobody tried to get them out. All of the bodies were undressed, the women were in underwear. The river was called the Laba."

Alexander continued his life in this small village, swimming in the Laba River. This was the first time that he had spoken to people who weren't from the village. It was the first time he had left his silence.

Chapter 11

THE LAYERS OF PLANKS

Childhood in Villegaudin, immersed in a Bressan countryside that was virtually unchanged in the 1960s, seems so close, so present, and so far away all at once. Everything was stable, or at least cyclical; like the purslane seeds my grandmother Victorine planted in the spring around our cement terrace, always in the same spots, to bloom amid the gravel. There was the green bench, the wooden wing chair that we always had to repaint after the thaw. The wisteria blossomed everywhere, its interlacing branches transforming the facade of our house into a Manet painting. The ancient roses, tiny but so sweet-smelling. The first cuckoo song in the spring forest, heard from afar, that brought good luck to those who happened to have money in their pockets. The big ditches around the moats of the château on whose grounds my family lived, its two beautiful stone lions reigning for eternity.

Everything remained, everything was renewed.

As Catherine Deneuve says in *Indochine*, "Youth is believing that things don't have to come apart."

Never, ever, had anyone explained to me that one day we would have to leave; we were one with this place. No one had even told me that we had to die. Ever. For me the Château de la Marche would always be "*chez nous*." This meant that when we heard the approach of any motor, be it a car, a truck, or sputtering motorbike, we looked up to see who could possibly be coming; an unfamiliar vehicle was an event.

At eighteen, like many young people, I kept a diary. I ended it with these words: "I'll write about just one week because my life is a succession of weeks." This was country life before tractors or television. Everything, absolutely everything in life, was a function of repetition, repeated acts generation after generation, time without end. From the outside, this might be termed "habit and custom." For us, it was simply life.

I picture myself with my cousins, shouldering pitchforks, going into the fields full of freshly cut green hay drying in the sun. I can still smell it, still hear the scurrying of little gray mice fleeing at our approach. I can taste the blackberries from the brambles. We learned life by observing it, or rather, we were immersed in a universe where objects, actions, and seasons were all of a piece. And objects were one with actions.

When, much later, after years at the university, I came as an adult priest to the Ukrainian or Moldavian countryside, I would suddenly find myself mesmerized by the smell of a room recently whitewashed, a smell I recalled so well from a distant time and place. I was moved by the sight of a farmer throwing corn to her chickens, a gesture I knew well but had forgotten, buried as deeply as if under concrete. Not to mention the daffodils and red tulips in a freshly tilled garden, with pink peonies planted at the entrance and a dog chained to the gate. I had already seen all this. This was home. This was us.

No doubt that is also why I felt my own self come into question every time a peasant described a crime scene in which a familiar object or farm tool would appear but wouldn't be serving its intended purpose in village life. It might be a shovel, a table, a pitchfork, a bowl, a chair.

Often, one of these objects would appear in isolation; isolated from its proper use but also from the person who had transported it. In the rural world, an object doesn't exist by itself; it is always attached to a certain know-how.

The first time I had such an impression was at Rawa Ruska. It was in front of the mass grave in the hamlet of Borove where they killed the last 1,500 Jews from the ghetto. The villagers told me the story on several occasions. I went back many times. They all recalled that the German shooter had put down his guns, apparently Mauser rifles, on a table several yards from the ditch. A farm table in a field.

Many also remembered a black box on this same table, also belonging to the shooter. The box contained mints that the neighborhood children, especially the youngest ones, would sneak while the shooter was busy killing the Jews. A box of candy on a farm table in a field . . . Where did this table come from? And this box? And these mints?

All the witnesses recalled two chickens, bought in the village, that the Germans had grilled themselves for fear of being poisoned by the farmers. But where did these chickens come from?

At the beginning of our research, I was so surprised to discover these familiar objects displaced in this way that I didn't have the wherewithal to ask where they came from.

However, when I heard people talking about wooden planks, it was too much. Many witnesses, especially in western Ukraine and in Belarus, described wooden boards placed over the ditches. The Jewish victims, already beaten, had to stand on these planks to be shot so they would fall directly into the ditch—dead, in their death agony, or sometimes only wounded. There could be just one plank, or several, or, as in Bogdanivka,[1] a full walkway where four rows of Jews could be lined up to be felled by machine gun and fall into a ravine. No doubt, this was one of the most deadly killing grounds for Jews in the East, for 45,000 victims were murdered around Christmastime in 1941.

It was not during the actual interviews but much later, as I read the translations, that the question took root in me. Something didn't sound right. In the testimonies, the planks seemed to come out of nowhere, as if by magic. But who had actually carried them and why wouldn't anyone talk about it?

The answer took years of investigation to discover. Surprisingly, it was easier for witnesses to say that they had seen Jews from their windows, carried their dead bodies, or taken their clothes than it was to explain where those wooden boards came from.

But why? I figured that someone had been requisitioned to bring the planks and someone else to put them over the grave once it was full of bodies. I thought of this particular person as akin to the man who lifts the guillotine blade between beheadings. We're not talking about the murderer or the victim but about a crime technician, like a stagehand who transports the flats for theater productions from location to location, only the production in question was the spectacle of putting one's Jewish neighbors to death.

Who were the transporters and layers of the planks?

In order to understand, I had to listen again to the accounts of several witnesses. They mentioned the boards as being placed across the ditches for many of the executions. The Jews were forced to go forward, one by one, or in families or groups. Even if the planks were not an official element of the killings, there are mentions of them in German depositions as well. Twenty-four years after the fact, Ostap Hucalo, the Ukrainian mayor of the small town of Bolekhov, near Ivano-Frankivsk, recalled the massacre of two thousand Jews—men, women and children—in the local cemetery in 1943.

"A board had been placed over the ditch on which the Jew had to go naked. I still remember that the Jewish families held hands on the plank. Then they were shot in the head from behind and then they fell into the ditch. There were a few Jews down in the ditch who had to lay the dead bodies in rows."[2]

Planks were also used in Belarus, in the districts of Disna, for example, where Fadei, a witness to an execution of local Jews, explained, "Planks had been laid across the ditches. The Jews were beaten as they were brought to the ditch, in groups of five, forced to undress, and pushed naked out onto the planks. As soon as the victims stepped onto the planks, they were cut down with salvos of automatic weapons fire and fell into the ditch. Then a new group of five Jews followed."

The use of planks for the shootings was very often accompanied by extraordinary violence in forcing the Jewish victims to step forward and stand, sometimes in family groups, in order to be shot. The number five suggests that the shooter in this village was using a Mauser rifle, with a five-bullet clip. How many times in the vicinity of mass graves have we found little cartridge clips into which the shooters loaded five bullets?

In Berejany, in Ukraine, we met a neighbor who had observed an execution. "From the second floor of my house, I watched the atrocities committed by Hitler's soldiers through a pair of binoculars. I saw people get undressed, walk on a plank that lay across the ditch, and be shot by a shooter with a machine-pistol. These executions were horrible to watch."

The use of binoculars by neighbors was quite frequent, as it permitted them to watch, risk-free, from home.

It was on August 20, 2005, in Iltsy, a small Ukrainian village in the Ivano-Frankivsk region, while questioning Fedor, that I was again attuned to a deafening silence. Although the villagers spoke easily of the way the planks were laid out at extermination sites, the silence remained total around the identity and actions of those who procured them, transported them to the ditches, and then took them back to the farms after the crime. It was especially quiet around those who moved them around during the actual execution.

I hadn't understood until this point that the planks were mobile. Unconsciously, I had perceived them as a fixture, like gallows or a guillotine. A stable instrument for killing that didn't require a continuous human presence. Or local responsibility.

Fedor explained that the function of the plank was in fact quite different. We met him in a peculiar fashion. We were with the whole team scoping out the elderly people in the market at Iltsy. I watched our researchers circulating among the colorful booths, speaking to one old woman after another. From afar, I noticed a heavyset farmer coming toward the market with a basket of tomatoes under her arm. As soon as we approached her, she let on that she knew all about what had happened here during the war, but that we would have to wait to speak with her until she had sold all her tomatoes. We waited. Once her basket was empty, she got into our van and guided us along a dirt road to her hamlet. Upon arriving home, she simply told her husband to put the cow in the stable. "Go ahead, talk to them, and I will go take care of the cow." It was then that we understood she had led us to him, this serious little man in blue overalls who had seen the execution of the Jews up close.

Fedor put his cow's lead in his wife's hands, climbed into our van, and took us to the edge of what had been the ditch, to the place where there had been planks . . . and people laying planks. He started to speak softly, with a somber air. Almost immediately, he talked about the ditch and the planks, plunging into his memories.

"If the pile of bodies was too high, they moved the plank farther along. . . . They would move the plank so that the level would be uniform and there wouldn't be bumps. . . . Five or six people could walk on it without it breaking."

So there wouldn't be bumps. . . . This expression resonated from my childhood. It was used for wheat, potatoes, or cabbages. On my grandparents' farm in Villegaudin, after we carried the harvested wheat in burlap sacks into the granaries, we would make a pile about three or four feet high. Then, with shovels or rakes, we would even out the surface so that there wouldn't be bumps. We did the same thing in the beet silos.

Fedor spoke of the plank and the Jews' common grave the way we talked about a wheat or cabbage harvest.

After realizing what Fedor was referring to when he talked about the common grave, I made a decision: to ask several women farmers how they filled ditches with silage. They explained to me that the best way to protect food from frost on farms was to bury it at the bottom of a ditch, in the garden. I pressed them to know concretely what this entailed. I even convinced one of them to bring me and my team down to the bottom of a ditch, or *iamy* in Russian.

After climbing down a small metal ladder, we found ourselves nine feet below ground, in darkness. We were in an empty ditch that could be filled with potatoes or cabbages once they were gathered next autumn. I refrained from explaining why I was so interested in how these ditches were dug on farms. As our time with this farmer was winding down, she lifted her arms in the middle of the street and proudly exclaimed, "In Ukraine, we say there is no good farmer without three ditches in his garden." This hearty saying was a revelation to me. The *iamy* are an everyday part of the Russo-Soviet landscape.

And planks? Do peasants also use planks? And for what purpose? Thinking aloud, I asked if ever planks were put down perpendicularly over the ditches during ensilage.

Svetlana, our interpreter, explained to me that in certain regions, Ternopil in particular, the potato ditches were very narrow, a bit like trenches. When it came time to sell the potatoes that had been stored in the ditch over the winter, planks were laid across the ditches for the customers. From these planks, they lowered their baskets on a rope down to the bottom. There, the seller, or one of his employees, would fill the basket, after which the client pulled it back up. I was told this technique protected the vegetables from being stepped on.

Were the Germans aware of these local agricultural practices? It's easy to believe, when we consider how numerous the *Volksdeutsche* were in the *Einsatzgruppen* or the German police brigades. There were also Soviets in the *Volksdeutsche*; they knew the local customs. At the end of this interview with the farmer about the potatoes, one of our Ukrainian aides, Micha, who had been listening attentively, burst out, "So, the Germans ordered the peasants, 'dig a ditch like you do for potatoes'!"

This hypothesis remains to be proven. Yet I still cannot help but think that most of the Jews killed were shot on the edge of common ditches, or on planks, and that both ditches and planks were integral parts of Russo-Soviet peasant life. The German occupants recycled rural customs for their criminal ends.

The task of laying the plank, far from being innocent, is crucial to the organization of the killing operations. The layers of planks have to stay on site during the entire execution, close to the shooters. They cannot leave the side of the ditch. And they cannot act alone. There must be at least two of them to carry boards solid enough to support the weight of five people. Who were these men laying planks?

A few years later, in May 2009, in the village of Novossilka, not far from Ternopil, the enigma cleared a bit. Patrice was conducting the interview. Anna, a very serious woman, belonged to a family who worked in the Soviet administration. She spoke with composure, sitting on a long bench against the wall of her house, her face framed by a blue linen scarf. She had her two-year-old grandson with her and never took her eyes off him. Our entire team had the same goal: to discover who transported the planks.

Anna was eleven when the events took place. Not only had she seen the ditches being dug, but she also saw the planks as they were laid. During the interview, she spoke without digression. "The Germans would go into any house. They took the young people to go dig; they had to bring their own shovels and dig. And they went. They dug three ditches, and then they put down planks. I was there and I saw everything."

For the first time, I was hearing a witness to the transportation of the planks. In this village, the requisitioned diggers were also the ones laying the planks. They traveled not only with their own shovels but also with wooden boards from their farms. If it was so simple, why was there so much silence surrounding them?

Patrice had an intuition that Anna knew more than she was saying and would be ready to disclose it. He went for it. "Were the planks that were laid over the ditches put down on the day the ditches were dug or on the day of the shootings?"

"It was when they were shot. It was the day they were shot that the planks were brought and put across the ditches. There were two planks on each ditch, one on one side and one on the other side. In all, there were three ditches and six planks. I remember it like it was yesterday. The Jews stood on the planks, and the Germans shot them.

"And had the planks come from the village?"

"Yes, from the village, from someone's house. Yes, in the village . . ."

The plank was most likely brought from a barn, to the ditch, and then back from the ditch to the barn afterward, after the crime.

Much later, however, on March 4, 2014, Geoffroy Lauby, from the Yahad team, met Alexey in Lokitka, in the Ivano-Frankivsk region. He had watched the shootings of the Jews from the safety of a house, through holes in a wall. Alexey recalled not only the planks but also the barked German orders to the Jews to stand on them.

"Yes, they were brought on foot. The Germans had dogs escorting them. There were also soldiers on horseback. The columns of twenty, thirty, or maybe forty people who were surrounded by guards with rifles. Those who couldn't walk were beaten. . . .

"The ditch was ready and the plank, too. They brought the Jews to the cemetery and started the shooting right away, ordering them to move one by one with a '*Noch einmal, Schneller, Feuer*,'[3] faster toward the ditch to be shot."

"So, they were slaughtered one by one?"

"Yes, yes."

The men in charge of the planks were standing amid the cries of "*Noch einmal*," "*Schneller*," "*Feuer*." Sixty years after the fact, I am hearing these orders repeated by a seventy-year-old man. They are still deafening. I hadn't imagined the Germans yelling out orders for each Jew who was shot. The memory of these cries and these orders repeated for each Jew murdered in Lokitka underscores how these plank carriers had to work in the thick of the screaming and violence, at the very heart of the criminal process. The villagers' silence surrounding these requisitioned men could only be, to my mind, an attempt to cover up their unfathomable proximity to the brutality and noise of the crime.

While our investigation has progressed enormously, with almost four thousand interviews as of this writing, no witness has ever admitted to carrying or moving planks on the day of the shootings.

PART THREE

THE DAY

Chapter 12

THE DANCE

April 28, 2013, Paris

The phone rings; it's a Ukrainian number. Patrice is calling me. "In Osipovka, the village where we were working today, near Jitomir, the Jews had to dance before they were shot."

Forced to dance before the crime, but why?

And then, when I asked him who the witness was who told him about this dancing, he sent me a written message.

"As I told you, Andreï and Natalia found Maria in Iossivka while they were looking for witnesses to another shooting. Maria hadn't seen the shooting they were talking about, but she had seen another shooting, one we weren't even aware of.

"Maria's house, like Maria herself, is a study in contrasts. Bright colors, extreme cleanliness, with a dignity to her manner and yet an obvious fragility as well. Her health is failing. As she speaks of a certain Yankel, she tries to mask her emotions. She wants to talk, but she has neither the heart nor the strength."

As soon as Patrice is back in France, I ask to hear Maria's recording.

Music is rare at shootings, to say nothing of dancing! It's impossible to imagine that an orchestra, or even a musician like the one at the gate of Birkenau, would come set up on the sidelines of a common grave. And yet, a couple of examples come to mind.

There was the Ukrainian village of Novozlatopol, in the Zaporojie region, where in 2006 we interviewed Marfa, who left an indelible impression. She was handicapped and so heavy she had to lean on a stool or chair at all times. She invited us into her home, where she had prepared a large pot of soup.

As a child, from her family's farm, she had seen carts and drivers arrive to transport Jews to the district police headquarters.

I can still see her, concentrating intently, counting on her gnarled fingers as she spoke the names of the Jewish neighbors to whom she had barely been able to say goodbye.

She testified along with her husband; he had climbed with friends up on the roof of a Jewish house next to the village pharmacy and from there had had a clear view of the shootings.

"The story is that there was a musician in the neighboring village. He played the *bouben*.[1] He was requisitioned several times to play during executions. He couldn't stand it. It was the only reason he was there. Of course, he didn't want to do it, but he was forced to. While he played, they banged on metal objects to make more noise."

So, in Novozlatopol, the German police would go early in the morning before the shootings to requisition a Ukrainian village musician. They dragged him from his farm and forced him to play his *bouben*, next to the police headquarters, beside the common graves that had just been dug. He was made to play in a futile attempt to mask the noise of the guns firing. He played loudly while the young Ukrainians requisitioned to guard the Jews hit tin cans to drown out the screams.

In Novozlatopol, the traditional Ukrainian instrument that is beaten like a tambourine was repurposed to camouflage gunshots and cries.

In Rawa Ruska, the people of Borove, where I discovered the first mass grave, also recalled music-loving Germans from the time of my grandfather's imprisonment. They listened to the music of their homeland to alleviate boredom while the Jews were digging. They had a gramophone set up at one end of the village. It was on a folding table, near the ditches. As at a campsite, one German would play the harmonica while another sang.

All the while, a few Jewish men were digging what would become the tomb of the last 1,500 Jews remaining in Rawa Ruska. Each time I went back to Borove, I thought about this German music ringing through the forest just before the crime.

Graveside music might at first seem almost utilitarian for the murderers, a way to block noise. But according to our witnesses, it was not very common and was not a widespread policy; it was a local decision.

"Forced dancing," to the best of my knowledge, is even rarer. Here is the story that Maria—born in 1933 in the village of Mokrovo in the Brest region of Belarus, now frail in mind and body—was able to tell us.

"They assembled all the Jews from the surrounding villages in one place. It was on a bridge. They summoned musicians, who were ordered to play, and the Jews were forced to dance. Everyone, without exception, big and small, young and old. I remember one old man with a long beard. He was crying, and the Germans kept clubbing him to make him dance. They had also brought together all the inhabitants of the village and forced us to watch the Jews dance. Everyone was crying; the villagers knew the Jews well. They were friends. It was very hard to watch them suffer. Everybody had to dance, the young children, the adults, the old people. They all held hands. If anyone stopped, they were instantly beaten. This happened before our eyes."

A forced dance show. The Germans who had come to Mokrovo made the Jews dance on a bridge. And they forced the villagers to come see. The bridge still exists. It isn't long and connects two villages. But why dance? Why such violence against those who weren't dancing? And why did the whole village need to be there? Did the general public need to witness German dominance to the point of seeing Mokrovo Jews turned into mechanical dolls?

I don't know. The story is exceptional. To try to understand, I listened again to Maria's interview. As I watched our video of her, I was struck right away; her face was virtually immobile, but her anxious eyes moved right to left across the camera. Her voice was soft, measured, and precise. She spoke calmly and without guile. Behind her were two piles of large, pretty pillows, covered in some sort of netting. I recalled that my grandmother Victorine piled her cushions in the same fashion on the beds at Villegaudin, veiling them in gauze against ever-present, annoying flies.

Maria was ten at the time of her story. She hasn't forgotten the names of her friends.

"I remember a Jew named Yankel very well. He had three children: two girls, Bassia and Lioussia, and a son, Dodia. . . . They lived on my street. There were only four streets here: Baranivska, Doubrivska, Tchotyriiska, and Zemlianska Streets."

Several times, she brought up Yankel.

"He sold tickets at the train station in Doubrivska. His wife was Ukrainian, her name was Tania. . . . It was very common! Ukrainians married Jews, and Jews married Ukrainians." She spoke with a certain nostalgia. These were the memories of a ten-year-old girl.

"Yankel was a nice man. When we kids would go see him, he would take a big handful of matzoh[2] and distribute it among the children." It is quite frequent in the stories of young Soviets who lived in the Jewish kolkhozes to hear about Pesach, or matzoh. Some of these non-Jews even still speak Yiddish. Patrice was quick to ask Maria if she still remembered the matzoh recipe.

"Do you know how to make matzoh?"

"It's a light dough. I know that it takes a lot of kneading and that you add very little water so that it will be firm. The girls said you had to knead for so long that your arms would hurt from doing it."

Like a child, Maria took up her story again and described the setting up of the local government by the German occupation.

"Two weeks after the Germans arrived, they announced a general meeting in the village. Everyone was there, including the Jews. This was where the *staroste* and the *sotnik*[3] were chosen. Both were selected from among people who were not originally from the village but had settled here in 1937 after the Poles had been deported to Kazakhstan. A man named Dratch was named *staroste*, and Litvinov was named *sotnik*. I remember the police, especially an officer named Zeremensy, singing 'Ukraine Is Not Dead Yet.'"[4]

Since this was the first time we had heard a witness use the term "*sotnik*," Patrice asked for clarification, "What is a *sotnik*? Is it different from a *desiatnik*?" Maria explained, "It's the same thing. . . . There was only one *sotnik* and one *staroste*."

This was not a question of simple intellectual curiosity. Patrice wanted to know who had assembled the Jews on the day of their execution. Maria clarified, "It was the *staroste* who announced that we had to assemble. All the villagers came, the Ukrainians, the Poles, the Jews. . . . Nobody thought that something terrible would happen."

It was to be a gathering of the entire village, a general meeting— what could be more ordinary?—in the local "club." This club, the sole substantial building ensconced in the village center, was the Soviet-era locale for culture, festivities, and political meetings.

"A German . . . flanked by a *Volksdeustche*, arrived from Baranivka with his adjunct. We sang our song. Then they announced that Germany needed our help, that we had to dig ditches, etc. They also said that all the Jewish men had to gather the next day So they gathered, believing they were actually about to be put to work. Yankel was more suspicious than the others; he realized that they weren't being taken away to work, and he fled."

Here again, to my surprise, Maria listed the names of the Jewish men summoned to the club and then shot. "I can name them all: Yankel, Doda, Mounik, Roiterman, two people, Maïté, the two young Meiers. . . . In all there were about fifteen men. They didn't bring anything with them. They were summoned, loaded into a truck, and told that they were leaving for work."

At several points during our interview, Maria returned again to the memory that she absolutely wanted to talk about: the dance. What she described was surreal; the Jews, mostly women, the elderly and children, made to dance in the club. And all the villagers brought to watch.

"They danced for a while. Then they were whipped so they would dance faster, which made the villagers watching begin to cry. They pitied the poor Jews whom they'd lived beside for several years now. The murderers started to threaten the villagers. They said that if anyone wanted to join the Jews, they could take him away too. There was a policeman from Baranivka playing music."

The policeman hummed to give rhythm to the dance. "He didn't really play an instrument, but he made music with a comb that he used like a harmonica. He made noises with his mouth. All the Jews, without exception, had to dance. First, they gathered them in the clubhouse, then they made them go outside. They had to dance surrounded by guards before the captive eyes of the villagers.

"The point was to frighten us. We had heard that they were going to shoot the Poles too, right after the Jews. The Poles were terrified. The Jews danced for close to an hour. They were exhausted, but every time they tried to stop, the Germans cried, "Dance!" and threatened them with whips so they kept going.

"The Germans pushed the older children to dance, but didn't touch the younger ones, who stood here and there in little groups."

Here Maria recalled an old crippled man.

"All the villagers were taken to watch. Our neighbor, Pess, a very old man, couldn't stand up on his own. So they tied him to his wife and forced the two of them to dance. That moment has always stuck in my memory. . . . They were bound together with a large belt, and they were dancing. . . . When it was time to go to the edge of the ditch, the man literally couldn't walk. So he and his wife were loaded onto the cart that followed the column of Jews and brought toward the site of the shooting."

I stopped the video. The dance wasn't simply a cruel and absurd game preceding the crime. The German viciousness was turned on the weakest. And the awful show was performed for the villagers, who had no choice but to watch. The murder of the Jews became a municipal event. There was a public dance followed by a public massacre.

To understand that the German shootings were far from traditional military executions, all we have to do is consider the fate of Mr. Pess.

"So, when the men were taken away, the Jewish women and children stayed in their houses?"

Maria replied, "Yes, they stayed quietly in their homes, as if none of this was their concern. There were quite a few mixed families; a lot of Polish and Ukrainian women were married to Jews and had children with them. These women got favorable treatment, and nobody harmed them, but the children of mixed couples were considered Jews and were exterminated."

She had seen her Jewish neighbors summoned by the Germans, first the men. Then it was the women and children and the elderly who were taken to "the club." She spoke of them all with great emotion.

Certain memories—repeated humiliation and cruelty—block out thought. The dark inventiveness in the sadism of genocidal murderers can seem limitless. I started the video again. Patrice, his voice calm, continued to ask questions, and Maria let her memories rise one after the other. The names of several families came up repeatedly. Her neighbors had become like toys to be switched on, broken, and finally destroyed.

Hatred, anti-Semitism, and the license to kill do not make all killers alike. In this village, the crime was transformed into a form of public amusement.

Chapter 13

THE COOKS AND THE SHOOTERS

Paris, June 10, 2013

Spring is slow to come and is over quickly. A compact mass of gray clouds swallows up all the light. Our morale is affected. One of the Yahad's five investigative teams is back from the Ukrainian region of Jytomyr. As with each return, after seventeen long days of listening to old men and women share their memories of mass killings, the team has to adjust to the regular day-to-day of Paris, with its traffic jams, its metro, its tricolor traffic lights, the rapid steps of its pedestrians, its shop windows. In short, they have to adjust to life.

Alexy, the young Ukrainian who is the head of this team, calls me. He needs to talk. Among other things, he tells me that this past June 4 he met the daughter of a cook who had to prepare food for the shooters. Her name was Galina.

Several days later, I received the video of Galina; life had not been kind to her. Her hardened face was protected by a tight red scarf; she was rather small, and she had trouble walking. Around her left calf was a sort of white cloth bandage. She lived in one of those old public housing buildings that survive from the former collective farms, the kolkhozes. A sad gray concrete bungalow shared by four grandmothers, each one poorer and more diminished than the last. Once she was seated on a "bench" outside, her back against the house, she told her story without hesitation. Her neighbors, one after the other, approached, perhaps to support her, perhaps also to learn, because none of them had been there on the day the Jews were murdered.

I was desperate to see the video. In this kind of meeting, certain details can escape the interviewer. Alexy's description rang true. Poor Galina spoke as best she could, relying on her knotty hands to help communicate what she could not say with her too-simple words. She wasn't sitting on an actual bench but on a board propped up on two wooden blocks. Behind her was a brick wall painted with lime. To the right of her were some abandoned tools. The whole scene reeked of misery. Yet she had put on her Sunday best, as they say in Bresse, where I come from.

When she was asked if she had seen the Germans, she didn't beat around the bush. She spoke directly: "Yes, when they shot." The Germans she had seen were killers.

Some Jews had been sent to work in her collective. And then one day, some Germans all dressed in black appeared. One of them called out to Galina's mother, "Hey, you, woman, go make us something to eat. We're going to be hungry after the shootings."

I raised my eyebrows: so, in occupied Russo-Soviet territory, one could requisition a cook with a few words tossed off brusquely, the cold, routine words of criminals who were obviously not on their first job.

Galina's mother worked in the collective's canteen. Later, the canteen would become a warehouse, then it would be abandoned and left empty. We've lost count of how many remains of dismantled Soviet collectives we have come across in the middle of immense prairies as we travel endless potholed roads. They are like shipwrecks in the middle of fields, vestiges of an abruptly vanished universe.

I listened attentively as Galina continued her story. It seems that as a child she went back and forth between the mass grave and the canteen where her mother worked. She said she mostly saw the beginning and end of the shootings. "There was only one who shot. The other Germans stood beside him. He yelled loudly. . . . He screamed at my mother: 'Get going, give us something to eat!' And my mother said to him: 'It's not ready yet.'"

This was the first time I had heard about phrases exchanged between a German gunman and the village cook. The gunman gives orders, she replies the way a canteen worker of today would to a rushed client. Galina spoke about it with the rough vocabulary of a simple woman, a member of a collective who has worked hard.

"Yes, it was at the edge of the grave, and we brought him food. . . . He shot them one by one. . . . His gun was big. . . . They were single shots. When he was done shooting, he walked around the ditch, and he shot inside to finish off the ones that were still alive."

She explained in her own words how they murdered mothers and babies: "They took them like this, fired, and then threw them in. First, they killed the mother, then the little baby. They only cried out once before they fell into the ditch."

When the shootings were over, the Germans first stopped by the well, not far from the canteen. Before they ate, they had to remove the spots of the Jews' blood. The well doesn't exist anymore; it's been filled in since that time. No trace of it remains.

Galina repeated several times the orders screamed at her mother.

"He was in uniform. He screamed loud! He yelled at my mother to make something for them to eat. . . . Yes, yes, in German: '*Makta, gut! Makta* eat!'"

The German seems to have addressed her mother with the same injunctions several times, including at the end of the meal. "They shot, and my mother cooked. He came up to my mother and yelled. My mother said to him, 'Why are you yelling? Don't you like the food?' He replied, '*Makta, gut! Makta gut!*' My mother said to him, 'There is no *gut!*' And they left."

They washed their blood-covered boots and cleaned off the traces of the crime on their faces. Then, with their leather boots still wet, they went to eat. In the canteen.

THE COOKS AND THE SHOOTERS

This is a story of terrifying simplicity. I think, as I listen, about Galina's mother, busy cooking as fast as possible, with Germans screaming at her while from just a few feet away she can hear the shots and the cries of the Jews falling one after the other. Surely, she had learned to cook so that the workers on the collective could get their strength back after hard work in the fields. But on this day, it was neither the harvest nor the gathering of potatoes or beets. It was the murder of the Jewish neighbors.

The cold pragmatism of the killing units is chilling. Can it really be that for mass murderers a routine crime is simply bracketed between an early morning coffee and a meal served at a local canteen? They talk about it as though it were a hunting party. This raises so many questions.

And what of the cook who has to fill the correct number of plates for the shooters and their auxiliaries, and have everything ready by the end of the fusillades? The genocidal criminals killed the Jews, then barked at the cook.

Galina's account touches me: the Germans' verbal abuse of the "little people" in the village is yet another manifestation of their urgency and their violence.

Quite a while ago, in July 2006, I met Hannah, the niece of another cook. She, too, was conscripted in the early morning before the shooting started. She lived in Romanivka,[1] in eastern Ukraine.

The weather was good. She told her story sitting down low to the ground, on a tree trunk that had been stripped of its bark. She spoke kindly, punctuating her words with "my son," as she looked at Andrej, who was translating at the time. It was as though she were speaking to one of her children. Yet her delicately spoken words revealed a very dark universe.

Apparently, there was no canteen in Romanivka. The Germans wanted to eat outdoors, with a view of the grave. Or, more precisely, they wanted to alternate between shooting and eating. This meant the shooting lasted quite a long time.

The Jews had been forced to dig a hole not far from the grave. It was a pit for a fire over which they could suspend a cooking pot. The wood for the fire had been torn out of Jewish houses. The food, a cow and a goat, was stolen from a Jewish farm. The cooks were Russian women, not Jews, conscripted in the early morning. The animals had been killed and prepared by the townsfolk. The tables and chairs were borrowed from the village primary school. In short, it was an open-air kitchen for an improvised banquet.

Several times our witness repeated, "I remember the Germans conscripted my aunt to do the cooking. They only wanted to eat big pieces of meat, they didn't like the little ones. Then, some of them would shoot the Jews while the others ate and drank. Then those who had eaten went again to shoot the Jews, and those who had been shooting came back to eat. They killed people in groups of twenty-five. Mothers held their small children in their arms."[2]

Hannah herself, a young, black-haired girl of ten, became a waitress for the day, serving at a murderers' banquet. Curiously, the way the table was set remained a vivid memory for her. She recalled the iron nails that had been hammered into the trees so firmly that the shooters could hang their guns on them while they ate. They alternated, two by two, between the banquet table and the common grave. The Jews waited, naked, stripped of their belongings. The meal was washed down with alcohol brought by the Germans in their trucks. While the Germans ate, the Jews agonized.

With her mind's eye on both the table and the grave, she talked and talked. "I don't know anymore what time their orgy ended. They were drinking, singing. They were drunk. They were shooting at the same time. You could see little arms, little legs that spilled over the edge of the ditch. There was one woman who was very fat. They shot her several times, but she didn't fall into the ditch, so they had to go up to her and push her in."

It was so hard to listen! I lowered my eyes. It was terrible to glimpse the two faces of the crime at once: the shooting of the Jews and the meal of the killers. And difficult too to listen to someone who served a meal only feet away from the shooting of Jews.

For Hannah, the two were one: the meal to be served and the murdered Jewish neighbors. The killers became guests, and the guests killers. The meal seemed to last as long as the crime. There was no separation. In Romanivka, the shooters ate, drank, and shot. Between the table and the common grave, there was no barbed wire, no door, not even a partition, not even a thicket.

Is this what a genocidal human being is like? Capable of murdering an entire population while at the same time, in the same spot, forcing people to serve them big pieces of meat?

I am reminded of the German gunmen in Borove, not far from Rawa Ruska, who brought a box of mints to freshen their breath during the shooting. I recall the one who had cold cuts and vodka set up on the same table as his rifles, while the Jews paraded before him to be shot.

These scenes, which are so hard to hold simultaneously in one's mind, were in fact not even remotely separate. The genocidal man lives, circulates, murders, eats, and drinks in the same human territory as everyone else. In order to fathom his behavior, we try to picture it as happening elsewhere. Yet his strength resides not in separation but in the inscription of his crime in the very heart of our society, be it rural, urban, traditional, or modern.

He isn't coiled within our humanity like a serpent in its nest. He participates fully. This is surely the thing we cannot bear to acknowledge and that makes him both invisible and public at the same time. We cannot see what we cannot stand to see together.

Of the 3,900 witnesses interviewed by the time of this writing, only two described the setting up of kitchens for the criminals. Did we miss something? Is it possible that we forgot to ask if the canteen was functioning on the days of the shootings? Especially when the shootings lasted several days? I decided to clear my conscience with more research.

THE DAY

I consulted the archives concerning the site of the biggest shoot-ing, or at least the best-known in the territory of the former Soviet Union: the Babi Yar ravine, in Kiev, Ukraine.[3] Could we find any trace of the installation of a kitchen for the shooters in this small valley, where the killings lasted at least two days without interruption?

The answer was not long in coming. Three alarming texts from the same trial, one from a chef in Babi Yar, another from a supplier, the third from a shooter. Three links in the murderers' "food supply chain."

Babi Yar is a pretty little valley situated today in a large leafy park in Kiev, the capital of Ukraine. If you go into the park and gradually ascend the path, your steps will lead to a sort of precipice. There is a beautiful menorah in black metal, not far from a large, gaping hole. This is the spot where more than thirty thousand Jews were murdered by bullets on the 29th and 30th of September, 1941.

These were the Jews of Kiev. Several days before the shootings, posters appeared all over the walls of the capital. The Jews had to leave their houses and apartments in order to be deported.

ALL THE JEWS IN KIEV AND THE SURROUNDING AREA MUST PRESENT THEMSELVES ON MONDAY, SEPTEMBER 29, 1941, AT EIGHT IN THE MORNING ON THE CORNER OF THE MELNIKOVSKIA STREETS (NEAR THE CEMETERIES). THEY MUST BE IN POSSESSION OF THEIR IDENTITY PAPERS, THEIR MONEY, AND THEIR VALUABLES, ALONG WITH WARM CLOTHING, LINENS, ETC. THE JEWS WHO DISOBEY THIS ORDER AND ARE FOUND ELSEWHERE WILL BE SHOT. CITIZENS WHO BREAK INTO THE APARTMENTS ABANDONED BY THE JEWS AND STEAL THEIR BELONGINGS WILL BE SHOT.[4]

More than ten thousand of them went toward the station, thinking they would be taking the train. The German units corralled them into what could only be called ravines of death. As they approached the valley, the Jews went through a barricade, manned by the Germans, which prevented them from crossing back, like a fish trap. Then they had to leave their baggage, their jewels, their clothing.

Every Jew—man, woman, child—was murdered by a person armed with a gun. More than thirty thousand victims saw their killers, while each killer looked into the eyes of each of his Jewish victims. In broad daylight. Thirty thousand personal crimes.

A long time ago, I interviewed some Ukrainian women from Kiev who lived next to the Babi Yar ravine. They had gone up onto the roofs of their houses, or into their attics, in order to watch. These interviews took place at the beginning of my research. I didn't know at the time that, at the scene of the crime, there were a lot more people present than the gunmen and the Jews; there were also cooks and suppliers.

Today, more than ten years later, recalling this ravine that I visited so often on days of national mourning, I sift through the archives.

A German, a certain Georg P.,[5] was questioned in 1967, because he coordinated the kitchens at Babi Yar. He testified, "I was a *fourrier*.[6] It was a lot of work. . . . We got to Kiev at five in the morning. . . . We had to organize a kitchen and dining room. There was no water and no electricity. . . . My task was to get the kitchen working and to organize the supplies. I didn't have anything to do with managing the ammunition. . . .

"The *Aktion* was already prepared. . . . Everyone had his orders. . . . I don't know anything about the executions. I wasn't outside. . . . We heard that an action would take place. We had to organize more provisions than usual. . . . H. came to tell me how much food to organize. . . . I don't know who transported the provisions. . . . It was the same day as the action. Usually, I had to coordinate the feeding of one hundred twenty people. For those two days, it was for four hundred. There was no distribution of alcohol on these days. There was only a little rum in the tea. I learned only afterward why I had to prepare so much. There were open-face sandwiches and tea."

Thus, I understand that at Babi Yar, beginning at dawn, while the assembling and undressing of Jews for execution has already begun, a man, a German off to the side, is busying himself in improvised kitchens.

For him, a mass shooting is foremost a question of supply, of mouths to feed, the mouths of murderers. He is ordered to prepare food for four hundred, for the killers and their acolytes.

Georg P. seems, in his role as cook, to be used to mass murders. He has already had to do similar work but for smaller executions. In an improvised locale, off to the side of the ravine, he is busy furnishing sandwiches and tea with rum.

He talks about a dining room that he needs to install, which means he isn't far from the ravine. The shooters must have had to come out and sit down to replenish their strength before heading back to the shootings.

Part of the food seems to have been delivered to the site. He isn't the one responsible for the delivery. His job is to prepare the food. Another German, a certain Oscar C.,[7] during the same trial, will tell the story of the delivery of the supplies to the crime scene. Oscar C., with his van full of food, takes the same route as the Jews walking toward their death through the streets of Kiev. He crosses the German roadblock, sees the mound of suitcases that the Jews have been forced to leave behind; he drives on toward the site of the shootings, where he drops off the bread, sausage, and grog.

"*Obersturmführer*[8] M. came to see me, saying that he needed me to transport provisions. P. had given me bread, sausages, and tea. I transported it with my Ukrainian driver. I saw a long convoy of people. It looked like the migration of a whole population. When we got to the barricades, there were comrades at a table. They were writing down names and numbers. This was where the baggage had to be handed in. There were already mountains of suitcases when I arrived. . . . I went on one hundred meters [one hundred yards] past the barricade onto a plain of about three hundred or four hundred meters. At the end of the plain, you could see the edges of the ravine. We could see the barriers, and I could hear the shots. The Jews were led there by men in uniform, either Wehrmacht or SchuPo,[9] I can't remember anymore, but in any case, it wasn't our commando. I called over one of our men to give him the provisions. . . . I hadn't transported alcohol to the ravine. It's possible that there was rum in the tea. It was cold that day."

Yes, it was cold. . . . This is the first time I read a statement from a German whose only concerns are the cold, hunger, and thirst of the murderers; the column of Jews he passes in his van seem transparent to him. While thousands of Jewish families were beaten and forced to strip before being murdered, the delivery man seems mostly preoccupied with making his delivery on time, even though nothing, not even a wooden barrier, separates him from the Jews he doesn't see.

One of the shooters, Viktor T.,[10] as part of the same trial, describes what happens in the ravine, just a few feet from where the provisions are dropped off. Murder in all of its horror. Butchery. With breaks every ten to fifteen minutes so that the murderers can warm up with rum-spiked tea that the head cook has prepared and had delivered to the edge of the ravine.

"The next day, they put us into trucks early and we left. . . . I found myself in a very wide ravine, like the anti-tank ravines we would dig. There was a curve in the ravine. . . . What I saw there was the worst thing I ever saw in Russia. I hadn't shot [anyone] before. People were packed lying down like in a tin of herring. I don't know how many layers there were already. I had to go down into the grave. They were bringing people who were half undressed. There were soldiers sitting on the edges, reloading our guns and tossing them to us. It was horrible to be standing among those stacked cadavers. It's indescribable. It was horrible. And that was where we had to shoot. We were relieved every ten or fifteen minutes. It was very long. During our breaks, we got hot grog, or something of the sort. In any case, it had alcohol in it. On the other side of the ravine, I saw countless clothes and jewels. They called it the 'jewelry store.'"

Here we have the summary outline of the food chain for the killers of Babi Yar on the day of the genocide: Georg P. is busy in his kitchen;

143

bread to cut, to butter, sausage and tea with rum to heat. Oscar C delivers it all, driving alongside the columns of Jews. And Viktor T., along with many others, fires into a ravine that, for several days, has been turned into an extermination site.

Across from Viktor T. is what they call the "jewelry store": the place where the Jews are robbed of their jewelry and their personal belongings. Above the ravine, along with the loaders refilling the magazines to throw down to the shooters, is the food and grog that are available at breaks every ten to fifteen minutes.

A pretty little green valley transformed into a valley of extermination, without barbed wire, without a train, without tattoos. And yet, for a few hours, or rather a few days, certain spots are given names, like the jewelry store.

In Auschwitz too, they assigned names to certain places: Kanada,[11] Mexiko.[12] The murderers seem to dress up the landscape of their crimes, albeit furtively, like landscape painters, not hesitating to label the sites of their worst horrors with a certain elegance and humorous flair. The topography of crime is thus named by the murderers with words that cover over the crime scene in proper terms.

So, it seems clear: at Babi Yar, hunger, thirst, cold, and the killers' need for rest were taken into serious consideration in the planning of the crime.

On such blood-soaked days, one might have thought that the human extermination machine would forget to eat, drink, or rest. Such was not the case. Those who organized the mass shootings seem never to have sacrificed the comfort of their staff.

Chapter 14

THE CURIOUS CHILDREN

Curious children running through the streets exist in all civiliza-
tions but especially in little villages, where daily life repeats itself
ceaselessly over the course of seasons, through the cycle of sowing and
reaping.

I remember when, as a young professor of mathematics in Haute
Volta, Burkina Faso in 1983, I would pass through villages on my
blue motorbike and see hordes of children running everywhere. They
rushed out of their straw-covered huts, playing and crying loudly,
"Toubabou! Toubabou!" This meant "The white man! The white man!"
A white man on a motorbike was, for a few minutes, a great spectacle.

Most of the witnesses we spoke to in the villages of the ex-Soviet
Union had been part of the streams of children who followed in the
wake of the columns of Jews during the German occupation. They
would sometimes accompany them on the sidewalks of towns or run
to keep up with them through the fields of grain.

It is virtually impossible today to imagine the pain endured by men
and women being beaten as they were marched to their death simply
for being Jewish while their neighbors' children ran up and down
beside them, more likely than not just to watch the show. It is difficult
to visualize this coexistence, the juxtaposition of the mass murder of
one part of the village and the curiosity it excited in the children of

the same village, a curiosity that would be banal were it not focused on a crime of genocide.

Yet, it happened. I think back to April 2006, in Kamianka-Bouzka, a small town in western Ukraine. A man was standing there. A short man. Planted like a post in the middle of the road. He had a visor cap pushed far down on his head, like a jockey. We were interviewing him in a street that was still muddy from the previous night's rain. He said, "I was standing here where I am right now. I saw the Jews being killed."

I was listening distractedly. At the beginning of my investigation, it seemed improbable to me that a child could have come to watch the murder of the Jews as a spectator, like going to the circus. And yet there he was, straight as a post, describing the scene with big gestures.

Suddenly, a stout woman of about fifty, in an apron and a scarf that nearly swallowed her face, burst out of her house. Three other women followed. They walked toward me at a fast and furious pace and started to scream. I asked my translator what they were saying. Svetlana whispered in my ear, "They're saying, 'Don't take my kitchen garden! Don't take my garden!'"

I found myself in the middle; the old man dressed like a jockey to my right and to my left the three women coming toward me threateningly. In a flash, I understood: the dead were buried under the garden!

At the beginning of my inquiries, I would sometimes cut an interview short, because I was incapable of processing the unbearable contradiction between the ordinary lives of those who were not murdered because they weren't Jews, Gypsies, Communists, or handicapped, and the others. The proximity of villagers defending their kitchen gardens and those who lay buried beneath them was just too much.

There were many times when I asked the cameraman to stop shooting because I didn't want to, and simply couldn't, know any more! And then, little by little, perhaps hardened, but perhaps also animated by a combative flame that made me realize I shouldn't give in to terror, because terror is the strategy of mass murder, I have grown able to hear the unhearable.

Today, I know that when the Jews were gathered in the market square or along the main road, everyone in the village understood that they were heading for the mass graves that had been dug by local farmers on orders of the mayor, who had been *his* given orders by the Germans a few hours earlier. Now, I know.

I know that hordes of children, boys and girls, but mostly boys, rushed out from their farmyards, their schools, or the fields where they were working to play hide and seek with the police or the Germans, who tried to shoo them away like crows. I know, and yet I can't get used to it.

I have met these children, who have grown old now. Their words unnerve me and raise questions about the human capacity to bear the horror of genocide. Children who were witnesses to massacres.

It is May 28, 2010. We are in eastern Ukraine.

I will never forget Vladimir. I met him in one of those flat, rectilinear streets that make up the former kolkhozes. This one was called Novopodilsk, and it was an old Jewish colony in the Dniepropetrovsk region.

Dressed simply in a checked shirt and blue cloth cap, Vladimir has light eyes. He stands squarely in the middle of his farmyard, facing the camera. His parents were sergeants in the kolkhoz, which means they were chiefs of a unit of manual laborers. His mother was the milking sergeant, and his father was a sergeant in the fields.

In the oppressive heat of the Ukrainian summer, a storm grumbles in the distance. We see the lightning, hear the thunder, see that the storm is approaching, but I can't tell exactly how far away it is. David, our cameraman, is worried and keeps saying, "I'm scared of thunder!" Suddenly, one of the lightning bolts appears much closer. Hastily, we pile all our equipment into our van and ask Vladimir if he knows of somewhere in the village that would be sheltered from the rain where we could continue. Without hesitating, he points toward the center of town, indicating the school. It's a typical old Soviet school, a single story, raised up a few feet on concrete. A big bronze soldier by the door memorializes the dead of the Great Patriotic War.

The school closed its doors two years ago. Walking in, we find ourselves in a damp, cold hallway with a ruined ceiling, leading to deserted, silent classrooms. We set up in this dilapidated hallway. Vladimir starts to tell his story.

In his memory, the one execution that stands out the most is that of the village children with only one Jewish parent. They were called mixed-race children.[1] These children were in preschool with all the others, in the very building that is giving us shelter from the storm. A Ukrainian policeman came to the door with his horse and cart. He had orders to load all the half-Jewish children into the cart.

"The policeman came into the school. The teacher pointed out each of the half-Jewish children: '*Juden! Juden! Juden!*'"

We shivered. I swept my eyes over the classroom. This abandoned school with its moldy wooden desks was the site of an unbearable act of selection among students, in which the teacher was complicit.

The policeman loaded the children into his cart.

Vladimir's grandmother lived on the farm right across from the school. Apparently, she tried to stop the roundup but to no effect. The oldest of the children was six; there were also babies among them. Their young parents were at work in the kolkhoz fields and didn't witness the arrest. They didn't learn about the murder until it was too late, in the evening upon their return from the fields.

The horse and cart made their way to a mass grave that had been specially dug a few miles outside of town. Four Germans stood around its perimeter. Vladimir followed the cart across the fields. "There were grapes growing. . . . I went through the vineyards to follow the cart . . . and then, we saw . . ."

Vladimir takes some time explaining how he came to watch the whole scene. First, he describes how he was in the vineyards, stealing grapes, not far from the mass grave. We decide to take our van together to the scene of the crime. Standing on the site of the grave, I ask, "So, where were you exactly?" He points to some distant vineyards. I'm surprised. "But those vineyards are far away. How could you see from there?"

Flustered, he answers, "I came through the cornfield, to see. For us children, it was interesting."

Countless times I have heard this phrase, in Russian, Ukrainian, Moldavian, Polish: "For us children, it was interesting. . . ." Is a child always interested in watching, at no risk to himself, the murder of his schoolmates? Does the absence of danger for the child spectator, in conjunction with the absence of any barrier between him and the scene of the crime, transform murder into a compelling show?

It's true that the situation is unique; if you see a murder in the streets of Paris or New York, you are in danger. The murderer or his accomplices may want to kill you too since you are a witness. Your presence is unauthorized by the killers.

But in the case of the mass crimes against the Jews, the neighbors and children present rarely ran any sort of risk. The crimes became spectacles for a considerable number of Soviet children. And, of course, there was also pervasive anti-Semitism as well as Nazi propaganda justifying the murder.

I feel a mounting disgust for our species. The sort of nausea that makes you want to quit the human race. Yet I continue my dialogue.

"How many babies did you see have their heads bashed against the walls of the cart?"

"Twenty."

I close my eyes for a moment. I tell myself not to waver. But this man's calm is hard to bear as he recounts a double horror: the murder of the "half-Jew" children of his village coupled with the fact that he, a child himself, spent a whole day watching.

Many of the victims were the same age as this witness. I ask him if he knew any of the children killed. He stammers, "Yes." Yes, he saw four of his cousins shot. He barely remembers their names. Although he does recall that one was called Boris. He was one of the four children of a Ukrainian aunt married to a Jewish man. I ask if the children tried to run to escape being killed or at least acted scared. He said, "They didn't move because they saw how the babies' heads had been smashed against the walls of the cart and they were afraid of the same thing happening to them."

The interview lasts a long time. Vladimir has a little blue string around his neck with a cell phone attached, hidden under his shirt. It rings constantly. His wife is calling him, warning him to stop talking to strangers who may be spies. Finally, he turns the phone off. He wants to talk to us. Although his face betrays no emotion, his body seems to remember, as though he has never really left the cornfield by the ditch.

Vladimir's testimony resonates with me.

We know very little about the German units' murder of children with one Jewish parent, or *Mischlinge*. I had met Nina, a survivor from Crimea, who told me that her Gentile mother was asked to turn over her daughter while she herself would remain free. The murderers seemed to scrupulously follow the Nazi rules of selection regarding those they considered *Mischlinge*, and therefore condemned to death. But I never imagined that the children would be selected during class. Nor did I imagine the selection would be performed by a local policeman barging into school.

Later that evening, in the same village of Novopodilsk, another villager, Sergueï, tells us that his mother saw that policeman return covered in blood. "What did you do with those Jews and those children you had on the cart this morning?" she asked. Sergueï overheard the unvarnished response, "We didn't have enough ammunition, so I tore a piece of wood from the cart and crushed the heads of the children with it."

It is horrible to read the transcript of the SS chiefs discussing the murder of half-Jewish children during their meeting at the Wannsee villa[2] in suburban Berlin in 1942. But to be in the dilapidated corridors of the school where their selection took place, to go to the common grave where these children were murdered, is to truly understand and still not comprehend.

Vladimir is for me one of the most painful enigmas of my species. How can a typical child watch the murder of other children under the most horrific conditions with five or six of his friends, for an entire day? Did anti-Semitism block out the conscience of these children? Did it blind them to the point of losing all compassion and all sense of the other as a fellow member of the human race?

We know from the history of the Cambodian genocide how many children and young adolescents were party to the killings. Anti-Semitism and racism have a repulsive effect on the conscience of young human beings. Was Vladimir from an anti-Semitic family? Maybe, because he said on several occasions, "But they were only half-breeds!"

But I cannot shake off this other thought: it appears that when you live near the scene of a genocidal crime and you know precisely who is, and who is not, at risk of being killed, and that you are not part of the targeted portion of humanity, you can stay close and watch the crime without experiencing much stress.

Furthermore, those who commit the genocide never stop repeating, through every means at their disposal—posters, radio—exactly who it is they are going to kill. So, neighbors who have understood that they run almost no risk because they are not targeted not only sleep easily but are comfortable enough to come watch. It's as though they were cut free from all bonds of brotherhood.

It is said that because of televised reports of violence people cannot truly comprehend the gravity of mass murders once reduced to sensational numbers. I thought this too. But in little Soviet villages, the children didn't watch the genocide of the Jews on television. They went to the neighboring fields in order to see for themselves. The capacity to see the mass murder of others without taking any responsibility predates mass media. To watch others die murdered seems not just to leave them indifferent—it's an attraction. Sadly, those conducting the public murder of the Jews were well aware of this.

Chapter 15

THE CHILD WITH THE BULLETS

H er name was Violida, and she was ten years old on the day of the mass shootings of the Jews. The name of her town is hard to pronounce: Starokostiantyniv, in the Khmelnitsky region of Ukraine.

On January 10, 2010, in front of the camera, she spoke distinctly but with a serious air. The first thing she wanted us to know was that her father, who had left to study in Cracow, had been a victim of the Soviet purges of 1938. "My father had spent a year studying at Jagollenne University in Cracow and worked as a head accountant. In 1938, during the period of the great purges, the NKVD police came to get him, and, if the archives are to be trusted, he was shot on October 13, 1938. My mother was left alone, pregnant, with two children. She had studied at the conservatory in Kiev."

Violida was from an educated family that had endured repression long before the war. Perhaps this explains why her testimony was so precise, calm, and serious. She spoke of her Jewish neighbors with precision, answering Patrice's questions with a student's earnestness.

"Were there many Jews in Starokostiantyniv before the war?"

"Yes, many. They lived everywhere in the center of town and throughout the area from the Ikopot to the Chakhivka."[1]

"What kind of jobs did they generally do?"

"The Jews had all sorts of professions. There were tinsmiths and cart drivers. . . . As for the Jewish youth, they were generally intellectuals, lawyers, doctors, etc."

"Was there a Jewish school here?"

"Yes, there was a Jewish school and a Polish school."

"And a synagogue?"

"Yes, there was also a synagogue, but it was bombed on the first day of the war. The Germans weren't even here yet, but they were doing air raids and bombing the town."

"Were there Jewish children in your school?"

"Across from this house, there used to be two magnificent houses owned by the Kryjanivsky merchants who sold geese and pigs in Poland before the revolution. After the Bolshevik Revolution,[2] one of the houses became a school where I did my first year, in 1940. Our teachers were all Jewish women. The villagers called it the "Jids School,"[3] even though there were no Jewish children attending the school. My teacher was named Guenia Ronovna, and we liked her."

She described the arrival of the German troops in the same manner. Then, suddenly, the tone of her voice shifted. Immediately after the German soldiers came in 1941, she heard the rape of a young Jewish neighbor. "In the house next door, which is still here today, lived a Jewish family. They had a sixteen-year-old daughter. Two or three days after they got here, the German soldiers came late in the evening and spent the whole night raping this poor girl. All night long, we heard her screams, but we could do nothing.

"And then, about a month later, they started shooting the Jews in large groups. The Jewish quarter was called Sloboda,[4] from the word 'svoboda,' which means 'liberty,' because the Jews were free to settle here, and the street leading to Sloboda was called Slobodianska."

She continued to describe the parade of horrors she witnessed, up until the massacre of the Jews. She saw the biggest mass execution, which took place on Orthodox Christmas Day, from the roof of a barn. "Everyone had to be there. I remember that it was January 7, at Christmas,[5] and we climbed onto the roof of a barn and saw everything that was happening over there. The shooting lasted all day. They shot five thousand Jews."[6]

In listening to her words, I thought: *The Germans had to have been aware that they were murdering Jews among Orthodox villagers on their Christmas Day.* To connect the popular celebration of the birth of Jesus with putting their Jewish neighbors to death was yet another example of religious inversion.

"Yes, they started shooting very early in the morning. I remember that it was freezing, and from time to time we would go into the house to get warm, then go back out onto the roof again. Surrounding the village was an anti-tank ditch that the Jewish women had dug over two weeks at the beginning of the war. They shot the Jews in front of this ditch. I saw with my own eyes the way the Germans made them take off their clothes. The winter was harsh, and they were all red with cold."

On their Christmas holiday, how many villagers showed up to watch the murder of their Jewish neighbors? Did they then continue their holiday celebrations?

Her testimony resembled that of many Soviet children who had witnessed the shootings until, all of a sudden, she mentioned a young neighbor who was going back and forth between the village and the ditch with his sled. "My neighbor, who was sixteen at the time, carried boxes of bullets and cases of wine to the shooting site. The Germans drank the wine straight from the bottle and then shot the Jews with machine guns. Some of the Jews were only wounded, and they fell into the ditch still alive and died slowly."

So, there was a young Ukrainian replenishing the shooters' supply of ammunition and alcohol. "Vanya, the boy who was carrying the bullets, told us that there was a German sitting on a stool on the same side of the ditch as the Jews. He was shooting them in the back. As the anti-tank ditch filled up, he moved his stool. He kept moving until all the Jews were shot. Vanya brought the cases of ammunition and wine, and he unloaded them next to the shooter. Then, after a certain amount of time, he would return with more cases in his sled and unload them again.

"They forced him. He was in charge of the horses in the kolkhoz, and when the Germans asked the chief of police to send someone, he is the one they sent. The Germans ordered the *staroste* to find someone who could drive a sled, and Vanya was sent." The requisition had been simple: the Germans wanted someone who knew how to drive a sled. Vanya, the kolkhoz groom, not only saw the massacre up close but became an assistant to the killers.

"They got undressed in groups of ten or fifteen people and went over to the ditch. They lined up in front of the ditch, and the German shot them with a machine gun. The boy who brought the cases of ammunition was sick for several days afterward."

To my knowledge, it was rare that young villagers transported arms or ammunition. The archives show that this work was generally left to the Germans, who sometimes alternated between arming the shooters and being shooters themselves, as was the case at Babi Yar.

Victor T., a driver in *Sonderkommando* 4a, found himself in Kiev. There, Paul Blobel,[7] the coordinator of the murder of the Kiev Jews, asked all the drivers to come to the extermination sites and help with the shooting. Viktor T., improvising as a shooter, noticed that the armorers were not far from him. Their chief was called *Ladekommando*:

"I should also add that, during the execution, two or three men in the ditch were constantly refilling magazines and giving them to the shooters. To answer your question about the number of magazines I emptied, I have to say that I don't know exactly. As for the shout from Blobel and the other SS chiefs, I assume they were directed at the commando who was supplying the *Ladekommando*. He couldn't keep up, and we kept running out of ammunition."[8]

Only one witness ever talked about a child delivering ammunition. Is this really an exception, or have we failed to ask the right questions about who was requisitioned for transporting bullets?

Chapter 16

THE FORCED WITNESSES

Eastern Russia, September 2011

Rostov-on-Don is currently a large metropolis in Central Russia. This was the first time I had gone so deep into Russia. The city is pretty, with big boulevards, wide sidewalks, and intense traffic. In late September, a warm wind still blows over the Azov Sea.

On the day of our arrival, we were welcomed by Rabbi Lubavitch in his synagogue. The building was white, sandwiched between old two-story Russian buildings on a tiny cobblestone street. The rabbi introduced himself warmly. With him was a small, humble man; a historian of the town of Rostov.

Early the following morning, I was taken by the historian and a representative of the Jewish community to the site of the massacre. It is a large valley just outside town, where a massive white Russian memorial honors the "Soviet" dead.

Twenty-seven thousand victims.

At the foot of the monument was an immense bed of red flowers. The historian, noticing my interest in the flowers, said softly, "The blood of the victims."

We knew about this massacre from Soviet archives. But to be in the center of Russia and to see such proof that, far from Berlin, over a very short period of occupation, the Germans found the time to shoot 27,000 civilians, mostly Jews, is another form of knowledge.

What an obsession! I thought. To come from Munich, Hamburg, or Berlin, sometimes by train, sometimes by truck or car, in order to murder thousands of men, women, and children. The Germans went all over the world intending to track down and kill every last Jewish child.

We talk a lot about Babi Yar, for good reason. We talk a lot about Auschwitz-Birkenau, again for good reason. But who knows about all the deaths at Rostov-on-Don?

Before this silent plain, standing at the side of a heavily traveled road, I looked at the surrounding habitations. There were mostly postwar Soviet buildings. This place is surrounded by nice new houses, along with big Soviet blocs. At the time of the genocide, were there people living near the valleys of Rostov-on-Don?

Our Russian companions shook their heads, saying that the shootings took place day and night but that there were no witnesses. The archives corroborate this by telling us that the surrounding population was evacuated for the period of the murders.

I asked immediately, "How did they do it at night?" This was at once unusual and seemed technically impossible. My answer came: "They brought tractors from the kolkhoz and used the headlights." I wondered where the tractors came from and who drove them. A Soviet tractor doesn't move by itself. How many tractors did they need to light up this valley?

We stayed for a long time while our photographer and cameraman did their work. The site of the Rostov murders was sealed in a double silence. The silence of the Soviet monument bordered by blood-red flowers. The silence of the official absence of any witnesses.

And I daresay I believed it there. Maybe at Rostov, so far from Moscow, so close to Stalingrad, the Nazis did murder the Jews in secret. When we decided to investigate around Rostov, we knew it would be practically impossible to meet people who had seen the giant massacre.

Our work in the surrounding villages had shown us how unique the region was. Many of the peasants explained to us that they were Cossacks. Many of the merchants in the markets told us they were from Azerbaïjan. The investigation was fruitful, but we didn't meet one single witness to Rostov itself. We returned to Paris with a burning question: did the Rostov executions take place in secret?

A month later, another team returned to Rostov. I advised them to continue their investigations in the villages first, which is how, on a market day, they found Iegorlyskaya.

Marie, a researcher and student of history, told me the story.

"We decided to stop in the small town of Iegorlyskaya. We were walking through a market, several low wooden tables covered with decorative objects, colored cloth piled up on old wax mats. The stalls were tended by babushkas sitting on low stools and by men from the Caucuses. One after the other, the women all directed us to a certain Lydia who sat behind a small display of multicolored socks. It was late October, and the weather was not warm. We got to Lydia's table. She was sitting wrapped in an abundance of blue shawls. When she saw us, having surely been alerted beforehand by the other saleswomen, she immediately began telling us, in a feeble voice through the morning chill, that she had seen the shootings in the Rostov valley where she used to live. She seemed fragile as glass. She agreed to move with us into a less crowded corner of the market."

I watched the interview for a long time.

Lydia had insisted on standing for it despite her shortness of breath and watering eyes. The interview lasted no more than half an hour. She kept saying she couldn't take it anymore. She couldn't stand to remember anymore. She was no more than a child in 1942. At the end of the interview, a neighbor had to support her as though she were in great pain. Afterward, she went back to her spot, behind her little wooden table, an anonymous salesperson in a small market in Iegorlyskaya.

As a small child, Lydia was forced to watch the murders committed by the Germans.

Her family was suspected of ties with Soviet sympathizers. Her house was requisitioned by the Germans; her family was kicked out and had to live in their barn during the entire occupation. Lydia's story is that of many Soviet peasants who had to cohabit with the Germans in the outbuildings of their own farms.

"We were chased out of our home, and we had to move into the barn. The Germans lived in our house and ate everything we had. They left us nothing."

Their farm was part of a neighborhood of fifteen dwellings, near the valley that would become the valley of extermination. Not right next to it, though. She recalled that it was a twenty-minute walk to the ditches. Every morning of the genocide, at dawn, the German police forced them out of their houses to make them watch.

"Yes, the police came, made us go outside. They went to every house to bring people there, and before our eyes they shot old people and children." This happened for every execution. The Russian children in particular were made to stand and watch.

"In every household, there were children, and they were sent. All of them, they were all sent. . . . Every time the trucks came full of victims for the shootings, they dragged out the whole neighborhood."

And every morning, Lydia's mother tried as best she could to hide certain children in order to protect them from seeing.

"It took us twenty minutes to get there on foot. . . . There was my mother. My father and my older brother were at the front. There were a lot of us, we were twelve. My mother hadn't had time to hide all of us. . . . She hid some in the basement. . . . On the outskirts of town, there weren't many people. Only about fifteen houses. It was quick. A team would come and get everyone outside."

So, the forced march of the neighbors was not a one-time or improvised event. On the contrary, it was systematically organized as part of the process of execution. The Germans extracted the inhabitants from house after house and forced them to go to the extermination site. But why such organization and insistence? And why such emphasis on the children?

The neighbors and their children were not allowed to return home until the shooting was over. And all during the shootings, the police kept them close to the ditch. "They were behind us with dogs and automatic weapons. They had big black German shepherds."

Were the Germans trying to dissuade the Russians from joining rebel forces by forcing them to watch the murder of the Jews? Maybe, but why force the neighboring children to watch every day? Why mobilize armed police with dogs in order to make it happen? I can't help but think there was some sick pleasure derived from, on the one hand, murdering the Jews, and on the other, forcing Russian families to watch. In a sense, organizing a forced spectacle, mandatory family entertainment, children included.

It seems strange to me when I think of the thousands of children who, of their own free will, tried to find ways to see the shootings. What is the difference between a child who plays hide and seek with the guards or climbs a tree, and one who has to watch under armed threat? It seems to me that the major difference is in the perception of danger. The former knows that he runs no risk; he is on the right side of the guards. The other, because she is escorted by the police and forced to watch, is no longer a voluntary spectator. She herself is in danger.

Lydia's testimony has me thinking. The freedom to watch, without much danger, is an essential part of the pleasure. To run no risk and to watch one's neighbor condemned to death seems to provoke pleasure.

Last week, I was in Romania. There was a terrible traffic jam on a country road. Far ahead, a trailer truck had gone off the road. I was completely unsurprised to see the drivers of the cars that were stuck in the traffic jam get out of their vehicles to go look, and to take pictures with their cell phones. One of them came up to show me his shot: a car had been hit head on by the truck. Wounded passengers were still stuck inside.

What kind of joy is there in not having had an accident, in being free to move about, to walk or run, and to go gape at those who no longer have such freedom? The murder of the Jews was no car accident. Some died, and others lived according to the brutal will of the German masters at any given time. In a village, those who were authorized to live could not often resist the pleasure of watching others die before their eyes as victims of the racial laws of the Third Reich.

Lydia was another story. Forced, constrained, part of a family under threat, for her the shootings had nothing of spectacle about them. She was standing at the scene of a murder where she herself was within the zone of risk.

The local Russians didn't hide their enmity for the German units; they weren't passive spectators. On the evenings of the shootings, certain adults even seem to have tried to help save people who might have survived.

"And when the Germans were gone, there was an adult who took us, the children, back home, but the other adults stayed to see if there were any survivors, and they got them out and saved them. Some lived and some did not."

This was not the first time that a child who had been forced to watch shared memories with me. I had already heard a similar story in Lubavichi in the Russian region of Smolensk. This is the famous town where the Lubavitch[1] family originated. Here too, families, especially rebel families with their children, were forced to watch the murders.

Lydia, deeply troubled as a child by what she had seen, said with the child's words, "You know, it's something you can't talk about, a horror you've seen but can't put into words, and it stays inside to this day. We focused on the people falling and not on the shooters. When they were finished, they fired into the air to disperse us and everyone was supposed to go home, but people hid and came back to see if there were survivors. It happened."

The end of the forced spectacle was signaled by shots in the air. I couldn't believe it. Like the end of a game or a race.

Very simply, she added, "It was so horrible that my mother hid my eyes so that I wouldn't see." She spoke like the child she had been, with the memory of a mother who did what she could to protect her from the sight of the murders. The mothers and children of Rostov were made to witness. The witnessing was hard, the memories of it painful. "I can't," she kept repeating.

Today, it is still said in the former Soviet territories that the killings were done in secret.

Chapter 17

A GERMAN SOLDIER AS SPECTATOR

I look one more time at the yellowed photograph, so often featured in books and exhibitions, the image referred to as the execution of the last Jew in Vinnitsa.

A poor, kneeling Jewish man looks uncomprehendingly into the eye of the camera. An immobile shooter poses with his arm out-stretched, pistol in hand. Below are still bodies, apparently the Jews who have just been killed.

The German shooter isn't posing by himself with his victim. There are other soldiers—apparently, all of them from the regular German army, the Wehrmacht—who are posing with him. One even seems to have pushed others aside to be in the front row in the photo. They look serious, some with arms crossed, some more relaxed, with their hands in their pockets.

They are young.

I look at them the way I have often viewed snapshots of young Germans who've come for one day, perhaps even for a brief moment, to see the crime of genocide and be seen, or rather to be in the photograph. Immortalized forever.

Whenever I'm walking in Germany, in the streets of Berlin or Munich, I can't help but stare at every old man who might have celebrated his eighteenth birthday in a green uniform.

I know this is not fair. But each time I ask myself, did he see? How many saw? Because they were passing by on the road near the ditch on a motorcycle or in a car or train. Because their barracks were not far from the common grave. Or simply because, as in Vinnitsa, they went to see. The voices of Germans who looked, out of curiosity, are mostly absent from the archives.

I wanted to ask the burning question of what attracted them to the graves and ditches, the agonizing bodies of the Jewish victims, the pitiless shooters. I wanted to ask, what was it that you came to watch?

In the German archives, we found the deposition of one of these German soldiers. Josef F. was stationed in Kerch, a pretty little town in Crimea. From the port of Kerch, if there isn't too much fog, you can just see the Russian coast.

His account began with a hunting meal with a Lieutenant Schiller, and with Fi., another member of the SS stationed in Kerch.

"The second unit of the maintenance company, directed by Lieutenant Schiller, was located, in November and December 1941, in Kolongov, three or four kilometers [a mile and a half or two miles] east of Kerch. Since there were a lot of rabbits in the region and I had a hunting permit, Schiller often sent me out to hunt. Among others, SS-*Sturmführer*[1] Fi., also stationed in Kerch at the time, was invited several times to eat rabbit [. . . .] During one of these rabbit meals, at a point when Schiller had been called away, this *Hauptsturmführer* spoke to me, asking if I had strong nerves. If I did, I could come on December 4 to see the shooting of the Jews. I objected to the *Hauptsturmführer* that there was an order for the members of the Wehrmacht, that we had to immediately leave the zones where the *Sonderkommando* of the SS was active. Our sergeant had read this order in front of an assembly of men. . . . The order stated that we needed to leave any place where the SS was working. But the *Hauptsturmführer* told me I could come with impunity to the place where the Jews would be shot. If anyone asked me, I only had to say that I had permission from *Hauptsturmführer* Fi. Already at the time, the name *Hauptsturmführer* Fi. was known to me. I remember that Fi. had access to the Jewish apartments and that it was from these apartments that all the tablecloths had been taken."[2]

At a table covered in a cloth stolen from the home of a Jewish family, Josef F., the soldier, accepts the invitation to go see the extermination of the Jews. Fi. tells him how to get there.

"When I asked, Fi. described with great precision the place where the Jews were going to be shot. It was an old Russian anti-tank ditch, located between Hirschdorf and Kerch. Part of this ditch was in Bagerovo, to the west, in the direction of Hirschdorf, where our first unit was stationed. Since I often roamed the region, I knew it well. I knew right away which portion of the anti-tank ditch he was referring to. So I went there. As I went from Kerch toward Hirschdorf, the ditch was to the right of the road. It was dug into a slope, and on the side of its straight wall, it was over two meters [six feet] deep. The anti-tank ditch flattened out toward the west, so the deep wall was in the direction of Kerch. There was a mound of earth on top of this wall. Coming from Kerch, there was a narrow path to the right of the road. This path was on top of an embankment almost two meters [six feet] high. From the top of this embankment, you couldn't see the whole inside of the anti-tank ditch."

Reading this description, I gasped. Years ago, I had also been to this long anti-tank ditch. I recalled Maria, buttoned into a large coat, walking along with us despite the cold and pointing, "There, that's where Anna is, with her father, her mother. . . ."

She had seen the murder.

I took up my reading again. Josef F. continued his account of the rabbit dinner.

"To my question about the number of Jews who would be shot, Fi. answered that there would be two thousand."

With the date set, Josef F. now had only one problem to solve: how to procure a car illegally to get to the site of the shootings. He was going to have to sneak out a military vehicle because the ditch was quite far from his base.

"When December 4, 1941, came around, the only question for me was whether or not I could access the execution site I've described. We had a ban on using gasoline due to a fuel shortage, and we had no regular orders to go to that area. But I wanted to see what was happening in the anti-tank ditch. In order to have a pretext for a drive, I pretended to have a gas leak in my vehicle. The only way to verify and correct this kind of problem was with an extended drive. Since the yard at the base was not sufficient, I got permission from the warrant officer to drive for a while. So I drove at breakneck speed to the anti-tank ditch and parked my vehicle strategically on the side of the road, in such a way that it couldn't be seen from the road."

Josef F., soldier in the Wehrmacht, wanted so badly to see the murder of the Jews that he was prepared to lie to his superiors.

"I climbed up onto the embankment I have already mentioned and saw that a heap of clothes, furs, children's shoes, and hats were lying right there. I also saw piles of watches. Trucks full of men, women, and children were arriving from the direction of Kerch."

Next the soldier spectator coldly described the criminal "process" that he observed.

"The trucks arrived at the road and, after they had stopped, the people were pulled out by Russian civilians overseen by an SS guard. If they didn't go fast enough, they were hurried along with sticks until they were all assembled on the embankment. On the other side of the embankment, the Jews had to take off their clothes. If they didn't do this fast enough, their clothes were ripped off by the Russians and two or three SS guards. If the Jews hadn't known before, now they discovered what was to become of them. Some moaned aloud, but most of the older Jews clasped their hands and looked toward the sky. It was always the same image; they clasped their hands the way we do at home to ask for something and looked up at the sky. When the children had nice shoes, they were pulled off by the Russians and the SS."

Suddenly, an SS officer asks him to act, to participate in the crime. He is told to push the Jews toward the ditch. This puts him in the position of having to explain that he is only here to observe. It is hard to imagine a German soldier explaining to an SS officer that he has permission to watch the murder without participating.

"One of the SS officers there called me over so that I would take a stick and help drag the Jews to the shooting spot. I replied that I had nothing to do with this. Since he then tried to send me away, I told him I had permission to watch from *Hauptsturmführer* Fi. After that, he let me alone."

I thought: how many young Josef F.s got SS permission to watch the shootings?

"The firing squad was composed of five or six SS. Once they were in front of the shooters, the Jews had to jump into the anti-tank ditch and stand against the straight wall. From there, it all went very fast. As soon as they were all inside, there was firing and the people slid to the ground."

I was surprised by the strength of his memory. He recalled several Jews beaten forward with sticks toward the ditch.

"I noticed among the women a man who was obviously paralyzed. He was big and fat. He was dragged to the execution spot by two twelve-to-fourteen-year-old boys. The two boys took him by the shoulders but had to keep putting him down because he was so heavy. When they put him down, another Russian would hit and push them. Then I noticed a very handsome couple with two small children. The husband and wife were very well dressed. You could see right away that they were fine people. . . . This couple was in one of the groups that a Russian civilian was bringing toward the firing squad. The woman had a child of about one in her arms, and the couple was leading another child of three or four by the hand. Once they were facing the firing squad, I saw the man ask for something. He had probably asked for permission to hold his family in his arms one last time, because I saw him embrace his wife and the child she was holding. But at the same moment, the shots were fired and everyone fell to the ground. I watched those people all the way to the firing squad because they were such a handsome couple and they had two children."

Despite his memory of the handicapped man and the young couple with the children, he continued to call the crime a "process."

"It made a real impression on me. I can still describe the process with precision today."

His account of the murder of Jewish children is unbearable, especially where it concerns those children who survived their mothers by a few moments.

"Most of the time, the children knocked over by their falling mothers sat on the ground or on their mothers' bodies without really understanding what had just happened. I saw how they climbed on their mothers among the dead women. They looked around and definitely did not understand what was going on. I still have the image very clearly before my eyes: they looked up with their big eyes and scared expressions at the shooters. They were too terrified to cry. Twice I saw an SS go down into the ditch with a rifle and kill the children, who were sitting on the dead or on their own mothers, with one shot to the nape of the neck. As I've said, they weren't crying, but looking around in shock. I think he was aiming for the head with his gun. At least, he held the barrel not far from the head, because I noticed almost no space between the head and the barrel. The children I saw struggling to move here and there ranged from babies to children of two or three years."

Josef F.'s coldness, the precise details about the babies lost among the bodies, froze my blood. How could a young soldier, not a member of the SS, seeing a mass shooting for the first time, have actively wanted to watch children, babies, a young couple, a crippled old man, massacred before his eyes? How could he recount it so cold-bloodedly years later?

The end of his account provides some clues, or rather, it goes to the heart of my question: what did he see? A young Jewish schoolgirl speaks to him, implores him, in German:

"While I was watching the massacre, a young girl came up to me suddenly, grabbed my hand, and said: 'Please, please, they have to let me live a little longer, I'm so young. My parents have already fallen. We didn't have any radio at the house, and we didn't have newspapers either. The rich Jews left a long time ago with cars and planes. Why are they shooting the poor Jews? We have never insulted the Germans. Tell them that they have to leave me alive a bit longer. I'm so young!' The girl had her hands in front of her face, as though praying, and she was looking me straight in the eyes. From what I remember, she was still a schoolgirl or a student. She spoke German fluently, without an accent. She had brown hair and did not look at all like a Jewish child. One of the shooters with an automatic pistol saw us and called out to me: 'Bring her!' I answered that I would not do it. The girl, who had heard, begged me, terrified: 'Please, please, don't do it!' Since I was making no move to bring the girl to the firing squad, I saw the SS coming toward me. He had his automatic pistol ready at the hip. At this moment, all I could think was: 'Let's hope that the girl doesn't turn around, that she keeps looking me in the eye and that she doesn't see her killer approaching and have to face death.' I kept comforting her over and over, even though I could see the shooter approaching her back. The girl was still begging me and surely didn't hear the shooter coming. Once he was right behind the girl, he pulled the trigger. He shot her behind the ears and she fell to the ground in front of me, without a sound. I think she even fell on my feet. I will never in my life forget this image of the girl lying at my feet. Her right eye had been torn out. It was still held by the optic nerve and lay on the ground ten or fifteen centimeters [four to six inches] from her head. The eye was still whole. The shot had just ripped it from her head. I can still see that white globe today. Her head wound barely bled. I stood there as though paralyzed. When I saw the SS approaching, I assumed he was going to send the girl to the ditch to be shot. I didn't think he would shoot her right in front of me. When she was lying on the ground, the SS told me I could drag her to the other dead. This man made me so nauseated that once he turned around I spit behind him. Disgusted by the animal behavior of these people, I turned around and went back to my vehicle."

He had to be begged for salvation by a young girl in his native German; she had to look him in the eye in order not to see her killer coming, and collapse on his shoes in order for him to realize that what he was watching was murder.

What is the dark force that attracted Josef F. and allowed him to stay so long at the anti-tank ditch, to watch and remember certain victims, and also to recall the process? What made him watch and at the same time blocked him from understanding he was witnessing murder? His deposition dates from twenty years after the end of the war.

In Josef's deposition, from February 1965,[3] the fact of a soldier authorized to watch the killings is terrible, terrible for the former young soldier. Was Josef unable to admit to himself that he derived pleasure from watching Jewish children and their parents killed? The disgust he experienced so late is most likely linked to the fact that a young Jewish girl believed in him and spoke to him as her savior.

Chapter 18

THE TRANSPORTER OF CLOTHING

Inhulets, June 2, 2010

Inhulets is a pretty name that evokes little villages in Provence. But it is actually not far from the major industrial city of Dniepropetrovsk in northern Ukraine. Today, this village is very small, lost in the steppes. Before the war, it was what was called a "Jewish colony."

There were many of these to be found in eastern Ukraine; the Jews first came to farm at the invitation of the tsar. Later, under the Soviets, these Jewish villages became kolkhozes. Jewish kolkhozes! A little-known story. When I discovered a map of these Jewish kolkhozes in Ukraine, I decided to find out more. And especially, to learn about the shootings of their inhabitants. And so, one morning in June, we found ourselves in the deserted streets of Inhulets.

As our van turned this way and that through the little streets, I scanned desperately for the silhouette of someone old enough to have known the war and the Nazi occupation, maybe even Jewish inhabitants from before the war.

As we were starting down one of those banal streets of gray facades, I saw on our left, sitting on a long bench, a pale, immobile man who was very tall, dressed entirely in gray.

He had the air of one of those elderly people you meet in a French retirement home, sitting sadly. They wait, today just like yesterday, often without knowing what they are waiting for.

I asked the driver to stop and I approached the man along with a translator; he seemed so very still. To my surprise, as soon as we started talking to him about the past, his entire body, his mind, and his expression all seemed to awaken.

Yes, Yevgeny did live in Inhulets during the war. He saw everything. He was here for the execution of the Jews, he saw the ditches. He said he had even been requisitioned to transport their clothes.

I couldn't believe it: an old retiree, apparently alone, motionless and silent on an anonymous bench. Within him was a witness whose memory of the murder of the Jews proved quite precise. His family, who lived across from the bench, agreed to let him get into our van. With the camera rolling, we drove through the village or, rather, along the paths of his memory.

Right away, he guided us to the center of Inhulets, to what he called the theater. It was a large, flat, white building with big wooden doors that looked as if they had been shut for a long time. The sun was leaden.

Sitting on another bench, next to the theater, he told us his family memories with great nostalgia. He explained how his father and his whole family had come to live in this Jewish colony.

"How did we end up here? . . . At the time, the roof tiles of the Jewish houses were tin. After a violent storm, the roofs were torn off. My father was a skilled tinsmith, so the Jews came to offer him work. They brought him here to re-cover their houses with tin. [Here, the witness cries.] That's how we ended up in the Jewish colony. At the time, this colony was only Jews, there were no Ukrainians or Russians here, except for the miller, the mechanic who ran the mill, and then us . . ."

Yevgeny couldn't help crying. His family had left western Ukraine after having suffered under Soviet repression, long before the war.

His grandfather had been branded a kulak and had lost everything. I understood that for him and for his parents, the village of Inhulets, or rather the kolkhoz, had been not only a haven of peace but also a Soviet structure for reintegrating his family. His father was able to work and be admitted to a kolkhoz. The families of kulaks often remained tainted by their history and were rejected by the Soviet regime.

Yevgeny's entire universe shifted again when the German units came to Inhulets to exterminate the Jewish-populated kolkhoz, which was basically the entire village. "One day, there was a raid. The Germans and the police surrounded the Jewish territory and took all the Jews into the theater building. We have a big theater, it still exists . . ."

On that same day, Yevgeny, the son of a Ukrainian worker, found himself requisitioned, pulled into a criminal machine.

"Early in the morning, the sergeant[1] came to see me at home. At the time, I was working with horses, working the earth. The sergeant told me to harness the horses to my cart and to go to the front of the theater. By now, all the Jews had been gathered in the theater. They had been told to bring their things and their valuables because they were going to leave."

His words were interrupted by sobs. He wiped his eyes with a big white handkerchief. He went on to describe what happened at the theater door. Four other villagers had also been requisitioned with their carts, "When we arrived in front of the theater, there were five carts in all. The Jews loaded their things onto the carts, and then they were lined up into a column and taken away. The column was led by the Germans and the police."

In the very place where we were talking, he had had to wait for the Jews to come out of the theater, which had been transformed for a night into a prison. His hay cart was transformed into a transport vehicle for Jewish possessions: their luggage, their jewelry, everything they had brought with them.

I asked him calmly to explain where he waited with his cart, where his horse was, and where the other carts were waiting.

With his long arms, he showed us the exact spots. Then, without hesitation, he explained that the Jews put their things into the empty carts themselves and then waited to the right of the theater door.

Our photographer took shots of the theater doors, closed ever since; of the places where the carts waited, and also of the road on which the Jews walked toward their death. In silence, standing to the side, I looked at the theater, the doors, the road. Sixty years ago, the Jews, suddenly deprived of everything, couldn't know their murder was so near.

Yevgeny began to take us through his memory of transporting the goods of his Jewish neighbors on the day of their murder. Then he was quiet, his eyes vacant. He agreed to get back into our van and to guide us to the extermination site.

Certain witnesses speak coldly, with no apparent emotion, without so much as a tear for the death of their neighbors. Not so Yevgeny. He reminded us several times that he knew them all by name. Some of the Jews had been part of the kolkhoz for a long time. Others had arrived recently from western Ukraine as refugees from the war. They had tried to flee the Germans at the beginning of the occupation and thought they were safe in this Jewish village lost in the steppes. But that was not the case.

Nowhere in our research had we found even the smallest hamlet where the Germans didn't turn up to murder the Jews.

As we approached the extermination site, Yevgeny began to speak again.

"They went off to the south, in the direction of Chyroke. . . . There was a natural ravine there, and the ditches were already dug. The Germans had taken twenty-five Communists there. . . . They had dug an enormous ditch because there were many, many Jews. In fact, they dug two ditches separated by a path. That's where they took the Jews. The column stopped marching fifty meters [fifty yards] from the ditches and the Jews were forced to undress. They had to get fully naked, the women, the children, the elderly—all, without exception. I waited with the other drivers on the hill, and the Jews were in the ravine. So we could see perfectly what was happening below."

Yevgeny spoke more and more. He didn't seem to see us anymore. He saw the Jews there, where he had stood more than sixty years ago.

"Then it started. They brought the Jews onto the path between the two ditches, and the firing squad, posted on the other side of the ditch, shot them with machine guns. The naked bodies fell into the ditch. . . . We had lived in this village for a long time, and we knew a lot of Jews. We knew all of them, the women, the children, the old people. . . ."

Yevgeny cried more warm tears. For him, these were not Jews who were murdered but names and faces. Since the beginning of our investigations, I've been struck by the fact that those who cry and sometimes have to stop talking are usually the ones who recall names and faces. For others, their neighbors had become anonymous "Jews."

He cried and wiped his eyes several times but wanted to continue talking. This was the old man who, a few hours earlier, had been waiting immobile on his bench, facing the door of his house. He was speaking today for the first time.

He had to stay until the end of the shootings because he had to collect the clothes of the dead. It was only once the firing had stopped, and the bodies had fallen into the ditch, that the four carts could drive into the ravine to the place where the Jews had undressed.

"Once the shooting was over, it was a terrible sight, naked bodies every which way in the ditch. . . . I can't talk about it. . . . Some were still moving. Then they told us to bring our carts to the pile of clothes. They ordered us to load them onto our carts and transport them to Chyroke."

I knew he would have to hold his horses tightly because the smell of blood would make them desperate to bolt. The words that came next surprised me.

"We deposited the clothes stolen from the Jews in the church at the edge of the village that the Germans were using as a warehouse. We unloaded the clothes, and we left. I don't know what they did next with these things. There, I have told you everything I saw."

The church of a neighboring village became a storage site for the possessions of the murdered Jews, a warehouse for the clothes of the dead. For Germans, coming from a country deeply marked by Christianity, the local church had become a warehouse for goods stolen from murder victims. It was perhaps irrational, but when I heard this, I thought of German centurions: *Gott mit uns* (God with us)!

Sometimes during our investigations, when a witness is too upset or too tired from age, I hesitate. Should I interrupt the interview? But on this day, I had no hesitation. It was too rare to meet someone who had been requisitioned to carry the clothes and possessions of Jews and who was willing to talk about it. Everything that touches on the taking of goods seems to provoke silence. I have met and questioned many diggers and fillers. But this was the first time I had met someone who admitted to transporting Jewish possessions.

I also didn't hesitate because I grasped that this lonely old man was recovering some of his dignity in telling his secret so that it could be re-inscribed in our memory and in the memory of the human race.

This son of a tinsmith, grandson of a kulak, who had been welcomed into a Jewish kolkhoz, was for one day a small part of the machine that stripped his Jewish neighbors as they were killed.

Listening to him, I thought about how on that day, the Fascists had completely overturned his universe. His expertise, his horses, the carts of the kolkhoz that were meant for carrying stacks of wheat, and even the church in the neighboring village: his immediate world was suddenly transformed into what is often the least known aspect of the genocidal machine, a machine run by Germans and villagers alike, that robs, transports, and stores the goods of the dead Jews, down to the last item of clothing.

For stealing as well as for murdering, the Nazis came to the village empty-handed. Under Nazi orders, everything in the daily life of the village became tools for killing and stealing. The genocidal machine for stealing is just as human and made up of the village as is the machine for killing.

The sun began to set, and we had to leave. Our van passed by Yevgeny's house one last time. I turned to look for him, and I will never forget what I saw. He was sitting again, motionless on his bench, waiting.

Chapter 19

THE TEACHERS

In all the villages where we've conducted investigations, even the smallest, the school has been one of the most prominent buildings and the teachers have been people of note. I recall one we met during a frozen winter. I wanted to speak with her to ask if she knew where the old people lived. When I came into her classroom, I was surprised to see her standing in her anorak and her students bundled in their coats and mufflers. I asked if they had heat. The teacher showed me a hole in the wall, about one and a half feet long and eight inches high. I saw red coals. A brazier. Through their determination, teachers in these rural settings play a considerable role.

To this day, the witnesses we interview will often mention their childhood teacher. Although some went to school infrequently, others can remember proudly moving up through the grades.

For these children of the war, school, with its classrooms, its benches, its teachers, remains an important touchstone. And yet, I'd rarely thought about what happened in the village school on the day the Jews were massacred. What did the teachers say to the children? What could the children see from school? It's strange, as a former public school teacher myself; I could have raised these questions in every village. But perhaps this is the very reason I suppressed it.

In going over the long list of thousands of interviews conducted by Yahad, I rediscovered that of a certain Paulina. When she was young, she lived in Tchoutchmany, not far from Bousk, the capital of the district of western Ukraine. Tchoutchmany is a very small village not far from a lush forest. I remember Paulina because she was terrified during her interview and asked us not to bring any vans into her street. She was mostly afraid of her neighbor, a former nationalist.

It was only sitting on her couch, in the shadow of thick curtains that darkened her small house, that she began to speak openly.

During the war, after the summer of 1942, she worked as a teacher in a school in Bousk, school number 2. With her salary, she had been able to pursue studies by correspondence at the University of Lemberg. But on the day the Jews were executed in Bousk, she was still a student in the eighth class, or the last grade of high school. She relives all of her memories from the perspective of her classroom bench. Even when the Germans invaded, she was sitting in class.

"When the Germans came, I was in school in Bousk. . . . The school is still in the same spot today. It's the one closest to the Jewish cemetery, because there are two schools, and mine was number 2. I didn't live in Bousk. I lived here, and I went to school on foot. We left early in the morning when it was still dark."

One morning, she found the doors to her school locked. "One day, as we were coming to school, the German soldiers told us to go back home. The next day, we returned to school, and it's there that we were told that there had been shootings. For the rest of the week, they continued bringing groups or single people to the cemetery. These must have been people who had tried to hide."

The high school in Bousk closed only for the first day of the shootings. So this young girl would become a witness from the schoolroom.

"I remember seeing through the school window a woman with her baby being taken to the cemetery. Two guards were with her, one in front and one behind. I started to cry because she was taking such care of the child in her arms, whispering to him, holding him close. I don't know any more. I didn't see the shootings themselves.

"She was fairly young, about thirty or thirty-five. . . . Her child was a baby, less than a year old. She caressed him. She held him against her heart and murmured something to him. I started to cry thinking about how heavy her heart must be."

Paulina said she simply glanced outside during class. I thought, how could she stay sitting down, following along with one ear, taking notes, writing, while at the same time watching this mother and her baby walk to their deaths?

She continued her account. "Throughout the week, they would bring people they had caught. I didn't see things clearly. There was just that one time when I looked out the window. My seat at school was by the window and I saw this woman walking in the street outside school. I didn't see the rest. Such a tragedy!"

This is rare testimony from a high school student whose desk was by the classroom window and who watched what was going on outside during class. It is easy to imagine that the teacher, who would be standing, would see all the arrests and the violence committed against the hidden Jews. And he continued to conduct his class. This immediate reopening of the school transformed the students and teachers into witnesses to crimes. Apparently, neither the Germans nor the auxiliary police feared being seen from the high school windows. Thus, the classroom became a theater.

Just a few miles from Bousk, in the same year, 1942, in another school, a German teacher and her students saw not only the arrest of the Jews but their murder. From their schoolyard.

Twelve miles away, in the little town of Kamianka-Bouzka, Édith D. was a twenty-two-year-old German, or rather a *Volksdeutsche*, transferred in 1942 to the German school here. I didn't meet her, but I found her deposition in the German archives. She taught primary school to German-speaking children. It was in Kamianka-Bouzka that she would later marry the man in charge of the farm bureau.

She was never able to forget the day of the execution of the Jews, the *Judenaktion*, as she called it. Not only had the school not closed its doors on that day, but Édith was on duty in the recess yard. The German children were outside playing when suddenly there was a terrible noise.

"I myself saw several *Judenaktion* in Kamianka-Bouzka. One day, from the schoolyard, I heard a horrible shriek. The children could watch the execution process from the yard. We realized that a crowd of Jewish women and children were gathered on the land bordering the yard. Ditches had been dug on this land, and they were supposed to be for building bunkers. The group of women and children were guarded by SS men. The victims had to get completely undressed and were then taken in groups of six or eight to the edge of the ditches and shot by a firing squad. This was where the shriek I spoke of came from. In the moment, it was all I could do to shield the children from the spectacle."[1]

Édith D., the young teacher, had already witnessed other *Judenaktion*. On this day, her school wasn't closed and she hadn't been warned that another massacre would take place right next to her schoolyard. So she watched and let the children see what she called the process of an execution: the ditches dug, the guards, the undressing of the Jews, of women and children, their placement at the edge of the ditches, the shots, the deaths. She didn't decide to bring the children inside until the Jews started to scream. It was as though the cries broke through the "process" for her and her students.

First of all, it is barely believable, barely comprehensible, that an execution would be planned next to a German primary school. Unbelievable that the killers didn't ask for the school to close. Also unbelievable that the children and their teacher watched as though unable to tear themselves away from the spectacle of the murder of the Jews.

In Kamianka-Bouzka, in contrast to Bousk, the killers didn't even bother to close their own primary school on the day of the murder. What could possibly have gone through the mind of whoever coordinated this shooting to decide to hold it right next to the yard of a

Volksdeutsche primary school? Was the extermination of the Jews normalized to such a point of banality that it could happen on a school day in full view of young German children and their teacher?

Édith D. is not just a spectator. She watches and lets her students watch. The questions they ask her once they're back in the classroom are certainly legitimate. "Inside, the children—these were German children and *Volksdeutsche*—asked me what crimes the people who were shot had committed. I didn't give them an explanation. I simply told them that there was nothing we could do besides pray for these people."

The German students think they have seen death sentences carried out for crimes committed. Their teacher doesn't weigh in on the subject but instead invites them to say prayers, Protestant or Catholic.

Nevertheless, Édith D. kept her distance, at least according to her deposition; she states several times that she didn't approve of the mass crimes committed against the Jews.

This wasn't the case for the principal of another school, in Klevan, a small town not far from Rovno in Ukraine.

In October 2011, Iryna spoke at length to one of our teams. Her testimony was so surprising that I decided she should be interviewed again a few months later.

Iryna, who was twelve at the time, was at the village school on May 11, 1942, when the principal came into her classroom and proposed that all the students go see that very day how we kill our "enemies," which is to say, the Jews of Klevan.

What she recounted astounds me to this day.

"The principal came into our class and said, 'Children, if you would like to see how we do justice to our enemies, you can go.' Of course, we rushed over there! They had been taken to be shot. And so, we went to see that horrible scene."

The principal of the school, who was thirty, was named Kourianik. According to Iryna, he seemed annoyed to have to make this announcement, as though he had been forced. Nevertheless, he was the moral authority for these children, and he came to suggest that they go watch the murder of their Jewish neighbors. He called them "enemies," classic anti–Semitic terminology that accused the Jews of being enemies of the people. Twenty to thirty children from the school went; they knew where the ditches were because other Jews had already been shot.

"We were above and we watched. We were on this hill. . . . We went there to see better."

The children from Klevan arrived in advance. There were no Germans, police, or Jews yet. So they sat above on a hillside, comfortably, for a good view, as though on circus bleachers. "When we arrived here, there was still nobody. We waited. We knew that they were being brought here."

Iryna spoke at length. The Jews had to climb onto planks, there were the undressings, the shooter. She said she looked for her Jewish classmates but couldn't recognize any. She said she had cried a lot and looked a lot. Attraction mingled with horror.

What can be in the mind of a child, sent by an authority figure, encouraged by her friends, to go see the Jews, including her classmates—deemed enemies by the principal of her school—meet their death?

Sixty years after the fact, Iryna's statements remain ambivalent. She tried to see her Jewish classmates murdered.

"In fact, that's the reason I went there. . . . My goal was to see these two children, Routa and . . . I forget . . . and Voussik. I thought I would meet them here. . . . There were some children here, but I was so upset I couldn't recognize the ones I wanted to see. . . . There were lots of children. . . . about ten children."

She couldn't see her Jewish friends. And it seems she was fascinated by the German shooter. Her description of him, as a young girl admiring a young man, completely ignores the fact that he is a killer: "There was only one shooter. He was a handsome young German. . . . He was almost a child! He had a pistol attached at knee level, but when he approached this place, somebody handed him a machine gun that he started shooting with."

Iryna, with her wrinkled face, kept talking like the adolescent she had been. According to her, the Germans, including the shooter, knew that the children from the Klevan School were there, on the hillside less than a hundred yards away, watching. All the spectators that day were young students.

The principal himself didn't go to the shootings, nor for that matter did any of the teachers. Yet he had, perhaps involuntarily, mandated that the children of his school go watch their neighbors be murdered, like at a show.

PART FOUR

THE EVENING

Nikolai, Novozybkov, Russia (David Merlin-Dufey/Yahad-In Unum)
"There were carts in which they drove the children and old people, who understood they were going to be shot."

Maria, Mokrovo, Belarus (Nicolas Tkatchouk/Yahad–In Unum)
"They summoned musicians, who were ordered to play, and the Jews were forced to dance."

Alexander, Temirgoyevskaya, Russia (Markel Redondo/Yahad–In Unum)
"The carts left and we stayed where we were and played a game of reds and whites."

Iosif, Bibrka, Ukraine (Erez Lichtfeld/Yahad-In Unum)
"[The German] simply measured four meters for the length and four meters for the width, and he drew them with his shovel."

Vladimir, Novopodilsk, Ukraine (David Merlin-Dufey/Yahad-In Unum)
"The policeman came into the school. The teacher pointed out each of the half-Jewish children: *'Juden! Juden! Juden!'*"

Ievhenia, Yavoriv, Ukraine (Erez Lichtfeld/Yahad–In Unum)
"That was the day they liquidated the ghetto."

Yevgeny, Inhulets, Ukraine (David Merlin-Dufey/Yahad-In Unum)
"They brought the Jews onto the path between the two ditches, and the firing squad, posted on the other side of the ditch, shot them with machine guns."

Viktor is showing the location of the mass graves at the extermination site in Bronnaya Gora, Belarus, where more than 30,000 Jews from surrounding cities where killed. (Nicolas Tkatchouk/Yahad-In Unum)

Execution site in Ladozhskaya, Russia, where at least five hundred Jews were killed in December 1942. (Markel Redondo/ Yahad–In Unum)

The Yahad–In Unum team interviewing a witness. (Markel Redondo/ Yahad-In Unum)

Searching for witnesses in Moldova. (Markel Redondo/Yahad-In Unum)

Portrait of Claudius Desbois, 1943.

Chapter 20

THE FILLERS

Among the conscripted villagers were what they called the "fillers." The fillers filled in the graves dug by the diggers. They
make up the largest portion of the requisitioned people we have met
over these past ten years.

They were conscripted in their houses early in the morning by a
polizei, or by a villager sent by the *staroste,* or by an armed German.
Or else they were called to work later, sometimes on the road to their
fields. They came to the graves with their shovels. Often before the
massacre was over, but sometimes much later, after the killers had left.

From our interviews, it seems that the majority of fillers were men,
often older children, barely twelve years of age. Sometimes, though,
women had to fill in the graves. I can recall, among others, the member of a Crimean collective who was made to join the fillers with her
own shovel.

Most of the fillers had to wait onsite for a long time before they
could begin work. Some sat beside the ditches from daybreak. They
had been part of the digging team; they had dug out, either at dawn
or on the preceding night, the same ditch they would soon fill. Others had been called in as reinforcements during the shootings, while
the Mauser rifles or the automatic pistols were still firing on terrified
Jewish families.

Once it was time for the fillers to work, to bury the bodies of the Jewish victims, the Jews for the most part had already deposited their clothes, at least the best ones, around the outside of the ditches. Sometimes the Jews were made to throw their clothes in a horse-drawn carriage waiting nearby, sometimes simply on the ground. It was not rare for a jacket, pair of pants, or a pair of shoes to be given to a filler as recompense for his work in the evening.

When there weren't too many victims, a filler's work could be done in a few hours. But it could also last several days in cases where the ditches would swallow up more than ten thousand people. The fillers always worked in teams. Very rarely have I heard of a filler being sent alone with his shovel.

However, the fillers were not entirely like the other conscripts. Each of them was confronted not only with the bodies of murdered Jews but also with Jews who had survived the shooting and were in agony, or who had simply been thrown alive into the grave and were trying, most often in vain, to extract themselves from the mass of bodies, blood, and sand.

This is what immediately affected me upon meeting them. Their shovels full of dirt were, in fact, murderous.

One of them, named Samuel, in Dovbych, a small town in the Lvov region of Ukraine, has never left my mind. Young at the time, he went up close to the grave to look. He was one of the many Soviet adolescents whose curiosity got the better of them. This was how he was recruited by a *polizei* to become a filler. I listen again to his words, recorded ten years ago already. All the early members of Yahad can recall Samuel, with his white shirt and black pants. He was the first to clearly explain to us that he had been ordered to bury Jews alive. He was also, curiously, stirred by his own Christian feelings at the moment the *polizei* ordered him to start shoveling dirt.

"Me, I had come to see what was happening. A police officer came up to me and gave me a shovel. I remembered a religious commandment that said, 'Never dig a grave or it could be your own.' Seeing the people still moving in the grave, I started to feel bad, to stagger on the side of the ditch. A policeman I knew, a neighbor, came and pushed me aside so I didn't fall in. I couldn't stand on my legs anymore. My mother came a little later to take care of me. She talked to me and asked me questions, but I was incapable of answering. I stayed there for about three hours until the graves were already filled in, and the police were gone. We were still there. We saw the graves still moving. Then we went home."

Samuel saw "people moving." Many witnesses among the diggers remember seeing children's toys, hands, feet sticking out of the dirt. Samuel saw people moving. This is something else entirely.

Samuel is surely the one who made me realize that the filler is not in fact a conscript like the others. He must, of course, bury the dead Jews who have just been murdered. But also, and sometimes mostly, he has to bury living people, Jews who have been wounded but also Jewish adults, children, and even infants who have been shoved or brutally thrown down like dead dogs. And the filler's live burial will certainly finish them off.

Samuel mentioned a verse of the Bible that made it all the more impossible for him to shovel the earth.

The act of filling, even when forced, contributes to—or rather is inscribed in—the criminal act. The shooters shoot. The pushers, sometimes with leather gloves, sometimes with the heels of their boots, push the bodies of the dead and wounded Jews into the graves. The fillers bury both the dead and the living. Thus the filler is a conscript physically associated with the murder, more precisely with the very act of killing. And not all fillers would feel young Samuel's pain.

As our interviews progress, a range of fillers becomes evident. They situate themselves differently with respect to the victims and to their mandate to bury the living. Here again, behind the awful task of the filler, there lies a fully responsible man.

Some, like the young Samuel, will refuse or become incapable when they find themselves looking into a grave that is full and writhing. They will not fill. These witnesses are rare. Most of the fillers did not leave the grave before the end, often because they were forced to stay by the *polizei* or the Germans, but also because they were hoping for recompense from the killers, often in the form of clothes belonging to the dead.

At the extreme other end of the human chain from Samuel, in terms of responsibility, I recall a Ukrainian woman whom I did not film because she fled after she talked; although in truth, she didn't talk, she yelled. We were going toward an execution site with one of the witnesses we'd interviewed beforehand. The woman shouted out terrible words while waving her arms in the air. Words that have stayed engraved in my memory. Her mother had been called up to fill the Jews' common grave.

"My mother buried them, some still alive. She hit them with her shovel to finish them off." She screamed this violently in the middle of a group of neighbors, without any apparent regard for what the others might think. Maybe the neighbors already knew?

She was the only one, to my knowledge, after so many interviews, to yell such a thing. Yet I can't help but think that there were others who finished off the murders with their shovels. Between Samuel's panic and the shovel blows of this anonymous woman who "finished off" the Jews, we discovered an entire human panorama.

Living today in a city like Paris, we tend to think of Jew, *polizei,* and grave filler as separate beings, or at least as clearly distinct from one another. But above all, they were simply neighbors. Sometimes it would turn out that the filler knew the *polizei* who guarded the Jews leading up to shooting, as well as the Jewish family with all its children who waited, naked, beside the ditch. They were all, or rather they had all been, neighbors. And not just for the past few weeks or even years, but quite often for generations. Only the Germans, foreigners arriving by truck or car from the big city, were strangers to the villagers.

This fact of being neighbors would sometimes mean that there were words or gestures back and forth before or even during the crime. Some witnesses can recall the last words exchanged. Old neighbors who were talking together until some of them killed the others.

In March 2012 in Ukraine, Patrice interviewed one of these neighbors whose father, conscripted to fill in a grave, heard a *polizei* speaking to his Jewish neighbor before the neighbor was killed. Mykola lived in the small village of Toutchyne in the region of Rivne. He was the ninth boy in his family. His father was the chief miller in the village; he worked at the watermill. His father must have personally known most of the inhabitants. In a rural village in the 1940s, everyone needed the miller to mill grain or to buy flour.

"I forgot to mention that most of the workers in the mill were Jewish, Shats was the owner, Liouppe the accountant, Pinia worked as a night watchman, etc. As for my father, he was the head miller."

Many of the villagers in Toutchyne had told Patrice that Mykola was there on the day of the shootings. He had a nickname, "the artist," probably because of his especially unkempt hair. Mykola had a good memory for the past and could remember tensions and fights between the Jewish and Ukrainian children from before the war. "Sometimes these fights got violent and the mounted police had to intervene. I don't think the fights were religious in nature. Sometimes the Jewish kids called the Ukrainian peasants 'boors,' and the Ukrainians called the Jews 'Yids.'"

Rare, though, are those who have been willing to describe serious tensions between the two communities before the German occupation. Mykola described life in Toutchyne with plenty of vivid detail.

"The Jews were mostly engaged in commerce, just like today. For example, Khyzda, Khania, and Leika owned shops. There was a big market in town where the Jews sold provisions. It was also a fairground; there was a puppet theater and a circus with polar bears. I remember when we were coming home from school and we saw the heads of tigers and were very impressed."

He expressed nostalgia for his fourteen-year-old self at the time the war broke out without losing sight of the tarnished atmosphere of the village at the time. Names of Jewish families studded his child-hood memories. On the day of the crime, his father had to dig and fill, and Mykola had to come to the grave with food for him. Many villagers remember meals set up for the Germans beside the ditches; few mention that the conscripts were hungry, too, and that they were not fed by the German authorities. Often, it was a relative who brought them food on site.

Hearing this, I envisioned my grandmother Victorine during the harvests in Villegaudin. I could see her in the cool shade of an awning, preparing a heavy wicker basket with slices of sausage, two-pound loaves of bread, and fruit from the farm that she wrapped conscientiously in a big white napkin to keep cool. She would add a bottle of red wine and another of lemonade. Then my cousin and I would heroically carry the basket out into the fields of ripe wheat. I can still remember the smiles of the harvesters when they would see us arriving. I can't help but think that if I had grown up in an occupied Soviet village, I could have carried the same basket into a field of extermination. Simple, rural gestures carried out on the day of the crime against the Jews have often recalled similar repetitive acts, seen or performed during my childhood, gestures I might otherwise have forgotten.

So Mykola was not just the son of a grave filler. He was also the carrier of provisions to his father, beside the ditch where a number of Jews, by force of blows, were undressing to be shot. "When the grave was ready . . . the villagers, my father included, were requisitioned. And I went to carry lunch for my father. I remember Richter sitting on a chair beside the ditch."

Richter. Many times, Mykola will describe the behavior of Richter, the German who personally shot the Jews of Toutchyne. For Mykola, Richter was not a foreigner come from elsewhere; he was the German commander of the town and had a reputation as an extremely violent man.

"He was sitting on a stool at the edge of the ditch. The Jews went into the ditch, lay down on the ground, and Richter shot them from above. I can still see his silvery gun shining in the sun. He put two bullets into each person's neck. No one checked to make sure they were dead. They were immediately covered with dirt.

"Richter was right at the edge of the ditch, he saw the Jews lying down inside and had no problem aiming because he was very close. My father was nearby. He had to wait until the end of the shooting to fill in the grave. He could hear the Jews asking how they should lie down and the police answering, 'Face to the ground.'"

In fact, Mykola's father hadn't been directly conscripted by the police; he had put himself forward to replace one of his sons, "It was the *polizei* who came to get him. They wanted to take my oldest brother, but my mother started to cry and persuaded them to take my father instead. She guessed that it was to bury the bodies and she didn't want my brother to be traumatized by the blood and the cadavers. The police accepted and took my father.

"The Jews had to strip naked, climb down into the ditch, and lie down. Richter was sitting on a stool by the ditch. The *Schutzmann* brought the Jews, and Richter shot them in the neck with his pistol. As soon as the Jews were shot, they were covered with a layer of dirt and the next group was brought in. The bodies piled on top of one another. It was horrible."

And then, suddenly, Mykola stops designating the naked bodies of "the Jews" condemned to die but evokes his neighbor, a young mother with her baby. "My neighbor was among the people shot. In fact, her house still exists. I remember that she was there completely naked with her baby in her arms. Our house was on top of a hill and we could see clearly what was happening there. . . . The *Schutzmann* searched for Jews everywhere and rounded them all up. Once they had grouped a large number of Jews, they brought them toward the ditch. I saw two *Schutzmann* bring a group of two hundred Jews. They didn't say anything. You could just hear a low moaning that made me shiver. I don't know if you can imagine the horrible sound of the moans of people condemned to death. It's horrible."

Here Mykola began to cry. "It's horrible." "*Strachne*" in Russian. Countless times have I heard old people, former Soviet children, cry while repeating "*Strachne . . .*"

Like young Anna in Medzhybizh, Mykola could still remember the sound of the footfalls of the Jews walking toward their death. This hum of two hundred people resonated for a long time in my head.

One of them even recovered his name in Mykola's narrative: Tevel was a former neighbor, just like the *polizei*, who himself had a name, Kostiouk.

"I'm going to tell you something else that happened. In this spot, there used to be the house of the shoemaker, Tevel. We knew him well because my brother was his apprentice. The Jews were already gathered next to the ditch when suddenly Richter had to leave. He left on a motorcycle, and the *Schutzmann* stayed to guard the Jews. As soon as Richter was gone, the Jews started talking to the police. Tevel addressed the policeman Kostiouk, saying: 'Brother, give me a cigarette!'"

As he speaks, Mykola himself realizes that his story sounds unreal; a police officer, here to help the killer, conversing calmly with the shoemaker he's guarding before he's to be murdered. They speak together because the German authority is no longer present. The grave filler watches, listens, and waits along with the people he is going to have to bury in the coming minutes. And Mykola, a child, watches them all.

I don't know why, but I hadn't realized, before hearing this testimony, that very often all of the people around the grave were neighbors. The village Jews, their neighbors who had become police, and the neighbors conscripted to work, as well as those who came as spectators. Neighbors. No doubt, I would have liked to think that these people no longer had any human connection, that no words were exchanged between them on the day of the crime. I would have liked for there to be only Jews, Germans, collaborators, and spectators. Black, white, and gray. But on the day of the crime, everyone—*polizei, conscripts, Jews, and spectators*—are all part of the same Soviet village.

It is unbearable for me to think that the Jewish shoemaker Tevel will shake the hand of the *polizei* Kostiouk before climbing into his grave. With great emotion, I recall this passage from Robert Anthelme's *L'Espèce humaine* (*The Human Species*): "There is no ambiguity; we remain men, and we will finish only as men. It is because we are men like them that the SS will ultimately be powerless before us."[1]

Mykola recounts this scene: "It was a surrealist painting, the *Schutzmann* speaking in a friendly way to the Jews. My father was sitting beside them with his shovel. He was looking at his friends whom he was going to have to bury soon, and I was watching this scene from behind the bushes. Once Richter returned, the Jews had to undress. Tevel shook Kostiouk's hand and climbed into the ditch. I also saw my neighbor go into the ditch holding her baby in her arms. Richter sat on his stool and started to shoot. I think he hit the baby first, because the baby started to scream so loudly that I couldn't stand it. I wished I had a weapon to kill Richter. It was horrible."

It was Richter's temporary absence from Toutchyne on the day of the crime that would allow the villagers a few moments "among themselves."

"They waited near the ditch and talked. The Jews called the *Schutzmann* 'brother,' as they were all sitting and chatting together. But as soon as Richter came back, the behavior of the *Schutzmann* immediately changed. They stood back up and ordered the Jews to stand up, too. The Jews had to undress. Then Tevel shook Kostiouk's hand, asked him for a last cigarette, and went down into the ditch. But the thing that touched me the most was the screaming of the baby hit by the bullet."

Mykola has not forgotten the payment offered his father at the end of the day.

"After the shooting, they gave my father two or three pieces of clothing, but I don't know what happened to the rest of the clothes."

Mykola himself inherited a jacket with some gold in the pockets.

"My parents had ten children. We needed clothes. I remember that they gave us a jacket. When I put it down, I heard a jingling. When I looked closely, I noticed an interior pocket. I found five rubles in gold. The Jews often hid money in the lining of their clothes."

The life of the neighbors took up again after the massacre and included the few surviving Jews; Mykola, dressed in the jacket of a murdered Jew, met one of the surviving Jews in the street. "After the shooting, there was a so-called amnesty for the Jews to come back to town. I remember I was wearing the jacket that had been given to me when I crossed paths with a Jew in the street. I was so ashamed of wearing this jacket, because I knew where it came from, that I threw it away."

I know very well that the Soviet requisition was coercive. The members of a collective could hardly refuse to participate in its work. And I know that the Germans took advantage of this collective structure to have free labor on hand. But I cannot help but ask myself certain questions. To be forced to bury your Jewish neighbors, dead or alive, then to live with the few who have survived while wearing the clothes of the dead . . . It is somehow harder to bear genocidal human fracturing deep in a Soviet village than to hear Nazism screamed and hammered out by Himmler on a podium in Poznan.[2] How many Soviets had to bury their own neighbors with their own shovels right after having spoken to them?

I cannot end this chapter without sharing a final memory of Mykola's of a young Jewish girl, sitting on top of a pile of bodies, screaming in Ukrainian:

"I want to see my mommy! Take me to my mommy's house!"

The little girl cried out in Ukrainian and not in Yiddish, because around the grave, Ukrainians were all she saw.

Chapter 21

THE SALE

His name was Nikolai. We interviewed him on October 26, 2010, at his home in Novozybkov, in the Briansk region of Russia. He would reveal himself to have an exceptional memory.

It was autumn, and the leaves were becoming more and more crimson and swirled in gusts of wind. Nikolai had a very long white beard, and his silver hair and light eyes gave him the allure of old faces in ancient Russian paintings. Patrice conducted the interview. The room was badly heated and decorated with several flags. Svetlana, who was translating, kept her hat on and pulled down over her ears to protect against the cold.

Nikolai lived on the street where the train station was during the war. This station would play an important role in his story.

Even though he was originally from Koursk, he had spent most of his life in this little town of Novozybkov. His father had abandoned the family, and he had grown up with his mother and sisters. He had known the local Jews, of whom there were more than three thousand according to the 1939 census.[1] In fact, as a child he had learned to read the Talmud with a friend: "I had Jewish neighbors, and I had a very good Jewish friend named Dvorkine. We were very curious about everything at the time, and we asked him to bring us the Talmud, and he did bring it and he translated it. He had a garden, and we met there and discussed the Talmud."

I had met and interviewed many villagers from the former Soviet Union who still spoke Yiddish. They had learned it working with Jewish families, or else from being a "Shabbos goy."[2] One of them even wanted to do her interview in Yiddish.

But this was the first time I had come across an old Russian man in a small town who had studied the Talmud, which was written in Hebrew and Armenian, with his neighbor as a translator!

He told us about the war, his war. He was seventeen when it broke out. And since he lived by the train station, he saw German trains carrying starving Soviet prisoners. With tears, he described the first dead people he saw: Soviet prisoners who had fallen out of trains and were shot.

His story was strange, or rather unique. It was winter of 1943, and he went to his uncle's house. "For the Jews, I was an eyewitness. My uncle lived in Kakhovka. I was taking him potato peelings for his cow, and I was walking toward the station. There I was stopped by a German, an armored soldier who said to me '*Komm, komm.*'[3] I was on a sled. He ordered me to take his suitcase, put it on my sled, and to take it along with him to the house where the German soldiers were. I took him." Nikolai's words evoked the German objective of colonizing the Soviet territories. During this period, a German would consider any Russian villager at his disposal.

Nikolai, in his sled, with his passenger and the suitcase, came right up against a German roadblock: a column of Jews en route to extermination. The Jews of Novozybkov were shot in midwinter, on January 18, 1942. According to Soviet archives, 950 people were murdered.[4] They were killed by *Einsatzkommando* 8.[5] Nikolai speaks of a thousand people. He describes the column in simple words.

"When we are a ways away from the station, I see a column of Jews that they're taking to be shot. In front, there are four SS, obviously the big chiefs with the military stripes and crosses, big strapping Germans. They call out to the tank driver and yell at him, almost hit him, and give him the order not to move from there. In short, we let the column they were taking to be executed go by. There were carts in which they drove the children and old people, who understood they were going to be shot. Their legs no longer carried them and so they were driven in carts."

So they waited, Nikolai and the German officer, for around twenty minutes, watching the column of Jews go by. Then traffic resumed. He spoke like someone who has seen so much death and so many crimes that a column of Jews walking toward their graves was first and foremost a traffic jam. "We started up again to do what we had to do. We lived near the station, and it was very close to the place. We heard the firing of automatic weapons."

His testimony could have stopped there as far as the murder of the Jews was concerned. He did not go to the ditches to watch. But once evening fell, it was very cold and the Germans returned from their shootings. On their way home, they went into Nikolai's house to warm their feet.

"Since we lived near the station, they came by our house. They had boots that didn't fit, they were cold and came into our house to warm up."

To hear him, the Germans were regular guests in his house. I don't think the Germans could go into any house to get warm without some risk. In this one, there was no man in the family. It's also possible that the proximity of the house to the station got them used to each other, so the family had no choice. Nikolai recalls with precision something that happened in his house.

"And one night, a young SS, about the same age as me, showed up, and my mother and my aunt said to him: 'You should be ashamed, you who are so young, to do things like this, to shoot people.' And he answered: 'We're not the ones who shoot. It's the Russians.' And he explained how this happened. First, they ordered the Jew to undress and to keep on only their underwear. Then they patted down the underwear because sometimes the Jews sewed in coins. And while they were being searched, a woman escaped just like that, in her underwear, through the forest. She escaped execution."

Nikolai's eyes grew misty. What happened next in his house leaves me speechless.

"He had a handkerchief where he had put teeth, rings, objects of value, maybe four hundred grams [almost a pound], and he offered them to us, but my aunt refused. I asked him: 'Are you the one who took these things?' He said: 'No, they were confiscated from the Russian police.' Our people, the Russian police."

So, I thought, on the very evening of the murder, when the Jewish bodies were barely in the ground, a young SS officer returns having collected the gold teeth and jewelry of the dead and tries to sell them to the neighbors, without hiding it from the other Germans who are there to get warm. This isn't a furtive sale on the fly, but a sale around a home fire. Probably it was easier to sell gold there before returning to base.

Stories of jewelry stolen by Germans during the executions are quite common. The neighbors see them fill their pockets and bags with jewels as well as expensive clothing.

But an SS officer who resells gold the same night to the Russian neighbors of murdered Jews! I thought about it in the simplest terms: this SS was looking out for his own interests. He killed the Jews out of Nazi ideology, but he hadn't forgotten to help himself. The story also showed that somewhere in the village someone was extracting golden teeth before the Jews were shot.

This German SS didn't live in the village. He apparently couldn't care less if the local peasants knew that his motivations were as venial as they were racial.

Nikolai was the only witness who described an intended sale that took place in his home. I can't help but ask myself: how many others saw this and were silent?

PART FIVE

THE DAY AFTER

Chapter 22

THE AUCTIONS

April 2009, Brest, Belarus

I t is still cool in Belarus, yet everywhere there is a feeling of spring. The scene seems unreal to me: I am in the middle of a pedestrian street in the center of Brest with the entire team. The camera is on its tripod on newly mounted nonskid pads. The town of Brest bears the imprint of historical combat. On June 22, 1941, the day of Operation Barbarossa,[1] the German army attacked the town, destroying the Soviet lines of defense. But the town and her citadel organized a resistance that held against the attack until July 8, 1942. Since then, Brest and her citadel have become symbols of the resistance of the Soviet people against Fascism. Who in Russia has not heard of the Citadel of Brest?

Facing the camera, Vladimir, originally from a little village not far from Brest, is calm and almost immobile. He recalls: "I'm going to tell you everything in detail about the first days of the war. The 21st of June, 1941, I was at home. The war started at four in the morning. In the month of June, this is the shortest night, so the night was ending when the war began. The entire frontier around Boug[2] was lit up by missiles; as soon as the missile fire ended, the combat started. Three kilometers [a mile and a half] from our village was an airfield where they immediately burned all the planes and tanks of gas. The fires

203

started to spread, and people were fleeing everywhere in their underwear. That's how the war began."

Though he didn't live in the center of Brest, he heard the shots and was fully aware of the town's heroism. "We lived not far from Brest, next to it, and we heard the sounds of combat here for a month. The fortress resisted for a long time. The Germans went off in the direction of Minsk, but Brest continued to fight. Sometime later, everything started to calm down and the Germans started to set up here. They installed their power."

This is how Vladimir began his account. Everyone here carries his own memories and bears his own scars from the Great Patriotic War.[3] It was only after having set the scene that he began to talk about himself and, in particular, his life as a prisoner.

"I spent the entire summer of 1942 at home. In the autumn, the Germans summoned me. They took me and brought me here, to Brest, where they put me in prison. Later, from this prison, they took twenty-five people and put them in this building here."

His testimony sounds all the more anachronistic among the young passersby, often in couples. Young people crowd into the hall of what is now the town's main movie theater to soak up the clichés of Western freedom. Women in blue smocks sell buckets of popcorn. It feels like a little piece of the West parachuted into this country where kolkhozes are flourishing again.

While the crowd hurries in so as not to miss any of the show, we stay planted firmly on the sidewalk outside, the camera fixed on Vladimir's face and gestures.

Vladimir celebrated his twentieth birthday in 1947. He had already known war, camps, and forced labor. His youth was battered under the bootheels of the German occupants.

We had met Vladimir randomly in the street. Seeing an old man, our researchers had started to ask the usual questions: "What year were you born?" "Where did you live during the German occupation?" "What did you see?" Vladimir was willing to testify about the war in Brest as well as about the extermination of the Jews in the ghetto. With his sharp black eyes and his leather—or leatherette—cap pulled far down, he talks. As he remembers, he relives.

He points out the building, the famous movie theater. He explains that it was built over the walls of Brest's former synagogue. I can hardly believe my ears. While he speaks, I look through the windows of the theater, I listen to the sound effects coming from inside, and suddenly it all seems different to me. Then Vladimir takes us inside. Together, we go down a small staircase toward the restrooms. There, in a hallway, we can see the foundation walls of the synagogue. The Jews have become like the Mayans of Belarus. We look for traces of them beneath new construction. Seventy years ago, rather than kids hurrying in to see a movie, there were others rushing into this place. They were eager to see the "Kabbalat Shabbat" on a Friday night. I can hear in my mind the melody, *Lekhah dodi liqrat kallah, p'nei Shabbat neqabelah*.[4] A little saddened, we climbed back up the stairs of this movie theater encasing the former synagogue.

Through word and gesture, Vladimir tried to explain what the ghetto of Brest was to him. Occasionally, he had to repeat himself several times in order for us to grasp what he was saying because it was just so strange.

He brought our team to the former site of the gates to the ghetto. He knew this place by heart. He had been locked in a building right behind the spot where we stood.

Vladimir was part of a team of twenty-five Soviet prisoners who were forced to "clean, store, and package" the goods of the Brest Jews after the shootings. There were mostly clothes and shoes, but also pillows, cloth, and sheets.

"A German came with a translator and told us that today we were going to the ghetto to clean up."

The band of prisoners had to go into the empty dwellings, carry the Jews' possessions outside on stretchers, and, after cleaning them, put them into crates.

"You know, crates where we would store butter, square crates like that." Vladimir shows the size of a crate with his hands. "So they made us fill the crates with the Jews' things. There was a lot of cloth, shoes, and other things, and we packed it all up. Afterward, we took it all to the market. There were two markets here. One was in Pouchkinskaya Street, and it was smaller. The other one, the main market, was in Moskovskaya Street, and it was bigger."

Not only was the sale of Jewish goods not hidden or discreet, camouflaged, but it took place in broad daylight at the center of Soviet life. To this day, these bazaars remain vibrant places of commerce and social interaction. In the place where everyone went to make daily purchases, the possessions of murdered Jews were sold shamelessly at auction. Given the presence of the Germans and the way the sale was conducted, no one could be unaware of the origins of these crates and their contents.

The crates were transported by truck through the streets of Brest. They had been shut, and then sent to market where the buyer couldn't open them until after he had paid.

But before this happened, Vladimir and the other prisoners had to clean everything, "The Germans forced us to clean everything, the good clothes, the not-so-good clothes, the different shoes."

And the contents of the cases could vary considerably. "People had to make deals after they had paid."

Not only did Vladimir pack up the Jewish goods, he was part of the team of salesmen hawking the merchandise at the market. His role consisted of holding up the crates to show the customers in order to get the auctions started.

"We would hold up a case, and the German next to the truck would cry out, 'This crate cost five marks, who will give more?'"

So the German played the auctioneer.

"This German could get the price up to ten, fifteen, or twenty marks."

Vladimir recalled that the sale of the Jewish goods was successful overall. There were no crates left over. He himself was able to scrounge some shoes to replace his own, which were "falling apart." He is embarrassed to tell us this and tries to give an explanation, "Here we could find Bata[5] shoes, from Poland, which were very sturdy, and so we wore them ourselves, too."

Could these shoes be considered a payment from the Germans for a job done? This is not unthinkable, especially considering other testimonies confirming that requisitioned workers could often freely take goods and shoes. After thousands of interviews, Vladimir remains one of the only ones to describe in such detail the organization of the auction of Jewish goods in a town as large as Brest.

As a prisoner who conducted these sales under German constraint, his lack of personal responsibility probably made it easier for him to tell the story than it would have been for those who had freely participated. He spoke at length. Onlookers gathered silently around us, to listen to him.

Listening to Vladimir's testimony, I am reminded of another witness to an auction that took place in the village of Romanivka, in the Jitomir region of Ukraine. Anna Pavlovna, an old woman in a blouse with giant purple flowers, described the sale of Jewish goods in the days following their shooting by Ukrainian police:

"They took what they wanted. They had taken all the horses, the carts, and the clothes belonging to the Jews."

On the day after the shooting, they sold the clothes at a sort of fair. The clothing market was held in the primary school that was transformed into a bazaar. It's impressive to think that over the course of one night the police were able to collect the clothes, sort them, classify them, and alert all the villagers to the fact that the Jewish goods were for sale.

"They had opened the windows of the school. In each classroom, there were different things. In one were the women's clothes, in another, the men's clothes. They had gotten young people from the village to sort the clothes. They sold them through the windows."

For the furniture, a large number of requisitions were needed over a very short time. They needed people to sort, to transport, and to unload. It took three days to get the furniture out of the Jewish houses.

"Our village was big. There were more than a thousand Jewish houses to empty."

It took a village-wide effort to get the Jewish furniture out of the houses and into the schoolyard where it was sold. "They brought furniture, then sold it. They brought more furniture and sold that, too. They went from house to house, loading this, loading that. Then they came back to the school and unloaded everything.

"It was the police who did this, along with the strong young people, the adolescents. . . . They used the kolkhoz carts."

In one week, using the basic materials of rural life, carts and horses, more than a thousand Jewish homes were emptied and everything had been sold. I imagined the villagers coming to the little school with their own carts, pictured these muddy streets teeming with carts full of furniture, coming and going. This wasn't pillaging, it was a sale!

Most of the Jews murdered here were farmers. Their livestock was not abandoned for long: "The livestock came and went freely in the village. The cows mooed because they were swollen with milk. It wasn't the Germans who came to take them; it was the Russians. They took them, killed them, and sold them."

I know from my own rural roots that anyone on a farm can become a butcher, especially when it comes to killing a pig. But from there to catching the animals of all the Jews in order to kill, butcher, and sell is quite a step. There again, the coordination among the villagers can't help but leave me with questions.

It takes not only efficiency but also know-how based in longstanding habits and customs to explain the extraordinary reactivity of the police aided by the requisitioned population. And we should not forget that similar auctions had taken place six years earlier, when families disappeared or died out during the Great Famine[6] and also during the persecutions of the kulaks.[7] A very old witness in the Krivoi Rog region of eastern Ukraine lived through both of these earlier "catastrophes" as well as the auctions during the war. He first told us about an auction during the purge of the kulaks.

"There was a man who lived right over there, and he was dispossessed."

"When they confiscated someone's house, what did they do with the furniture?"

"There was a special sale. . . . My father went to this sale. There were many men like this man in Ukraine, and their goods were sold at this sale. They sold to the person who would pay the most; it was an auction. I know that my father bought a table and a cot. We were poor. . . . All these things were sold at a low price, I know it. And so, this man's things were also taken there. . . . The sale took place in Krivoi Rog, because my father had a horse at the time and I know he went there. They sold good clothes as well as furniture. Everything they had taken from the kulaks. Because they took everything from the kulaks! They even sold the house. . . . They sold the animals! Yes, yes, yes, they confiscated everything! As for the horses, local people bought them."

There is striking similarity not only between the facts but also between the terms used by the witnesses to both the de-kulakization and to the stripping of the homes of murdered Jews. On the day of the murders, did the police and the Germans simply tap into a long-standing Russo-Soviet village tradition? Each villager knows what he is supposed to do in life but also is guided by custom in all his tasks. Gestures are repeated throughout the seasons. Everyone knows, for example, how to work together on harvest days, how to gather potatoes, or how to catch a pig, kill it, cut it up, fill its lungs to make them pretty, and reward the workers with morsels of meat.

Is it possible that these village habits and customs allowed such rapidly organized sales of furniture, clothing, and animals to take place in times of the "disappearance" of portions of the local population? That it happened thanks to—and because of—these non-improvised, habitual ways? For example, the expression "good clothes" is troubling. I've heard it many times from the mouths of peasants in reference to the sorting of the good clothes belonging to the Jews from those of little value. The speed is equally troubling, and the way the witnesses describe it as nothing spectacular—on the contrary.

Did the Nazis understand how to tap into local rural customs? Or were they relying on their own experience of selling Jewish goods at auction outside Soviet territory? Should we interpret the auctions as German initiatives in Soviet territory,[8] similar to what they had done elsewhere? Or is the genocide of the Jews by the Nazis inscribed somewhere in the heart of Russo-Soviet village traditions?

What is clear is that the auctions of Jewish goods in villages and certain big towns are an established fact. However, whether they are more rooted in Nazi tradition or in Russo-Soviet customs of repression will always be an enigma to me.

Chapter 23

THE COATS

The years have passed. Yavoriv,[1] this village in the Lviv region, a small Galician town, is far from our other research sites. It is distant in time, too, early January 2009, and yet I have never been able to forget it. It's not so much the place that stays in my mind but rather a villager named Ievhenia. Why has her image persisted? I don't know. Perhaps because she wanted to speak inside the village church. Memory, after thousands of interviews, has kept certain faces and certain words while completely forgetting others.

Ievhenia was an educated person, a teacher. We met her as she was walking down the sidewalk, wrapped in a thick fur coat, her head covered by a stylish brown fur hat. Although retired, she had kept the keen eye and firm voice that had taught many generations of children from the region.

She refused to speak in her home or in the street, but insisted on going into the church, inside the walls where mass had just been celebrated. This was a rare if not unique circumstance. I should add that we had arrived in Yavoriv on January 9, the day after Orthodox Christmas.

Having asked the permission of the parish priest, we set up in the church. Ievhenia had her back to a decorated Christmas tree, and we faced her in a semicircle. The building had just emptied out as mass had recently finished. The sweepers, parishioners who had tied on their aprons, cleaned up pine branches scattered all over the church so that everything would be in order for the following day. I can still hear the scratching of brooms on the floor.

I remember being bothered by this tree sparkling behind her in the lens of our camera. I asked if she would mind moving so that we could see icons behind her instead. It seemed less bizarre, less indecent, and more appropriate to someone who had seen Jews murdered.

I can still hear her voice, her structured speech, as though she were conducting a class. As she told us what she had seen, she couldn't help but instruct us. She explained how the Ukrainians had believed Hitler's promises of independence and only later understood the horror that came with them. But what, exactly, had she seen?

Right away, she placed herself as a member of the local petite bourgeoisie. This is rare in the former Soviet Union, where anyone perceived as bourgeois risked deportation.

"My father was the head of a bakery, and my mother never worked. In our family, the women did not work. The village women worked or tended livestock. But our family was bourgeois, and my mother never worked."

As the baker's daughter, Ievhenia was an important figure in the village. The bakery was two blocks from the church. She didn't mind telling us that, during the war, the bakery supplied German stores as well as the shops owned by locals. The Germans ordered not only bread but also pastries. German colonial life in Yavoriv had its perks.

"It was the only bakery in town, and the Germans would come place their orders. My father made bread specially for them because they only wanted the best. . . . They ordered pastries, croissants, and brioches, while the villagers had gray bread. . . . The bakery didn't sell bread directly. We delivered to stores, and people came with their ration tickets to get the bread in these stores."

Listening to her, I recalled another bakery, in Belzec. The baker there also served both the Germans who worked in the extermination camp and the local population. She kept repeating, "Thanks to me, people ate white bread all through the war. With the flour provided by the Germans from the camp."

In Yavoriv, the Ukrainians' bread was gray. Ievhenia recalled the ghetto with its fence, right behind the church in which we were talking. I remember wondering if that wasn't the reason she wanted to speak here, as though sheltered yet so close to the former ghetto.

Her testimony, her words, were accompanied by vivid gestures. With her black-gloved hands, she spoke without hesitation of the "ambiguities" of neighbors who had housed Jews . . . and then denounced them.

"There was one Jewish family that went into hiding with people. The father was a pharmacist, and they had a little girl, Ziouta. The daughter and mother hid with one family, and the father hid somewhere else. The people hiding them denounced them. When the Germans went to get them, the girl took poison that her father had given her and died on the spot, but the mother didn't have time to take the poison. They put little Ziouta's body on a cart and the mother walked beside it. They took them to the cemetery and buried both of them there. So, there were good people who hid Jews and others who denounced them. I also think the Jews paid a lot to the people who hid them. Some took the money and then denounced them."

This too I recall as though it were yesterday. It is uncommon for a witness to talk about the neighbors' terrible choices. Some hid Jews for money, others denounced them, and sometimes they were one and the same.

But when I go back in my memory, I see that it wasn't the pretty church or the scratchy brooms interfering with the recording, nor was it her testimony itself, despite its uniqueness, that has left such an impression. It's something else, one of her memories that has taken me years to process.

She spoke of herself without awkwardness or embellishment, except when describing her tears at the burning ghetto. Suddenly, she was no longer the teacher, and she had to take her handkerchief out of her pocket. She was remembering a coat, her own; a coat from during the war. I should add that I had asked a question that somehow seemed to put a tangle in her narrative thread. She had gone into the ghetto.

"Was the ghetto surrounded by barbed wire or a wooden fence?"

"The ghetto was not well sealed off," she replied. "In places there was wood fencing, in others some barbed wire, in others nothing at all. But there were guards all around it. Once I went into the ghetto because the Jews were great seamstresses and my parents had put in an order with a tailor to make me a coat. On this day, I had to go into the ghetto to pick up my coat, but as I was approaching, I heard shots. The Germans had surrounded the ghetto and weren't letting anyone in. That was the day they liquidated the ghetto."

She had been able to get into the ghetto easily to order a custom coat from a Jewish tailor. But she never got to see the much-anticipated coat. The ghetto was liquidated before her eyes. And yet this was the memory that made her cry! The memory of this coat, lost forever, brought tears to her eyes sixty years later. It was as though, suddenly, this loss, so insignificant in comparison to the murder of the Jews, became her most potent childhood memory.

Her story is not isolated.

Another account that we discovered in the German archives tells of something similar. The subject is Berta, a German civilian working as an interpreter in occupied Ukraine in the service of the ZHO.[2] She was stationed in Kamaniets-Podilsky, a big Ukrainian city in the Khmelnitsky region. She gave her deposition in 1959, sixteen years after the fact.[3] It happened that the house where she was lodged with her chief in Kamaniets-Podilsky during the war had a view of the ghetto. "My chief, Mr. H., and I lived in a little house facing the Jewish ghetto.

THE COATS

"In autumn 1942, Mr. H. knocked on my door early one morning and told me that they were going to get the Jews from the ghetto and asked if I wanted to see. I declined and stayed in bed."

Apparently, Berta is not a morning person. She is not willing to get up earlier than usual just because the ghetto is being liquidated under her windows. So, by the time she leaves for work, the ghetto is lifeless. Nevertheless, she will go in because she too has objects with the Jewish artisans.

"On that day, I went on foot to my office as usual. The next day, I went to the ghetto and it was empty. The ground was covered with cushions and other objects from inside. All of a sudden, five Jews approached. They were trying to make a good impression because they were scared. Mr. H. and Mr. K. were with me. We'd come into this ghetto to get watches and other items from Jewish artisans, things we had given them to work on or fix.

"I had a fur coat made for myself by the Jews, but I didn't find it. When I couldn't find my coat, I complained in writing to the local police chief, a party member, and all of a sudden, my coat reappeared. I don't remember anymore the name of the police chief, but I would recognize it if someone said it. If I recall other details later, I will be sure to communicate them."

Ievhenia and Berta, two women, one Ukrainian and one a German civilian; one cried for her coat as she watched the ghetto burn and the other complained because she couldn't find her fur coat after the liquidation. Neither one worried about the Jewish tailor or seamstress. As for Mr. H and Mr. K., they were looking for watches they were having repaired as well as other objects.

Ievhenia, Berta, H., and K. remain, above all, men and women concerned only with their possessions. They had had sufficient confidence in Jewish artisans to entrust them with commissions and objects to fix, taking advantage of the discounted prices, if not the free labor, of those imprisoned in the ghetto. Apparently, people can sometimes recall a lost item with greater emotion than they can summon for the victims of murder.

On a day of genocide, a person can not only prove indifferent to the murder of her neighbors but seemingly motivated by one interest only: her own.

Chapter 24

THE PATCHWORKER

My childhood was a universe of manual jobs. Everything was made by hand. That world has been swallowed up today by big industry. In 1980, I went to Africa as a professor of mathematics. Three years later, on my return, I realized that my artisanal and family universe had faded.

We were poultry people. We bought chickens, ducks, and guinea fowl on Bresse farms and brought them back to our "plucking house," as we called it. On a given afternoon, it took no less than six or seven people, each one with their own small job, to pluck the Bresse chickens. How could I ever forget my grandmother, Marie-Louise, sitting on a straw-bottomed chair, holding a big white plastic bucket? How could I forget the women sitting at the back of the plucking house, each with a small, well-used knife, who checked each bird and scraped off any remaining down? How could I forget my grandfather, who folded each Bresse chicken before it got cold and stapled the beautiful tricolor medals to the animals' necks with the inscription that was our coat of arms, "Poulet de Bresse"? The plucking house was noisy, mostly because of a machine with metal discs that tore out the feathers.

Once a week, I went with my grandmother to Mme Gouillon's house, at the other end of the neighborhood. She made mattresses and pillows with goose and duck feathers. She and her husband worked in an odd place. It was a building that had been used as a sentry house on the border between the free and occupied zones during the war. It was at the end of a bridge. This little house, with its pointed tile roof, was still intact in the spot where the Germans and the French police controlled traffic. I went there each week to see Mme Gouillon stitching the pieces of striped material that would become mattresses.

Next to my parents' house, in Chalons, there was a dim shop run by the Denis sisters, two spinsters always dressed in black, with cardigans and knitted hats. They made funeral wreaths with beads of all colors. Their door was next to ours, a door with a bell that crackled. I went almost every day with my brother. We sat down with the sisters on very low straw-bottomeed chairs. All around us were rolls of wire. And there were buckets of red beads, green beads, yellow beads, and blue beads. We threw the beads into a little centrifuge and held the wire close. The green beads became branches; the blue and yellow ones became flowers. Then we pinned on a piece of paper with the name of the family that had placed the order and displayed the wreath in the shop window.

I have so many memories of this time and place: the woman who repaired flat tires, the bakers across from us, the *charcutier* with his workshop for making sausages. Everything, or almost everything, was handmade in public, not behind the walls of distant factories. These sorts of jobs still exist on a small scale today in certain villages in Eastern Europe. But they are going out on the tide of modernity.

Nevertheless, one can still find a blacksmith to adjust the shoe of a draft horse, sweepers with "village-made" brooms, seamstresses under little awnings in the middle of an open market, cooks who go each day to the municipal canteen with their blue-and-white aprons tied and their white chefs' hats. The small trades and the farmer's life make up the village. I was so surprised, during my research on the Shoah, to discover that a number of these jobs were deemed necessary and requisitioned on the day, or the day after, the execution of the Jews.

I recall, among others, a patchworker.

July 29, 2007

We had arrived early that morning in the village of Zabolottia, near the Volhynie in northwestern Ukraine.[1] The street was sprinkled with red, green, and yellow houses. The surrounding fields were freshly harvested, a tableau vivant, a van Gogh.

Irina was there with us, sitting on a low wooden stool. She was agitated. Her phrases were choppy. Her memories wouldn't leave her in peace. Curiously, Irina talked little about the execution itself and more about the day after. After the execution, she told us, a German originally from the village, a *Volksdeutsche*, returned there to requisition female labor. He stopped at Irina's house and summoned her to accompany him on foot. Eventually, she found herself sitting with a dozen other young peasant women from Zabolottia inside the *Kommandantur*, which today has become a school. She had been led into a room where the Jews' possessions were all piled up: comforters, sheets, quilts, covers, pillows, as well as clothes of no value. The German ordered her to do some sewing, or rather mending.

At this point in her story, Irina's hands began to tremble.

"There were a lot of clothes. . . . The Germans had collected all the damaged clothes and put them in this room. It was completely full. They requisitioned us to patch the holes."

Patch the holes: I think I am hearing my grandmother. She spoke in simple terms, recalling the repetitive movements as though it were yesterday, "The clothes were in a pile. We took them, repaired them, and threw them in another pile."

According to her, the clothes were of poor quality. "We sewed for a day and a night."

Why did the Germans want to have local peasants patch quilts and used bedding from Jewish houses? Who were they destined for? Were they going to be resold to the villagers? Or given to the *Volksdeutsche*, the Germans who had been living in the Soviet Union before the war and whom the troops of the Reich had decided to help in order to consolidate their occupation? Apparently, the clothes had been gone through before the arrival of the menders. Only the clothes of poor quality were left, says Irina. Most likely, the valuable ones were taken by the Germans at the crime scene.

Irina's memory of her night of patchwork still distressed her, sixty years later. She kept repeating that, that night, she had committed a theft, a very minor theft considering the circumstances. She had kept for herself three buttons from a quilt cover—the use of quilts is traditional in Soviet territories. Her incessant memory of this futile guilt about three buttons may have been a way of expressing a deeper sense of culpability at having patched the bedding of the dead after their murder. Maybe, but I'm not sure.

Even the smallest theft of Jewish goods by neighbors after the crime was strictly forbidden by the Germans. Did she feel bad because of having stolen three buttons from a murdered Jewish family or because it was illegal and punishable by the German regime? I have met too many witnesses able to talk about the murder of the Jews without discomfort. It was legal to kill Jews, but it was not legal to steal their goods.

Even sixty years hence, the laws put in place during the genocide seem to determine the feelings of guilt and innocence of the neighborhood. Law, even the law of a genocidal dictatorship, would appear to trump conscience. Human beings are quite adept at telling themselves that if something is legal, they can't be guilty.

Chapter 25

THE SANITIZER

His name was Stepan. It was April 5, 2007; it's as if it were yesterday. Memory, like the heart, has its reasons of which reason knows nothing. I have never forgotten the mixture of misery and dignity emanating from Stepan. There was a huge sadness that seemed to consume his entire being, a melancholy he had borne ever since the Second World War.

Propped up on his cane, walking with great difficulty, he insisted on being filmed standing, in his jacket. On his left pocket was an impressive strip of Soviet decorations. Younger people laugh at these decorations. But for Stepan, these multicolored medals attested to a certain dignity, signaling a past that for him had not disappeared. His speech slow and very difficult, his skin weathered by the years, he very much wanted to speak and to remain standing. It was almost as if he were testifying at the helm of history.

It was still cool that April in the small Ukrainian village of Rakv Lis.[1] Red tulips were starting to flower in gardens here and there, a harbinger of spring.

Stepan was twenty when the Germans occupied the region. But he didn't want to talk about his war. He wanted to talk about the executions of the Jews of the ghetto of Kamen-Kachirski.[2]

It was summer. For reasons I don't know, he was requisitioned several times. Maybe because he was among the poorer people in the neighborhood or maybe also because of his age, he was one of the young men considered available for any work.

First off, along with twenty other villagers, he had to dig the ditch. "The police came to my house and told me to go dig in this place. They gathered us all together. There were twenty of us, and they brought us there and gave us the dimensions. If you refused to go, you would be killed on the spot. You had to obey."

Stepan dug, but, according to him, he was not at the execution. He was well informed, however, as his brother-in-law was a member of the *polizei*. I sensed in his eagerness to talk that he wanted to tell us something else and was anxious to know that we would hear him out. At the time, it's true that I wasn't used to hearing such horrors and I frequently cut interviews short.

With clipped phrases that were almost injunctions, he guided us into his memories. "Those who weren't hit died smothered by the ones who lay down on top of them to be killed. The blood was more than a meter [three feet] deep." I knew that most Jews died of hemorrhage, but to hear Stepan speak of three feet of blood was something else.

And suddenly, his words fell like stones. "So, they made us bring lime in wagons, and we put it into the grave. It was summer."

He had said it. Stepan had been one of the hands requisitioned to perform one of the most hideous tasks, drying up the blood of the Jews that seeped out of the grave. While he was speaking, I would not, could not, visualize what he was describing. The only image that came to me was that of my grandfather, Émile, throwing lime on the body of a dead calf that had been put in a hole some distance from the farm. But I didn't want this image.

I had already heard other villagers, men and women, explain how they were made to get ashes from the hearths of their farms and carry them in wheelbarrows or buckets to dry up the blood that was running out from the ditches. This was the case in Borove, not far from Rawa Ruska. "The blood was running into the street," the neighbors recalled, "so we had to bring ashes."

But what Stepan was telling me was even worse, because the number of dead was so great. He wanted to recount something that for us was absolutely horrific, and yet it was his job as a conscript. "The grave was filled in. You could ride over it in a wagon. We poured lime onto it because there was more than a meter [three feet] of blood, and the Germans were worried it would make people sick. It was summer."

He had to get the wagon from his farm, to hitch up his horses. He had to search through the village, emptied of its Jewish population, and go into the now deserted house of a Jewish lime merchant. "Actually, we put it in the bathtubs that we took from the houses of Jews. They had their businesses, their houses. They were the ones who made the lime to whitewash houses and to fill in holes in the walls. . . ."

The lime sold by a Jewish merchant to fill in holes in the local cob walls became the lime to clean up Jewish blood. The personal bathtubs ripped out of Jewish houses became anonymous tubs for transporting the lime to the mass graves where the Jews had been murdered. For a few days, the entire village seems to have been transformed into a human slaughterhouse. A slaughterhouse needing to be sanitized after a crime.

Stepan vaguely remembered the size of the grave. "It was as deep as a man is tall and about twenty meters [sixty-six feet] long, maybe more. You know, we thought they were going to kill us there, but they sent us home and that was all."

Hearing these measurements, even though they were approximate, I could understand why Stepan was emphasizing the level of the blood.

He gave a few more details.

"It was liquid lime. . . . It was in big ditches."

In the Soviet Union, I thought, a ditch can have many uses. It can hold potatoes, beets, cabbages, but also lime. Stepan, his eyes downcast, had revealed the terrible secret he had been carrying for such a very long time. He had been forced to work for a few hours in the human slaughterhouse of his Jewish neighbors.

There were conscripts before the crime, conscripts during the shooting, conscripts after the murder. A labor force accustomed to Soviet pressures did not seem to have any means of refusal. Thus, when evening came, the Germans could go home. The human slaughter-house, set up in the morning, disappeared from the village landscape by nightfall. And along with it went all traces of the blood of its Jewish victims.

Chapter 26

THE METHOD

Already, night is falling.

The writing of this book is ending. I leave the new regional hospital in Chalon-sur-Saône, where my father, in intensive care, is quietly preparing himself for his final journey. While I was there, the doctor came into his room and asked him, "What was your work, Monsieur Desbois?"

My father started in on a long explanation that began with these words:

"My father was deported. When he returned, he weighed forty five kilos [one hundred pounds]. I had to stop working to help him. I couldn't leave him."

His account of his eighty years began with the deportation of his father, Claudius Desbois. I was astonished. I hadn't known that his life too had been marked indelibly by the deportation of the man he had such trouble recognizing on his return.

I leave the hospital pensive, sad, and surprised. My father is about to die and it is only today that I discover that, like me, his whole life he has thought about his father's, my grandfather's, deportation.

The TGV (high-speed train) takes me back to Paris. The unchanging countryside of my native Burgundy flies by. My thoughts take flight. They go east to village after village, archive after archive, investigation after investigation. No two murders, no two shootings were

225

the same. And yet there are constants among all the shootings. Perhaps there is no consistent method, but there is a kind of timed coordination in each mass murder. There is coordination among the shooters, the auxiliary police, the requisitioned personnel, the carts and horses, but also the cook.

I didn't know if I would find this coordination described in writing anywhere. Perhaps it was my own projection. When one is a math teacher, one can't help but search for the lowest common denominator. If there wasn't a method per se, it seemed to me that there was a recurring criminal savoir faire. Was this know-how transmitted orally or simply through habit?

After ten long years of listening and reading, one thing I was sure of was that from the perspective of a Russian, Ukrainian, or Belarusian farmyard, the minute precision of the Fascist crimes gave the impression that someone, somewhere, was keeping strict time. Who wore a watch? Who were the human metronomes marking time during the crimes committed against the Jews of a village?

To someone who hasn't been there, these may seem like banal questions. It's banal to start at six in the morning and finish at noon, or at five o'clock in the afternoon. As banal as office hours in Paris or New York.

But we traveled to these far-flung places, traveled many miles on muddy, badly paved roads leading to villages without running water. We searched fruitlessly for hot water to try to improvise a cup of coffee, watched the snow or rain weigh on our windshield, had one of our vehicles stuck in mud and needed to call on a massive tractor left over from Soviet times to pull us out. Come noontime, we could often find nothing but a little cold, wet bread along with a few tired tomatoes to eat. So when we left at night, our bodies and hearts heavy with cold and the weight of listening, we had to ask ourselves: How, in the 1940s, with less asphalt, less fresh bread and running water, could an armada of German trucks appear at 6:00 a.m. sharp? How could the neighbors of the Jews who were to be murdered not only be awake in the small hours of the morning but also be ready with their shovels to dig the ditch while it was still dark? How did the cook from the local canteen know precisely when to warm her wood-burning ovens and cook for midday so that the entire criminal team and its collaborators could all eat on time?

How many times at a little village restaurant have we waited more than an hour for a simple hot meal because, behind the counter, a woman calmly seated on a wooden stool was carefully peeling potatoes? How many hours have we sighed, aware that nothing, absolutely nothing could speed up the rhythm of these post-Soviet villages? How many times have our vehicles been slowed down by herds of cows returning home nonchalantly from the fields, their udders swollen with milk? Our drivers know that there is nothing to be done. Horns are pointless. For a time, the van has to move at the rhythm of a dairy cow.

Sitting at a computer in Paris, the timely efficiency of the genocidal crime can seem like a given. But when you have traveled so slowly through these same villages, the question of how such speed was ever possible becomes a permanent one.

I read through many Soviet and German archives looking in vain for a key or at least the beginning of an explanation. How could the Germans keep up the tempo of their daily criminal activities?

Then, one day, sitting in my Parisian office, I received an unexpected text from Olga, one of our Yahad translators.

Like a needle in a haystack, in one of the many Soviet commissions of 1944 was lengthy testimony from a person heretofore unknown to us. He was a Ukrainian who became the head of a Ukrainian police unit, of *Schutzmann*. His name was Fiodor Alexandrovitch Zaloga.

I had read numerous depositions from local police tried after the war by the KGB as Fascist collaborators. But this one was different. The man not only recounted his memories of the shooting of the Jews, he explained the process, with its distinct and successive steps and, most importantly, its precise timing. Schedule was omnipresent in his testimony.[1] On several occasions, he also used the term "method."

The villages and the town in which he admitted to having participated in crimes were not unknown to me. I had traveled through them several times. But who was this Zaloga? He was no longer a young man when the war broke out in 1941. He was already thirty-five, with a long career in the Red Army behind him. This was his thirteenth year in the Soviet military.

This is how he describes himself: "I, the undersigned, Zaloga Fiodor Aleksandrovitch, born September 17, 1906, in the town of Stalino[2] . . . worker, was in the Red Army from November 2, 1928, to August 5, 1941, the last rank in the Red army was captain. . . . 39th Armored Division of the Army No. 12."

So he had acquired not only a savoir faire along with military discipline but also combat experience, notably against the German army, and this experience lasted until August 1941, three months after the attack on the Soviet Union. At this point, he entered the auxiliary German police. What happened? How did Zaloga take such a sharp turn? How did he, a former soldier from the Red Army, become a Nazi police officer?

In fact, Zaloga did not go straight from the Red Army to the German police. He was injured in combat against the Germans and interned in a German prison camp at Ouman.[3]

"Between the 5th and 11th of August 1941, having been injured, I rested in the village of Niebylivka. . . . On the 13th of August 1941, all the injured were transferred to the prisoner of war camp at Ouman. I escaped on August 20 or 21 and came to the village of Vipacho-vka. . . . There I lived with my uncle, Zaloga Vassili Fillipovitch . . . between August 28 and September 25, 1941."

Rereading this, I realized that there was a six-month gap in his deposition, a blank unaccounted for. He did not join the police until March 1942. Why this silence? Was it forced? Voluntary?

In this, his story resembles those of many other auxiliary police in the occupied Soviet Union. A Soviet soldier made prisoner by the Germans and then recycled into the auxiliary police. But his motivations are not clear: was it in exchange for his life? To avoid being sent to a work camp in Germany? For money? Or out of a conviction to serve the good Nazi cause?

The fact is that in March 1942, he has to undergo training to become a *Schutzmann* in order to be what the peasants today still call a *polizei*. His superior is called Reich. "When I arrived in Kamaniets-Podilsky[4] on the morning of March 23, 1941 . . . Lieutenant Reich informed me that I, in fact, did have to do the *Schutzmann* training course." The training would prove bizarrely short.

"The course lasted from March 23, 1942, through April 4, 1942. After the course, I was named chief of police in the town of Smo-tritch[5] in the same district where I had been given the grade of non-commissioned officer."

Such a rank after twelve days of training! We often forget to what degree those who were called auxiliary police in the occupied Soviet Union were not professional police before the war. They were an improvised militia. What a notable difference compared with what happened in France! The French police who rounded up Jews in the streets of Paris were the official police of the French Republic before the war and often afterward. The *polizei* were not generally Soviet police prior to the war, and even less so after the occupation. There were few Soviet police, especially in the countryside. Certain members of the *polizei* had only been in their jobs for a few months on the day the Jews were killed. So the term *polizei* is misleading in that it suggests assimilation with the actual Eastern European police.

Zaloga says that after his appointment he was briefly made a prisoner of the Germans again, accused of cooperation with the Soviets and proximity to the Jews. Then he was freed from prison to fill an even higher position in the auxiliary police. The sequence prison–liberation–promotion was a common path for some of the most zealous collaborators with the Third Reich. "I received the post of commander . . . of the Second Company . . . of Doljok . . . and I had under me between one hundred and one hundred twenty *Schutzmann*."

It is only after having recounted the story of his astounding promotions leading to his appointment as a commander in the auxiliary police that he got down to the heart of the matter: the shooting of the Jews.

"The criminal activity . . . was the following: in autumn 1942, I participated along with my subordinates, around fifty people, in the shooting of the Jewish population, citizens of the Soviet Union, of the district of Staraïa Ouchista."[6]

He goes on to describe his participation in the shootings—but curiously, and this is what got my attention, he expresses himself in terms of method, protocol, and a process marked by precise timing.

At this point, I decided to look not only at his deposition to the Soviet commission but also the other declarations he had made during various interrogations. This is how I was able to trace the stages of what he called "the method." Zaloga doesn't give up a general method, but he does explain what he saw put into practice at Staraïa Ouchista.

The Night Before

According to Zaloga, everything starts the night before the crime with a phone call from the chief of police.

"As the commander of the company, the night before the shooting, the chief of police ordered me to send fifty *Schutzmann* from my company. At the same time, he had been ordered to verify that the chief of the section of Staraïa Ouchista had understood correctly that he had to assemble the *Schutzmann* from of his section in the village of Grouchka, twelve kilometers [six and a half miles] from Staraïa Ouchitsa."

He maintains that on the eve of the murders he didn't know the reason for this gathering. "He couldn't tell me over the phone what it was about," he states.

But it is fair to assume that an auxiliary police chief who has to mobilize policeman in the night and send them to sleep in a village forty miles away would ask himself the reason. Especially with this

230

specification: "We had received orders to take ten cartridges per gun, plus a machine-gun box in reserve."

The Route

So the night before the crime, he will drive with a team of subordinates to sleep in this village. The *polizei* will also bivouac for the night a short distance from where the murders will take place. Of course, none of the thousands of villagers that we've interviewed could have been at these police vigils. All of this took place out of their line of sight, outside the village.

Zaloga will recount in great detail his work assembling the *polizei*. He receives orders regularly, always by phone. The timing and cadence have a surprising precision.

"At the end of the day at around 5:30, I received another order from Lieutenant Reich. . . . We would be leaving by truck for the village of Grouchka immediately after dinner (the Germans dined at 6:00), and all the *Schutzmann* had to be ready at that time. After dinner, three trucks were ready to leave."

It's surprising. Six in the evening. It seems that the Germans' dinner, at its fixed hour, determined the criminal team's time of departure on the eve of the crime. The killers' mealtime does not vary. Doubtless, this is a function of German military precision. In any case, it is clear that the times of German meals frame the crime against the Jews in Staraïa Ouchitsa. A mass murder should in no way infringe on the regular eating habits and life rhythms of the German killers.

The Jews of Staraïa Ouchitsa will thus be shot between the Germans' supper the night before and their lunch the next day.

"The *Schutzmann* who didn't already have guns had them provided by the police. We received the order to take ten cartridges per gun plus a machine-gun magazine in reserve. The Germans took an automatic pistol and three machine guns. There were ten to twelve Germans, about fifty *Schutzmann* from the Krouzabik Company, and some of the *Schutzmann* from my company. The employees of the SD and the criminal police left separately. Upon arriving in Grouchka, we found *Schutzmann* from Zelenye Kourilovtsy and Privorottia."

A whole armada made up of German police, the SD, the German criminal police, and the police stationed in four separate locations will participate in the crime. Yet the Jewish community of Staraïa Ouchitsa was not very big. I think we would be quite surprised if we knew the number of German men and local auxiliaries who participated in the crimes against the Jews in the Soviet Union.

The German authorities travel by car and go directly to the village of Staraïa Ouchitsa in the middle of the night. Doubtless to ensure that everything is ready, most importantly the digging of the ditches and the hermetic sealing of the ghetto.

"Lieutenant Reich, accompanied by three policemen in one car, and the chief of the SD accompanied by four SD employees in another car, left for Staraïa Ouchitsa after having ordered the other Germans and the *Schutzmann* to go to sleep. When he returned from Staraïa Ouchitsa, Lieutenant Reich left in the direction of Kamaniets-Podilsky."

The Day, at Dawn

The distance remaining for Zaloga and his men to travel in the early morning was very short.

"The next morning at dawn, after waking up, we all left in cars, in two shifts, for Staraïa Ouchitsa. At about one to one and a half kilometers [a half mile to a mile] from Staraïa Ouchitsa, the cars were stopped, the *Schutzmann* lined up, and Lieutenant Reich, through the intermediary of Kroubazik, announced the goal of our journey and we received instructions to round up the entire Jewish population of Staraïa Ouchitsa and Stoudenitsa, to bring them to the shooting site, which was located not far from the road. After this, the chief of the district, Belokon, who was already there, reported to Lieutenant Reich that all would be done within the prescribed time and that everything was ready. From where we stood, at one hundred fifty or two hundred meters from the road, we could make out the silhouettes of the people digging in the earth. As I saw later, they were preparing a ditch that the local inhabitants, peasants, had to dig on orders of district chief, Belokon."

The clock of the crime springs into action. Everything will unfold with precision between four in the morning and noon. I follow along with Zaloga's tempo. His day could be called "The Day of the Genocide of the Jews of Staraïa Ouchitsa."

"At four and five in the morning, Belokon was already there with the locals who were digging a ditch one to two hundred meters from the road."

This requisition must have taken place the day before at the latest. According to our witnesses, a local administration would never go to farms during the night to wake up villagers and ask them to bring their shovels.

According to Zaloga, it's only now that the *polizei* are informed of their precise objective in gathering here. The announcement seems to follow a certain paramilitary ritual: the auxiliary police have to line up before they receive their orders. Once again, no witness we have spoken to has mentioned this type of speech or police lineup. This all happens at sunrise.

The Announcement

"The chief of police, Lieutenant Iakob, and the commander of the Kroubazik Company had the *Schutzmann* line up and announced to them that they had to round up all the Jews from Staraïa Ouchitsa and Stoudenitsa and bring them to the shooting site."

This is not exactly the announcement of the crime but of what they need to get done in the first hour of the schedule, between seven and eight: round up the Jews.

Why tell them so late? The German confidence in the auxiliary police is generally very limited. Did they want to avoid communication with the Jews in the ghetto? This is quite possible. Did they also want to be sure the auxiliary police didn't attack the ghetto to rob the

Jews or commit rape on the night before the murders? To my mind, this is also very probable.

"Together with the police and the criminal police, this was done between seven and eight in the morning."

Not only are the *polizei* fully complicit in the crime, because they drag the Jews from their houses after having seen the ditches dug, but what's more, all acts of violence against the Jews are permitted them in the interest of not slackening the pace of events. It's not a rounding up of the Jews but a veritable hunt. Listening to Zaloga, I can't help but think of the raids committed against the Jews in Paris, or in Bordeaux or Lyon, in the rue Sainte-Catherine. How many Eastern European police and ex-Soviet *polizei* participated fully, with their slurs and their blows, in the genocide of the Jews? I hardly dare to ask myself this question: in the West as in the East, could it have happened without the police and the *polizei?*

From Seven to Eight. Rounding Up the Jews.
What a euphemism! This "rounding up" is a violent raid on Jewish households.

"At the same time, a group of Germans and *Schutzmann* was formed and charged with checking all the Jewish dwellings and removing all those who didn't want to leave and all those who were hiding." The respect for schedule becomes paramount, for the Germans as well as for Zaloga.

"Everything had to be done between seven and eight in the morning," he repeated.

"During the rounding up of the Jewish population, many people who were hiding in the apartments were flushed out. The fugitives had already stocked their basements with food and clothing so they could hide out there. They also hid in attics, chimneys, under fake ceilings, and in the crawl spaces between ceilings and roofs, in barns, stoves, and dunghills. . . . Some men escaped by the roofs, jumping from the roof of a house that hadn't been inspected yet to one that had already been inspected."

For the first time in his testimony, we see Jewish resistance. Apparently, in Staraïa Ouchitsa, many inhabitants had planned to evade the liquidation or fled by the rooftops.

But Zaloga describes the violence that erupts when a Jew threatens to put the crime behind schedule:

"The sick people and the old men and women who couldn't walk to the square were brought, often carried by relatives. If they didn't have any, we ordered other Jews to help them. A woman aged sixty to seventy years old who was leaving her bedroom very slowly was bludgeoned by a policeman and a *Schutzmann*. . . . Then they threw her outside and ordered the other Jews to carry her, half dead, to the square."

Respecting the schedule was such an imperative that they could kill people who slowed the pace of the crime.

The Criteria for Killing

All of a sudden, Zaloga interrupted his story to explain at length, and with great precision, the Nazi criteria for establishing Judaism and in particular the criminal criteria for those who were half Jewish:

"It is crucial to note that a person was considered Jewish and was shot if he was related to a Jew up to three generations inclusive, in cases where the husband and wife were of different nationalities. I know of the following example: A Jewish woman who was married to a Ukrainian, their daughter who was also married to a Ukrainian, who herself had a daughter married to a Ukrainian . . . were all shot as Jews. A man or woman married to a Jew who was of another nationality was not shot."

Unbelievable. Zaloga knows the Berlin Nazi criteria for the crime. A low-grade member of the auxiliary police, at the end of the war, can recite by heart the Nazi guidelines for recognizing who had to be killed and who did not, particularly in mixed-race families. We so often imagine, when we speak of the *Einsatzgruppen*, that German chiefs commanded units that did nothing but obey. But Zaloga's testimony proves that there was in fact an understanding of the rules governing the genocide of the Jews even on the lowest rungs of command.

Zaloga takes up his story again. After the roundup of the Jews, the separation of men and women, and the selection of certain artisans who are not to be killed that day, three new orders are given.

The Roundup, Protection of Goods, Ordering of the Meal

"The chief of the SD, the chief of police, and the district chief all left by car for the execution site, having given the following instructions: (1) to send trucks to the village of Stoudenitsa in order to bring the few Jewish inhabitants there to the execution site; (2) to guarantee the protection of all the Jewish dwellings from pillage by the local population; (3) the district chief received the order to arrange a meal for between fifty and sixty people, the *Schutzmann* of Kamaniets-Podilsky and the Germans."

A triad of concerns: not to let any Jew slip through the cracks, to protect the Jews' goods from pillage, and to organize the killers' meals. We are in 1943. The killers are marked by their criminal habits. The Germans seem to control and coordinate a flowchart step-by-step, hour by hour, from the crime to meal. Zaloga does not mention any feelings of surprise; the murder, the confiscation of goods, the catering for the murderers, it is all of a piece.

I had often said in lectures that there can be no killers without cooks. I didn't quite know how right I was.

The killers, the auxiliaries, and the requisitioned population are mobilized by a single order. The murderers who have come from Germany, the police recruited in the region, and the local conscripts all have to work simultaneously. At noon, a hot meal will be served in the canteen, the Jewish houses will be protected from pillage, and the Jews of Staraïa Ouchitsa will be murdered, or perhaps only injured and buried alive, their bodies covered by shovelfuls of dirt from the fillers.

Zaloga mentions no delays on the part of the killers or the cook.

However, despite his methodical testimony, he neglects to answer an obvious question: how did the Jews assemble on time? How did they get dressed on time? How did they lie down in the ditch on time? How did they die on time?

Zaloga describes the execution as though the Jews themselves voluntarily respected the schedule for their own death. His narrative of the mass murder of the Jews leaves us to think that the victims were docile and played their part. In fact, respect for the precise schedule of the murder was maintained because, behind the sanitized terms for the procedure, the Jewish victims were subjected at every moment to violence and horror without limit. At every stage of the murder. Most of the time Zaloga describes the Jews as "docile." Nevertheless, his depositions betray the violence committed at every turn.

The Column of Jews

Zaloga relates the facts like this: "When the column turned and saw the ditch, a general outcry resounded, from women and men alike. No yelling, no insult, no beating or kicking could stop it. The deep cries of the men and the sharp, strident cries of the women mingled with the tears of children who wanted to be held. The screaming would die down briefly only to start up again even louder. It lasted for one hundred to two hundred meters, until they arrived at the site of the ditch."

The Circles of Guards

Zaloga himself is not far from the ditch because he's coordinating the second circle of guards. The term "circle" itself, clean and mathematical, masks or dresses up a mass of blows that rain down on the Jews in order to force them to advance toward the ditch:

"As the chief guard of the second circle at the site of the shooting, I personally saw how a policeman willingly joined the first circle of guards, not far from the ditch, and personally pressed people to get undressed before the shooting. Then they pushed the naked people toward the ditch where the shooting of the Jews was taking place. Those who didn't want to go or were walking too slowly were clubbed by the policeman and by the other Germans of the SD and the police. During all this, the people condemned to death wept and let out heartbreaking cries."

Again, any slowness on the part of the Jewish victims when it was time to walk to the ditch provoked beating. We are far from the image of Jews moving forward like sheep! All blows were permitted at all times. This was a large-scale massacre more than a military execution. A mass murder.

The Counter

Zaloga mentions a person whom very few witnesses recall: the counter. He draws a cross in a notebook for every five Jews killed. The counting of victims that takes places beside the ditch will allow the mobile units to make an accurate report to Berlin. Violence and rationality went hand in hand.

The "Chiefs"

In his description of the methodology, Zaloga doesn't fail to describe the behavior of the German authorities during the shooting. To the violence and the rationality, these leaders add laughter, satisfaction, and encouragement for the murder and the blows.

"Not far from the ditch stood the chief of police, Lieutenant Reich, and the chief of the SD, whose name I don't know, the two directors of the shooting, who, under the approving eyes of the regional kommissar, Reindel, gave the orders throughout. . . . With evil smiles on their lips, smoking cigarettes the whole time, they encouraged their subordinates, who were excited by the smell of blood, and laughed to see the blows connect as they rained down on the heads of the terrified Jews. Or, by contrast, they would watch silently with impassive faces the horrible sight of innocent people being massacred. From time to time, they would turn their backs to the ditch and speak in hushed tones, with their hands in their pockets and an air of satisfaction.

"After having been on site for almost two hours, Reindel, satisfied with what he saw, shook the directors' hands, saluted all the others with a hand gesture so as not to interrupt them in their work, smiled, said something else, and left by car to return to Kamaniets-Podilsky. The shooting continued."

The comportment of the men in charge of the shooting only amplifies the break with humanity that was revealed at the ditches: some laughed, some encouraged the killers in their work, some clubbed the victims, and others watched. The crime, with its combination of rationality, violence, blows, meals for the killers, encouragements, and greetings from the chiefs, all of it will effectively be over at noon.

The Search

That includes searching through the pockets and hems of the murdered Jews' clothing, collecting their jewelry, and the filling in of the ditch by requisitioned villagers. All this within eight hours.

It can nauseate you and make your head spin to think of the unity of the human species coordinating its actions at the side of a ditch. This was the method. Orders raining down for the tightest timing, absolute violence authorized and encouraged in the name of murderous efficiency and productivity, constrained by the short time frame of a half day or a day in a Soviet village.

The Jews were not sheep. They ran because of the murderous blows raining down. To the laughter and encouragement of the chiefs.

I cannot forget another deposition that I read years earlier. It tells the story of a German who also used the term "method." And it is so violent that I wish I could forget it.

It concerned the execution of the Jewish people of Sdolbunov, in Ukraine. A certain Wacker helps to round up the Jews. He talks about a method for avoiding delays. Here again, the term masks repellent facts.

"I can still remember the *Aktion* at Sdolbunov on October 13, 1942. I saw the way Wacker opened the door and pulled someone out. It was an old woman, with a small child in her arms, who tried to defend herself, saying, "Leave me, *Herr Kommissar!*" Wacker grabbed the child by the legs, swung him around several times and then hit his head against the doorpost. It sounded like an exploding tire. When the child was dead, the inhabitants of the house came out without any resistance, completely resigned. I heard how Wacker said to his comrades: 'It's the best method, we just have to understand this.'"[7]

To smash a child's head against a doorjamb thus became the method to eat on time. How many times have I heard witnesses describe with horror these same acts to effect the brutal murder of Jewish children!

Zaloga and Walter both leave out a category of people always present at these crimes: the neighbors, the spectators. It is because of these thousands of ordinary Soviet people, forgotten in most archives, that I decided to investigate their method. Because the Jewish babies, the Jewish women, the Jewish fathers and grandfathers murdered and thrown into ditches were human beings. Like us.

The End of the Killers' Day

Very often for the killers, the day isn't over yet; it ends when they return to the town from which they set out the day before. And that evening, there is a party, with plenty of alcohol accompanied by criticism or praise from their chiefs. Here again, the German depositions are about congratulations for having followed the process.

In Slonim, for example, the killers returned on time. Then the "process" was evaluated.

"At eight o'clock, everyone came back from where they'd been. There was a meeting with the *Gebietskommissar*,[8] in which they discussed the entire process for the whole day. A lot of praise was given out; the weak were reprimanded and told to do better in the future. . . . After that in the meeting, they drank and celebrated. The total dead for the day was between four and eight thousand Jews, men, women, and children."[9]

The evening event resembles a professional debriefing. But the work in question is nothing other than mass murder. The chiefs congratulate those who remained professional during the murder of thousands of Jewish human beings. Then there is alcohol and a party.

Tomorrow will be another day of genocide.

Zaloga could have stopped there. However, he goes on to deviate from his professional narrative. He departs from it not through inadvertence but quite deliberately, when he describes the collection of the Jews' goods and the personal thefts committed by the Germans at the scene of the crime, at the ditches and in public. Suddenly, the Germans' private life intrudes on the account of the crime.

"Under the direction of a German employee of SD, three to four *Schutzmann* started to shake out and inspect all the clothes and shoes of the victims. It was mostly the clothes they combed through, under the watchful eyes of other SD men. They followed this procedure because in folds, under linings, in the belts of pants, you could find coins and gold objects, bills (dollars, marks, ten-ruble Soviet bills), deeds for loans from the Soviet Union, and other documents. All this, along with lighters, pocketknives, leather pouches, cigars, and wallets, were put in a bag held by an SD man. The new things: dresses, scarves, boots, booties, coats, and cloth were taken by the Germans who ripped them out of one another's hands while swearing at each other. Then they packed up these things and sent them back to their homes or gave them as presents to their '*panienka*.'[10] For example, I know that the *Kommandantur*'s former cleaning lady, a certain Vera Dounina, was the mistress of the chief of police in Kamaniets-Podilsky, Lieutenant Jakob. On his recommendation, she was hired as a translator at police headquarters, the prison, and the work exchange. She lived in a two-room apartment and had clothing that used to belong to the Jews. I personally saw her wearing a scarf and a dress that Lieutenant Jakob had taken after the shooting of the Jewish population in Kamaniets-Podilsky in November 1942."

Sleaze comingles with horror. Starting on the day after the execution, certain villagers were dressed as Jews! In his deposition, Zaloga isn't shy about naming the girlfriends who benefitted from the Germans' favors and who wore, for all to see, the scarves of the women murdered by their beaux.

Zaloga resumes his narrative, explaining that some of the requisitioned people, especially the ditch fillers, were also rewarded with clothes.

"Once all the clothes were examined, and all the objects of value had been put into the SD chief's car, the chief allowed the *Schutzmann* and the peasants who had dug and filled the ditches to each take between four and six items. All the other things were loaded into trucks and taken to a warehouse or to the cooperative in Staraïa Ouchitsa, and, as I learned later, were sold to the local population. The Jewish houses, along with their furniture, were also sold to the local population. In short, everything they owned. However, some of the furniture was graciously given to the *Kreislandwirt*,[11] to the chief of the district, and to the chiefs of police and the border guards."

Zaloga describes the auction and the public sale of everything that wasn't taken by the Germans, officially or covertly. The theft of goods for personal use, especially women's clothing, at the crime scene, begs to be more broadly studied. It seems to sully the account of the method. It was as though, suddenly, the personal interest and greed of each killer, of his wife or local girlfriend, reemerged at the end of the day. It's as if, suddenly, Himmler's men were no longer just men obeying orders; obedience hadn't obliterated their humanity as thugs guilty of crimes like property theft from those they had just murdered. As if the murderers suddenly revealed themselves as the most unsavory of human beings.

After the trial, Zaloga was condemned to death for high treason. Here is the verdict.

THE METHOD

In the name of the Union of Soviet Socialist Republics

July 29, 1944

The Military Tribunal of the NKVD for the region of Kamaniets-Podilsky, held in the town of Kamaniets-Podilsky . . . without the presence of the accused and the defense, has examined in a closed hearing the affair of the accused Zaloga Fiodor Aleksandrovitch, born in 1906 in Stalino, of Ukrainian nationality, former member of the Ukrainian Communist Party, higher education unfinished, married, with a clean police record, accused of crimes as described by Part 1 of the Presidium decree of the Supreme Soviet of the USSR of April 19, 1943.

The Tribunal has condemned Zaloga Fiodor Aleksandrovitch . . . to death by firing squad and confiscation of all goods belonging to him.

The sentence was carried out a few months later, on November 30, 1944, in Kamaniets-Podilsky.

Neither Zaloga nor the KGB could have ever known that they would allow us, through their depositions and their verdicts, to understand the nature of "the method."

Conclusion

THE PHOTOGRAPHER

Berlin, January 2015

It is cold, or rather I am cold inside. I go down the three steps at the entrance to the German-Russian Museum in Berlin-Karlshorst. This is where, on May 9, 1945, the surrender of the Third Reich to the United States, the United Kingdom, France, and the Soviet Union was signed. The signing room appears intact: sober tables, simple blue tablecloths each decorated with four small flags, and, displayed in metal cases, the yellowed pages of the surrender that put an end to one of history's most abominable and massive crimes: the Second World War.

I'm moved. I have been to Berlin several times, but this is the first time I've been inside the immense, empty rooms of this museum, which today is maintained by Germany, Russia, Ukraine, and Belarus. All the texts are in Russian and German. I was particularly shaken by a display case containing the uniform of a Soviet prisoner of war. My grandfather's face comes back to me.

I am most touched by a temporary exhibit, on the second floor, of the work of a German photographer from one of the PK companies, the commando squads that followed the German units. A short film that shows the hanging of a young Belarusian girl dressed in white keeps passing before my eyes.

244

It was on the steps of this museum in Berlin that I recalled March 22, 2008, in Belarus. There, for the first time, I had found evidence of one of these photographers of genocide.

It was at the beginning of our investigations in that country. From our first steps on Belarusian soil, I tried to understand what I was seeing; the red flags, Marx and Lenin, the giant red effigy of the hammer and sickle on the outskirts of the airport in Minsk, the kolkhozes with their immense stables full of dairy cows. One of the last remaining Communist countries.

As we conducted our investigations, I learned as much as I ever had in my history courses on the Soviet Union about the execution of the Jews by the Fascists.

On that March 22, I was with the entire team in the small village of Prozoroki, not far from Vitebsk, the pretty regional capital. The wind was blowing so hard that sometimes I could hardly hear the words of Tadeouch, a very tall villager in a turtleneck sweater and checked cap, blessed with a memory that seemed prodigious to me.

This witness, interviewed seven years before the time of this writing, has stayed fixed in my memory as though he were the first one. He clearly described the Soviet deportations of villagers before the arrival of the Germans, the shootings of the Belarusian partisans by the Germans, and, of course, the shootings of the Jews that he had seen.

His testimony surprised me. Almost immediately, he wanted to explain to us in his hoarse voice who the *polizei* were. His words fell, precise and relentless. He got straight to the point in describing the active role of these "local auxiliaries" on the day of the murder of their Jewish neighbors. This was uncommon.

Many witnesses are generally ill-at-ease when it comes to discussing the presence of local police by the ditches. Tadeouch, on the contrary, talked often about the *polizei*, even going so far as to name them.

CONCLUSION

"Just after their arrival here, the Germans created a police force. The people who joined up with the police first were the ones who didn't like the Communists. Everywhere in Belarus, there were people who had suffered under the Bolsheviks. When the Germans came, these victims went into the police and took advantage of the situation to get revenge."

Tadeouch wasn't content to just talk about this; above all, he wanted to make us understand that in his village the *polizei* played more than a supporting role in the shooting of the Jews.

"They wore a black uniform with green stripes. They were paid fifty marks and given food rations. I remember that some of them, like Sklimovski and Logoch, who had participated in the shooting of the Jews, took great pleasure in counting by the dozens the Jews they had personally shot."

I tried to keep a noncommittal expression, sensing that maybe he was going to share something unexpected with us: "What was required to become a policeman? What agency did one apply to become a policeman?"

"All you had to do was put in an application with the police. It's interesting that, after the German retreat in 1945, all these applications fell into the hands of the Russians. This facilitated their search for collaborators. After the war, many of them took refuge in Poland. But since Poland became Communist, the applications could be used to find people there, too. The ones who had been in the police but hadn't done anything bad weren't arrested either here or in Poland. However, those who shot Jews were sentenced to twenty-five years in prison. They deserved it."

He finally got to the murder of the Jews.[1]

"Yes, there were Jews here. They shot the inhabitants of what was called the *mestetchko*.[2] Then they also shot the few Jewish families who lived near the Zagatie[3] station, which is about fifteen kilometers [eight miles] from here, as well as the inhabitants of a Jewish village near the station of Ziabki,[4] six kilometers [three miles] from here. The

Jews from these three villages were brought here and locked in the school. . . . The Jews spent the night in the school, and the next day they shot them."

I kept listening, waiting. Patience is often the key to a successful interview. As in many villages, carts, horses, and grooms were requisitioned here.

"There were a lot of inhabitants here, and almost all of them owned a cart and a horse. The Germans had given orders to the *soltys* to procure them ten to twenty carts that had to be kept ready at a stopping point near the local administration. Eventually, they were accompanied by a German and a translator who translated the orders: 'Come on, let's go!' The place is located near the local administrative building and police headquarters. They were told where they had to show up. Everybody knew this spot."

Were they summoned early in the morning?

"Yes. They had been given a precise hour at which to be at the *stoïka*. Later, they were told what they had to do, to transport things. They needed means of transport."

He came back to the *polizei*: "And on the day of the shooting, there were police everywhere: they were in the fields, blocking the roads."

But if, today, in the wide frozen streets of Berlin, I still remember the biting cold of Prozoroki, the dark color of its freshly turned earth, the grayish thickets off to the sides, it's because Tadeouch was the first to put me on the trail of the German photographers.

December 6, 1941, on the day of the crime, the Germans were not firing, they were taking photographs. Tadeouch told it very simply, as though it were obvious, even though I hadn't suspected it. To investigate a genocidal crime is also to make accidental discoveries. The interview continued as follows.

"Were there many shooters: two, three, five?"

"It was mostly policemen. . . . There were only three men from the Gestapo, who were members of the punitive detachment and wore insignias of skulls on their helmets and sleeves. These men were only taking photos for their report."

"How many shooters were there?"

"People said that Sendr and Logoch,[5] who were particularly eager, counted the number of people they had personally shot by the dozens. They were considered models to emulate."

"When they took photos, were they far from the ditch or up close?"

"They got up close to the ditch. . . . Our neighbors told us that after the shooting, when they started to fill in the ditch, they saw the Gestapo and the police drinking and smoking in the bushes."

I recall having looked at the bushes where the drunken Germans had hung up their cameras on the evening of the crime. There, over to the left, the ditch, the shooters, the *polizei,* and here, on the right, the Germans who were taking photographs.

Six years later, here in Berlin, as I get silently into the car that will take me to the airport, I remember the topography of the crime that was photographed in Prozoroki.

I had already seen, studied, and understood the importance of photographs in the crimes against the Jews. I especially recall having combed the streets of Lwow to find the spots where a photographer had stood and asking Guillaume to put his lens at the same angle.

In certain images, nothing had changed, not a tree, not a window, not a train track. Only the Jews and the photographers had disappeared.

It is one thing to use photographs in an investigation; it is another, for me, to rediscover the placement and actions of the photographers at the edge of the ditches. To retrace the steps of these Germans who, either as members of propaganda teams or simply for their own benefit, took the time to immortalize the scene while the Jews were agonizing in their grave. Since then, we have discovered other photographers, most notably in the villages of Lithuania.

THE PHOTOGRAPHER

Before Prozoroki, my team would try to figure out where the Jewish victims, the German murderers, the auxiliary police, and the neighbors were all positioned. Now we also ask "the neighbors" where the photographer stood.

Thus, the crime against the Jews was sometimes very public: public for the villagers, public for Germans in movie theaters, and public for families who received a snapshot, a trophy from their beloved criminal. The question only grows more insistent: how can a mass crime that is openly displayed and exhibited like a scene at a fair, and so often photographed, remain so little known?

Does this mean that when an excess of horror is exposed to view, or displayed in photographs or films, it stuns most people who see it, whether they're perched in a tree or sitting in a German living room? Does it simply feed their empathy for and engagement on the side of the criminals? Could there be a link between an overload of revealed horror and a well-kept secret? I am led to believe so.

In this sense, the secret and the spectacle of the shootings of the Jews are but two sides of the same event. The mass criminals of today seem to have learned this lesson; they claim credit for their crimes, even filming them and projecting their images crudely around our planet through social networks. The filmed and revealed horrors seem once again to stun and to multiply around the killers.

The writing of this book has forced me to measure how deeply the murder of the Jews was immersed in the rural immobility of Russo-Soviet villages: the same shovels, the same ditches, the same horses, the same paths, the same fences. And mostly, the same requisitions!

This inscription of murder in local immutability made it invisible even when seen by all.

The Russo-Soviet rural collective memory of the 1940s swallows up all specificity. The murder of Jewish neighbors takes place within the permanence of rural life, which will continue on course after the

249

crime, with the same carts, the same shovels, the same horses, the same houses, the same clothes. The Jews have been killed, buried under the habits of daily life. The landscape of the village has not changed. Rather, a portion of its population has simply been swallowed up.

AFTERWORD

Jerusalem, May 11, 2015

L eaning alone against a railing, I look again out at these white stones, polished by men and time, these stones I know so well. They have stood immobile here for many centuries. They are polished by joy, hope, and also pain. The light is diffuse under a fine layer of clouds. I have been invited to Jerusalem to speak about murderous anti-Semitism.

Today I am giving several lectures. A few weeks ago, I was speaking to a large crowd gathered at the University of Milwaukee. In a large, well-lit amphitheater, the faces of many young students looked eager for knowledge. But as soon as I spoke about the rape of Jewish women and the massacres of children, curiosity gave way to horror.

Horror.

The faces become tense, and the expressions grow alarmed. Some discreetly take out tissues. But horror rarely brings on a feeling of responsibility. On the contrary, it elicits a passing disgust, a disgust at knowing, then forgetfulness so as not to think about it anymore. So, I explain, I talk. I try to get my audience to keep thinking while learning the facts. And not to separate the "pleasant" world on one side from the knowledge of the criminal acts of the Shoah by bullets on the other side.

AFTERWORD

It took me a long time, many years, to live, breathe, and think with my eyes open. To listen, read, reread, question the neighbors to the crimes and search the archives in order to finally think, at least a little. Not only so that I could stand to know about genocidal acts but mostly so that I would not stop thinking once I knew about them. Not to be removed from oneself. To think while watching, to try to understand these acts, is already to resist.

When thought turns off, refuses to hear or see a genocidal act, we become half-conscious, perhaps without being aware of it, a spectator transfixed by the crime.

Purity.

There is no genocidal purity. Many believe, in good faith, that mass killers practice what they preach. It is true that when the Nazis called for the total destruction of the Jews, they tried to achieve it. It is tempting to think that the young SS, police, or soldiers were underlings, obeying orders, shooting human beings like robots faithful to Hitler's doctrines. Respecting, of course, the rules about purity of blood and righteousness that the Third Reich demanded of them. Notably the ban on sexual relations with "inferior races" and the duty not to take anything that belonged to the Third Reich.

It is tempting to believe that a totalitarian ideology confers on those who practice it a total adherence on a personal level. A totalitarian rectitude in life. The smooth speeches of genocidal leaders most often portray killing as a clean, surgical act, necessary to remove a dangerous part from the human race. The supposed purity of genocidal discourse is nothing more than the uniform cloak of a murderer. It not only authorizes him but also justifies and encourages him. The supposed purity of murderers is part of the pretense of a just genocide. They call themselves pure to justify their duty to exterminate those they deem impure.

A genocidal leader never incites simple underlings but always criminal ones: criminals who, by murdering, will effectively enact the genocide without, in so doing, extracting themselves on a personal level from the usual criminal motivations. In this sense, a genocide is also in part an organized and orchestrated mass crime that promises criminals the achievement of values that will save a country, a "race," or a political belief. This pretension justifies genocide with supposed "superior values." Genocide masquerades as a moral act.

To write and to think are my acts of resistance. They are indispensable preliminaries for reacting against a false genocidal morality. They are an act of insurgence in the face of the totalitarian discourse of those who coordinate genocide. To write and think in order to help resist the fascination and occultation that the genocidal act exerts on the spectator. The so-called justice of genocide fascinates and draws in crowds. A genocide, on the scale I am looking at, is, above all, human beings who murder other human beings while pretending to "save" a world from a danger. They "save" by killing, because for them the danger is the other.

I explain to the students in Milwaukee that, to write this, certain chapters made me sit motionless for months, as though incapable of saying the word "I." As though I were merely a conduit for the narrative repetition of what I had heard on the farms. To say "I" while listening to a witness to genocide costs a lot. What it costs is the price of personal responsibility in which I refuse to let myself be caught. Each chapter represents such a challenge.

I also explain that a moment of horror is most often followed by the will to live in peace and sleep well. How many times have we been horrified at the sight of a scene of mass crime that we have forgotten immediately? Forgetting the massacres of others is an integral part of democratic comfort.

And why is it necessary not to sleep well today, seventy years after the Shoah?

Quite simply, because our genocidal sickness, mass murder disguised as morality, is still with us.

AFTERWORD

The small screens of our computers can turn us into terrified and indifferent spectators. Yazidi women are sold in the markets of the supposed Islamic State; young Jordanian men are burned alive in cages; and on and on, here and there, not only in broad daylight but in the infinite space of social media, ricocheting over a silent sea of information.

The killers of Jews in France and Belgium, they too made sure to strap cameras on their bodies in order to save and transmit images of the faces of their victims, murdered Jewish adults and children. Crime scenes are sent and delivered to whomever wants to watch them. At home. For free.

For the last few months, I have been forcing myself to read, to study, but also to watch the recordings of crimes by the criminals themselves, especially those of ISIS. Some are almost unbearable. I ask myself, how can a cameraman, a sound man, hold their equipment, how can they zoom in on a man burning alive in a cage?

After more than ten years of research, I know that behind the purest, hardest ideologies, in the name of which is taught that it is virtuous, noble, urgent, and necessary to murder others, there is an appetite for gain and theft on the one hand, and on the other hand a sadistic will to commit violence, notably against women and children, who are never safe from the genocidal act.

Genocidal purity.

Leaders of genocides or mass crimes cry from podiums or pulpits in flawless discourses. After more than four thousand interviews of the neighbors of Nazi crimes, I can make this hypothesis: there is no such thing as genocidal purity.

Even if, for their killers, the victims are reduced to a pure object of the duty to murder, the murderers themselves are in no way the pure executors of some ideological justice. Genocidal murder cannot be separated from murderous appetites. Purity does not exist in mass killers.

But this is what they want us to believe, with their unified discourse, their rhythmic and triumphant music, and their infinitely repeated songs, their marching, their perfectly executed killings, their impeccably edited videos.

I understand, of course, that showing oneself to the camera with a human trophy at one's feet would seem to confer the illusion of superhuman power on that person who murders—justly, he will claim—other human beings. But a genocidal murderer is motivated by the same appetites as a common one.

Ideology authorizes mass murder and valorizes the criminal, but it does nothing to abolish his criminal appetites. How many houses have been looted, jewelry ripped from bodies, women raped, children tortured, in the name of the purification of our planet?

Some are believers. They set off with their backpacks the way others did seventy years before them in order to don black uniforms and join the ranks. The promise of being a superman, a "true man," pure and hard, is inseparable from the duty of killing others. The supposed purity of the genocidal superman is seductive.

If the Nazis couldn't keep themselves from raping Jewish women despite their insane ideology of blood purity, what can we think today of those who butcher, burn, and shoot in the name of Islamic purity? They are nothing more than criminals driven by insatiable appetites, the most powerful of which appears to be an idolatry of themselves, which seems, when it becomes criminal, the source of such pleasure that it demands to be preserved and perpetuated on film.

If certain Nazi executioners divided up the furs of Jewish women before shooting them,[1] what are we to make today of the thefts of goods by the Islamic State from conquered peoples? Purity does not exist among contemporary genocidal criminals either.

It is by unmasking the killer, wiping away the lie of the Aryan or Islamic superhuman, that we may be able to manage this pathology. Not simply repeating "Islamist" or "Nazi," as though they existed according to their own definitions, constitutes for me the first step in combatting them.

I have also learned that a mass killer is never alone with his victim, even if he appears to be in an image. It took many pairs of hands—voluntary, requisitioned, or forced—to ensure that the Jews were publicly murdered.

How many helpers appear onscreen when Islamists kill? When I watch a staged scene today in which men slit other men's throats against background music and prayers, I ask myself, who else is there behind that scene of genocidal crime? If there are images, there had to be at least a cameraman. A sound man. An editor. If there are clean, sharp knives, someone had to deliver them.

And who buries or burns the bodies? Where are the common graves of ISIS?

To reveal to the world the hideous faces of murderers disguised in the false garb of purity may permit one to hope that younger generations will rise up against the criminals as the just rose between 1941 and 1944.

My thoughts have flown very far. I watch, I listen.

It is a beautiful evening in Jerusalem. Birdsong fills the flowering laurels.

NOTES

Historical Introduction

1. One of the four *Einsatzgruppen* units that were responsible for the extermination of more than 120,000 people in Moldavia, southern Ukraine, and southern Russia. The *Einsatzgruppen* were the paramilitary units charged, following the invasion of Poland, with the systematic assassination of people classified as undesirable, such as intellectuals, Communists, Gypsies, and Jews. The *Einsatzgruppen* killed at least 500,000 Jews in Eastern Europe. They were divided into subunits, called *Sonderkommando* and *Einsatzkommando*.

2. This number includes 1.6 million victims in Ukraine (Alexander Kruglov, *The Losses Suffered by Ukrainian Jews in 1941–1944*, Kharkov: Tarbut, 2005, 360), at least 500,000 in Belarus (Yitzhak Arad, *The Holocaust in the Soviet Union*, Lincoln: University of Nebraska Press, 2009, 798), and at least 120,000 in Russia (Ilya Altman, *Opfer des Hasses*, Zurich: Verlag Gleichen, 2008, 348).

3. Other known methods of killing are poison, live burial, and death in mines or wells.

4. On September 29 and 30, 1941, the *Sonderkommando* 4a, a subunit of the *Einsatzgruppen*, killed more than 33,000 Jews in the ravine of Babi Yar in Kiev.

5. The trial of the *Einsatzgruppen,* which took place from 1947 to 1948 in Nuremberg, Germany, was one of twelve trials by an American military tribunal (*The United States of America against Otto Ohlendorf, et al.*). Twenty-four members of the *Einsatzgruppen* SS were tried, of whom fourteen were condemned to death.

257

NOTES

6. Trials of war criminals before the Nuremberg Military Tribunals under Control Council law no. 10, Nuremberg, October 1946–April 1949, Washington 1949–1953, volume IV/1, 490.

7. German term for an execution.

8. Interrogation of Herbert Wollenweber from May 14, 1970, BArch B162/1068, 4,312–13.

9. Interrogation of Franz Halle from March 2, 1962, BArch B162/5642, 493.

10. The name of the operation to exterminate the Jews and Gypsies of *Generalgouvernement* in Poland, between March 1942 and October 1943 in the three camps of Sobibor, Belzec, and Treblinka. More than two million Jews and fifty thousand Gypsies were killed.

11. A German state intelligence service between 1920 and 1944.

12. Report of October 24, 1941, a document of the Nuremberg trial PS-3047 (piece no. 4).

13. An incomplete Russian-language version appeared in Jerusalem and then in Kiev, Ukraine, in 1991. The first complete version was published in 1993 in Vilnius, Lithuania, and then in 1995 in France: Vasily Grossman and Ilya Ehrenburg, *Le Livre noir* (Actes Sud).

14. Complete name: Extraordinary State Commission for the Findings and Investigation of the Atrocities Committed by the German-Fascist Invaders and Their Accomplices, and the Damages Caused to Citizens, Kolkhoz, Public Bodies, State Enterprises and the Institution of the USSR. Material is also available on microfilm at the US Holocaust Memorial Museum.

15. George Ginsburgs, *Moscow's Road to Nuremberg*, La Haye: Martinus Nijhoff Publishers, 1996, 40. The archives of the commission contain 54,000 documents of proof of war crimes as well as four million other documents pertaining to material damages caused during the occupation.

16. Investigations were held in both West and East Germany.

17. Andrej Umansky is a Research Fellow at the Institute for Criminal Law and Criminal Procedure, University of Cologne, Germany, and is historical and legal advisor to Yahad–In Unum. He obtained a master's degree in French and German law from the Universities of Cologne and Paris I and another master's degree in the history of the Holocaust in Eastern Europe from the University of Paris IV. In 2016, he finished his PhD at the University Amiens, France, about the Holocaust in the Northern Caucasus in 1942–43.

NOTES

Introduction

1. Gallimard, Algiers, 1937.
2. Small town at the Polish border of western Ukraine.
3. The camp, Stalag 325, was created by the Germans in 1942 for French and Belgian prisoners of war who had either attempted to escape from a German camp or refused to work. By 1943, the number of prisoners in Rawa Ruska and its subcamps had risen to 24,000. In 1943, the camp was closed and the prisoners were transferred to other camps.
4. Maurice Chevalier (1888–1972) was a French singer and actor.
5. Aron Jean-Marie Lustiger (1926–2007), cardinal and archbishop of Paris, whose family is of Jewish origin.

Chapter 1: The Architect

1. George Smiley, an officer of British Intelligence, is a fictional character of John Le Carré.
2. The Ukrainian police was composed of men from the village or its surroundings, recruited and trained by the Germans immediately upon their arrival. At first, a commando of local police had to be made available in every town and in every district. Its size, depending on the number of inhabitants, was on average 150 to 200 men. At the beginning, the Germans recruited among former militia members, then quickly turned to candidates from the local population who would work more or less voluntarily. In July 1942, when the genocide was at its height, there were about 37,000 local police in the service of the *Reichskommissariat* in Ukraine and under military administration in the East, a number that rose to 100,000 by the time of the liberation. Comparable structures were created in other occupied regions of the USSR.
3. Small town in the Rivne region of Ukraine.
4. A portion of the Federal Archives (Bundesarchiv) can be found in the town in Bade-Würtemberg. It houses the files for the investigation and documentation of the Central Service of Investigation of National Socialist crimes, created in 1958, which to this day conducts preliminary investigations and coordinates German judicial institutions.

5. Deposition of September 24, 1964, BArch (Bundesarchiv), B 162/3433, 794*ff*.

6. Former German municipal police.

7. Legnica (Leignitz, in German) is a town in the southwest of Poland.

8. Small Belarusian town at the Lithuanian border.

9. Units of the local auxiliary police.

10. Abbreviation of the German word *Hilfswillige*, auxiliary volunteers.

11. Town in northwest Belarus.

12. District.

13. Rank equivalent to first lieutenant.

14. Acronym for *Sicherheitsdienst*, literally "Security Department." It was an intelligence service of the SS, central to the *Reichssicherheitshauptamt*, the central security office of the Reich.

Chapter 2: The Requisitions

1. Kolkhoz and sovkhoz were components of the socialized agricultural system that emerged after the Russian Revolution of April 1917.

2. Mayor and representative of the State in the communes of Ukraine before 1939. The German authorities borrowed from the system of the *starosta* by reinstating the pre-1939 mayors or by naming new ones. Their functions were limited and they were under the authority of the German administration. Their involvement in the executions varied from case to case but could go as far as an active and voluntary participation.

3. The *soltous* was the representative of regional power in a Polish commune.

4. Called either "*desiatskiy*" or "*dejourny*" (assigned a very specific mission). This was a person charged with specific functions of public and communal order for a limited number of households (often ten). This position had existed in the Russian empire since the seventeenth century. Appointed by the local government, the *desiatnik* answered to the mayor as well as the regional authorities. His work was not paid because it was considered a civic duty. This system was taken up by the Soviet Union and maintained under the German occupation. During the war, the *desiatnik* fulfilled certain duties relating to the executions, such as stockpiling shovels and organizing the labor force for the digging and filling in of the ditches. The orders given the

desiatnik, often with a threat of death if they weren't followed, were issued directly by the German authorities or by the mayor.

5. Ukrainian synonym for "mayor."

6. A traditional Romanian, Moldavian, and Ukrainian dish of yellow corn.

7. The term *Volksdeutscher* (literally, "member of the German people") was coined during the First World War for people whose native language was German but who lived outside the Reich and were citizens of another country. A special branch of government, the *Volksdeutsche Mittelstelle* (VoMi), was created in 1937 to facilitate immigration for *Volksdeutsche* into the Reich. During the war, the VoMi was in charge of registering all the *Volksdeutsche* living in occupied territories and giving them material aid. The VoMi worked in conjunction with *Nationalsozialistische Volkswohlfahrt* (NSV). Each *Volksdeutsche* had a special identification card, called a *Volksliste*, and official proof of the purity of their race. They had advantages over the local population, including access to special stores and extra food rations; sometimes the VoMi would distribute the clothes of executed Jews among the *Volksdeutsche*. Estimates of their number in occupied Ukraine vary between 350,000 and 500,000.

8. Kartakaï, a German colony in Berezivka in the region of Odessa. It no longer exists.

Chapter 3: The Diggers

1. Deposition from October 14, 1944, GARF (Gosudarstvenny Arkhiv Rossiskoi Federatsii—archives of the State of the Federation of Russia), 7021–67–78, 83s.

2. A Russian and Yiddish diminutive of Isaac.

3. Nickname for Ivan.

Chapter 4: The Night

1. Small Belarusian village, part of Poland until 1939, where the Germans carried out several *Aktion*, murdering more than three thousand Jews.

2. A town on the Polish border, better known by its former name of Brest-Litovsk.

3. Today the town is called Berioza.

4. Deposition of October 3, 1944, from the Regional Archives of Brest, 514-1-289, 14*ff.*

5. Probably a German policeman.

6. Deposition from December 7, 1960, BArch, B 162/3409, 670*ff.*

7. Jewish council. The *Judenrat* was an administrative body formed by force in the Jewish ghettos, by order of the Germans. It served as a liaison between the Nazi authorities and the population of the ghetto.

8. "Report from experience," from November 1942, document from Nuremberg USSR-119a, BArch B162/4949, 2*ff.*

9. Town in the south of Belarus where more than twenty thousand Jews were exterminated.

10. Acronym for Narodnii Komissariat Vnoutrennikh Diél (in English, the People's Commissariat for Internal Affairs). In the former Soviet Union, this political police force was created in 1934 to supersede the GPU and was itself replaced with the creation in 1946 of the MVD, or Ministry of Internal Affairs. The NKVD played a crucial role in the Great Purge of the 1930s, when hundreds of thousands of people were arrested or killed.

11. Deposition of February 13, 1963, BArch, B 162/4956, 058*ff.*

12. Before 1939, this Polish village was called Zablocie.

13. Report from September 30, 1942, from the 11th Company of the 3rd Battalion of the 15th Regiment of the police, GARF 7021-148-2, 342–3.

14. Deposition of Alfred Metzner from September 18, 1947, Nuremberg document NO-5558.

Chapter 5: The Rapes

1. At the beginning of Operation Barbarossa in June 1941, the *Reichssicherheitshauptamt* received regular reports (*Ereignismeldungen* and *Meldungen aus den besetzten Ostgebieten*) from the *Einsatzgruppen*. A set of originals exists in the German Federal Archives.

Chapter 6: Barriers

1. Town in Occidental Ukraine, called Ivano-Frankivsk since 1962.

2. Small town in the region of Lvov, where, of 13,000 Jews, only four hundred survived.

3. Deposition of November 12, 1973, BStU (*Bundesbeauftragte für die Unterlagen des Staatssicherheitsdienstes der ehemaligen Deutschen Demokratischen Republik*—Federal proxy for documentation for the Stasi of the former East Germany), MfS HA IX/11 ZUV 40, vol.1, 46*ff.*

4. Diminutive of the name Demiane.

Chapter 7: The Column of Jews

1. Jewish religious movement founded in the eighteenth century in Eastern Europe.

2. Personal counsel to the Archbishop of Lyons.

3. This thesis blamed the Jewish people for the crucifixion of Jesus Christ. In 1959, Pope John XXIII suppressed the critical language (*perfidis et perfidiam*) in the Good Friday prayer. This decision was made official in an announcement by the Vicariate of Rome on March 21, 1959 cf. *Les Eglises devant le judaïsme*, official documents from 1948–1978, texts gathered, translated, and annotated by Marie-Thérèse Hoch and Bernard Dupuy, Cerf, 1980, ch. 58, 351.

4. The apostle Judas.

5. "Broken," or "destroyed," in German.

Chapter 8: The Girl in Love

1. During the siege of Leningrad, between 1941 and 1944, more than a million civilians died of cold and hunger.

2. Bathroom in a small cabin.

3. Diminutive of Samuel.

Chapter 9: The Director of the Trucking Company

1. Deposition of October 1, 1945, BArch, B 162/19726, 8*ff.*

2. The *Kreishauptmann*, head of the *Generalgouvernement* district, was first SS-*Untersturmführer* Wilhelm Rebay von Ehrenwiesen; as of the summer of 1942, it was SS-*Untersturmführer* Joachim Nehring.

3. Späth was never found after the war.

Chapter 10: The Transporters of Jews

1. Until December 1920, the city was called Iekaterinodar.

2. A town in the region of Krasnodar. Until 1848 it was called Armianski (Armenian town).

3. One of four *Einsatzgruppen* units that exterminated over 120,000 people in Moldava, Ukraine, and Southern Russia.

4. "Kids are great!!"

Chapter 11: The Layers of Planks

1. Small village on the bank of the Boug river, in the Nikolayev region of Ukraine. More than 50,000 Jews in the vicinity of Odessa and Bessarabia were first deported to Bogdanovka and held in pork slaughterhouses. After a typhoid epidemic, at least 45,000 Jews were executed, with the help of the Romanian police, by the Ukrainian police and the *Selbstschutz* units, made up of *Volksdeutsche*, between December 21 and 23 and December 28 and 31, 1941. The bodies of the dead were burned.

2. Deposition of May 4, 1965, BArch B162-5835, 1082*ff*.

3. In German, "Again, faster, fire!"

Chapter 12: The Dance

1. Similar to a tambourine.

2. Unleavened bread, eaten at Passover.

3. Synonym for *desiatnik*.

4. The Ukrainian anthem to this day, composed in 1863 by the Greco-Catholic Ukrainian priest, Mykhaïlo Verbytsky.

Chapter 13: The Cooks and the Shooters

1. Beginning in the nineteenth century, Jewish colonies were created in eastern Ukraine, among other places, in order to encourage Jewish immigration. After the Bolshevik Revolution, from 1924 on, other Jews came to occupy these former colonies. Even while they were integrated into the local social and economic fabric, these Jewish agricultural colonies formed a distinct community in rural Ukraine.

2. Hanna's testimony can be found in *Porteur de mémoire* (Bearer of Memory) (Paris: Michel Lafon, 2007), 127*ff*.

3. September 29 and 30, 1941, the *Sonderkommando* (special detachment) 4a, subunit of the *Einsatzgruppen*, killed more than 33,000 Jews in this ravine.

4. Anatoli Kouznetsov, *Babi Yar* (Paris: Robert Laffont, 2011), 93.

5. Deposition of Georg P. from October 6, 1967, BArch, B 162/17909, 362*ff.*

6. Noncommissioned officer charged with supplies and logistics for the unit.

7. Deposition of Oscar C. of October 6, 1967, BArch, B 162/17909, 355*ff.*

8. SS rank, equivalent to lieutenant.

9. *Schutzpolizei*: subdivision of the regular police force of the time.

10. Deposition of Viktor T. from October 6, 1967, BArch, B 162/17909, 367*ff.*

11. Warehouses in which the Jews' goods from Auschwitz-Birkenau were stored.

12. Unfinished addition to Auschwitz-Birkenau.

Chapter 14: The Curious Children

1. *Mischlinge*, in Nazi terminology.

2. The Wannsee Conference, on January 20, 1942, held in a villa in Berlin, brought together fifteen of the leaders of the Third Reich to work out the administrative, technical, and economic details of the "final solution" to the Jewish question.

Chapter 15: The Child with the Bullets

1. The Ikopot and the Chakhivka are rivers near Starokostiantyniv.

2. The October Revolution in Russia, also known as the Bolshevik Revolution, started with a coup led by Lenin and the Bolsheviks in October 1917.

3. "Jid" is a term for Jew. In Occidental Ukraine, it was not pejorative until recently. It was a common term, preferred over "ievreï," which was considered Russian. It is still in use, especially in the countryside.

4. Sloboda is a typical village name in Russia, Belarus, or Ukraine. The name is derived from the old Slavic word for "liberty," and can be translated loosely as "free colony."

5. According to the Julian Calendar, Orthodox Christmas falls on January 7.

6. In total, eleven thousand Jews were executed in Starokostiantyniv.

7. Paul Blobel (1894–1951), an architect by training, was responsible as the chief of the *Sonderkommando* 4a for several executions in Ukraine,

such as that of at least 33,771 on September 29–30, 1941. Between 1942 and 1944, he organized "Operation 1005" which consisted of erasing the evidence of the mass executions committed in occupied territory. He was sentenced to death in Nuremberg in 1948.

8. Deposition of June 25, 1960, BArch, B 162/5641, 1*ff.*

Chapter 16: The Forced Witnesses

1. One of the major branches of Hasidism.

Chapter 17: A German Soldier as Spectator

1. SS grade equivalent to captain.
2. Deposition of February 13, 1965, BArch, B 162/986, 1,662*ff.*
3. He gave his testimony on February 13. 1965, in Gissen, as part of the preliminary file for the trial of the men of *Sonderkommando* 10b of *Einsatzgruppe* D, conducted by the public prosecutor in Munich (primarily against Alois Persterer, who was head of the SK10b).

Chapter 18: The Transporter of Clothing

1. The head of a team of workers in the kolkhoz.

Chapter 19: The Teachers

1. Deposition of October 23, 1967, BArch, BAL, B 162/20009, 516*ff.*

Chapter 20: The Fillers

1. Paris: Editions Tel Gallimard, 1957, 332.
2. Himmler's speech in front of SS officers in the town hall of Poznań, Poland, October 4 and 6, 1943, in which he openly defended the necessity of the Shoah.

Chapter 21: The Sale

1. The last census before the war in the USSR was conducted in 1939.
2. Yiddish term for a non-Jewish person who helps the family on the Sabbath by performing forbidden tasks, like cooking or lighting candles.
3. "Come!" in German.

4. GARF, 7021-19-2, 142.
5. Subdivision of the *Einsatzgruppen* operating in Belarus.

Chapter 22: The Auctions
1. Military operation named for the Holy Roman emperor Frederick I, or Frederick Barbarossa, when the Third Reich invaded the USSR during the summer of 1941.
2. River originating in Ukraine that passes through Belarus on its way to Poland, where it flows into the Narew.
3. Soviet and Russian term for the Second World War.
4. Song sung on Fridays at dusk in the synagogue to welcome the "Sabbath fiancée" at the beginning of the evening service.
5. Shoe factory.
6. At least 2.5 million people died between 1932 and 1933 in Ukraine and Southern Russia.
7. Campaign of repression between 1929 and 1933, directed against peasants who owned significant amounts of land.
8. In all the German townships, the auctions were organized by the local fiscal authorities.

Chapter 23: The Coats
1. More than five thousand Jews died of cold and sickness in the Yavoriv ghetto or were executed in several *Aktions*, the last of which was in April 1943.
2. Zentralhandelsgesellschaft Ost, a semi-private enterprise with more than 20,000 employees that helped direct agricultural economies in occupied territories.
3. Deposition of October 16, 1959, BArch, B 162/2883, 789*ff*.

Chapter 24: The Patchworker
1. Several hundred Jews were killed there between 1941 and 1943.

Chapter 25: The Sanitizer
1. Small village near the town of Kamen-Kachirski in Volhynie, Ukraine.
2. More than 1,800 Jews were killed between 1941 and 1942. In November 1942, four hundred Jews were able to escape from the

ghetto of Kamen-Kachirski. Some of them, like Jack Kagan, were able to join up with Jewish rebels like the Bielski brothers. See Jack Kagan and Dov Cohen, *Surviving the Holocaust with the Russian Jewish Partisans* (London:Valentine Mitchell, 1997).

Chapter 26: The Method

1. An inquest was made against Fiodor Alexandrovitch Zaloga (1906–1944) by the Ukrainian KGB. His file (No. 11259) is in the archives of the SBU of the Khmelnitsky region, and one copy is in the RG-31.018M section of the archives of the United States Holocaust Memorial Museum. Other testimonies from Zaloga can be found in the files of the Soviet Extraordinary State Commission of the district of Kamaniets-Podilsky, Ukraine, in the Russian Federal Archives in Moscow (GARF 7021-64-799).
2. Former name of the town of Donetsk.
3. After a major defeat in a battle near Ouman, more than 60,000 Soviet soldiers were made prisoners of war in August 1941.
4. Former town of Podolie, today in eastern Ukraine, in the region of Khmelnitsky.
5. Region of Khmelnitsky, Ukraine.
6. Village in the region of Khmelnitsky, Ukraine. On July 23, 1942, eight hundred Jews were executed.
7. Deposition of Hermann Graebe from January 29, 1960, BArch, B 162/5221, 61*ff.*
8. Chief of a district in the zones of civil administration in the occupied territories.
9. Deposition of Alfred Metzner on September 18, 1947, Nuremberg document NO-5558.
10. Mistresses.
11. The district head of agriculture in the civil administration zones of the occupied territories. One of his duties was to receive shipments of farm products.

Conclusion: The Photographer

1. Several hundred Jews from Prozoroki and neighboring villages were put into the ghetto. On December 6, 1941, about four hundred Jews

were executed. Many inhabitants were able to escape and join the Soviet rebels.

2. "Small place," in Russian.
3. Station near the village of Lomachy.
4. Station in the village of Ziabki.
5. Belarusian auxiliary police.

Afterword

1. Deposition of Jakob G., a member of *Einsatzkommando* 10b, from November 23, 1966, BArch, B 162/989, 2,311.

INDEX

INDEX

INDEX

INDEX

INDEX

INDEX

INDEX

INDEX

INDEX